BOLLYWOOD'S INDIA

BOLLYWOOD'S INDIA

A Public Fantasy

PRIYA JOSHI

Columbia University Press
New York

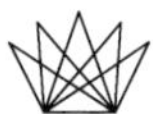

Columbia University Press
Publishers Since 1893
New York   Chichester, West Sussex
cup.columbia.edu
Copyright © 2015 Columbia University Press
All rights reserved

Library of Congress Cataloging-in-Publication Data
Joshi, Priya.
    Bollywood's India : a public fantasy / Priya Joshi.
        pages cm
    Includes bibliographical references and index.
    ISBN 978-0-231-16960-8 (cloth : alk. paper) — ISBN 978-0-231-16961-5
(pbk : alk. paper) — ISBN 978-0-231-53907-4 (ebook)
    1. India—In motion pictures.   2. Motion pictures—India—History—20th
century.   3. Motion pictures—United States—History—20th century.   I. Title

PN1993.5.I8J673 2015
791.43'0954—dc23

2014042100

Cover design: Jordan Wannemacher
Cover image: Based on a publicity poster for *Deewaar* (1975)

References to websites (URLs) were accurate at the time of writing.
Neither the author nor Columbia University Press is responsible for URLs
that may have expired or changed since the manuscript was prepared.

The dedication on page v is from "yes is a pleasant country." Copyright 1944,
© 1972, 1991 by the Trustees for the E. E. Cummings Trust, from *Complete
Poems: 1904–1962* by e. e. cummings, edited by George J. Firmage. Used by
permission of Liveright Corporation.

The epigraphs on page vii are from *Talking Films: Conversations on Hindi
Cinema with Javed Akhtar*, as recorded by Nasreen Munni Kabir (New Delhi:
Oxford UP, 1999), 35; and from Sudhir Kakar, *Intimate Relations: Exploring
Indian Sexuality* (New Delhi: Penguin, 1988), 27.

For Orfeo

*love is a deeper season
than reason;
my sweet one
(and april's where we're)*

There is one more state in this country, and that is Hindi cinema. And so Hindi cinema also has its own culture. . . . Hindi cinema's culture is quite different from Indian culture, but it's not alien to us, we understand it. . . . As a matter of fact, Hindi cinema is our closest neighbor. It has its own world, its own traditions, its own symbols, its own expressions, its own language, and those who are familiar with it understand it.

JAVED AKHTAR

[Fantasy is] another name for that world of imagination which is fuelled by desire and which provides us with an alternative world where we can continue our longstanding quarrel with reality. . . . Fantasy is the mise-en-scène *of desire, its dramatization in a visual form.*

SUDHIR KAKAR

CONTENTS

TABLES

ACKNOWLEDGMENTS

WRITING A BOOK ABOUT BOLLYWOOD is a bit like making a Bollywood film. There's a substantial time lag between idea and execution. Editing takes forever. Producers are hard to find just when they're most needed. And the stars—those ideas that glittered so enticingly in the dark screen of the mind—become hard to pin down just as the schedule for completion nears. The only reason the book and the film are ever completed is the willing collaboration of many who throw themselves into the project in which they passionately believe.

It is an honor to name the many collaborators of this book. Thanks first to my students at Berkeley and Temple whose enthusiasm and indulgence shaped my thinking as the project developed. Students in a 2005 Berkeley Freshman Seminar insisted that I include blockbusters after liberalization in the book, and the chapter on Bollylite is a partial reply to them. Students at the Bryn Mawr Film Institute came to Bollywood after full careers and lives elsewhere and took unscripted delight in the form and its many pleasures.

This book would not be *this* book without the many intellectual and practical resources Temple University provided. Conversations at the New India Forum were invaluable in keeping contemporary India front and center. Special thanks to Richard Immerman and Peter Logan of the Center for the Humanities for bankrolling the Forum, and to Arvind Phatak and Kim Cahill for extending the largesse from a CIBER grant to pursue the lines of inquiry we did in those heady years. A 2011 workshop on the 1970s and its legacies in India's cinemas focused many of the ideas that shape the present study. Thanks to the workshop participants, CIBER, and the College of Liberal Arts Research Council for making the event possible. Invitations to present portions of the argument at Brandeis, Bryn Mawr, Chicago,

Harvard, Hawai'i, Iowa, Madison, Old Dominion, and Penn provided lively occasions to sort out its claims.

Research in the humanities incurs considerable cost. Grateful thanks to the University of California, Berkeley, Washington University in St. Louis, Temple University, Temple's Center for the Humanities, and the Penn Humanities Forum for enabling archival trips to India and supporting the writing time to complete this book.

The research staffs at the Library of Congress Film Research Division in Washington, D.C., and the British Film Institute in London were extremely accommodating. The National Film Archive of India in Pune provided unmatched courtesies during several visits. Special thanks to the director, Mr. Sheshadri, and the research staff: Kiran Diwar, Shubhalakshmi Iyer, Urmila Joshi, Arti Karkhanis, and above all the legendary P. K. Nair, who founded the archive and provided immensely useful oral histories of the Bombay film industry in the 1950s and 1970s. Temple's Paley Library cheerfully acquired every obscure source requested, and its circulation staff took it upon themselves to flag and hold titles of potential interest for me—unasked. Kristina DeVoe's expertise made it possible to conduct research in the midst of full teaching terms: her clarifying questions frequently led to unanticipated areas of inquiry.

I was especially fortunate in my research assistants for sleuthing through the dense jungle of non-digitized sources and locating retrieval-resistant print materials: Daisy Duggan at Berkeley, Jason E. Cohen at Madison, Rich Gienopie and Daniel Ryan Morse at Temple were matchless in their genial partnership.

The community of scholars on Hindi cinema provided solidarity with this book and readily engaged its arguments by posing better ones of their own. The debt in the notes is one kind of payback. For the other kind are public thanks to many who are now personal friends as well: Ulka Anjaria, Kazi Ashraf, John Briley, Emma Bufton, Sumita Chakravarty, Sanjoy Chakravorty, Vikram Chandra, Gayatri Chatterjee, Anupama Chopra, Lawrence Cohen, Corey Creekmur, Kavita Daiya, Jigna Desai, Sara Dickey, Rajinder Dudrah, Rachel Dwyer, David Farris, Tejaswini Ganti, Ajay Gehlawat, Monica Ghosh, Sangita Gopal, Nitin Govil, Priya Jaikumar, Madhu Jain, Abhijat Joshi, Suvir Kaul, Sudipta Kaviraj, Sunil Khilnani, David Ludden, Philip Lutgendorf, Purnima Mankekar, P. K. Nair, Ashis Nandy, Veena Talwar Oldenburg, Swarnavel Eswaran Pillai, Satish Poduval, Madhava Prasad, Amaneep Sandhu, Harleen Singh, Jyotika Virdi, and Amanda Weidman. Behroze Gandhy and Rosie Thomas graciously provided permission and image, respectively, of the 1985 election poster that appears in chapter 3. Nasreen Munni Kabir opened doors in Bombay and Pune that would have been impenetrable otherwise. Her formidable research that established an archive of the industry has greatly enabled my scholarship. Nasreen's hospitality in London and her friendship since make her a fairy godmother to this project.

Hindi cinema is hydra-headed, and heartfelt thanks to those in the industry who spoke with me about the 1970s without insisting that theirs was the only account that mattered. Javed Akhtar was especially generous during his visit to Philadelphia and always made time for my questions about the industry. Shabana Azmi, Randhir Kapoor, Rishi Kapoor, Shashi Kapoor, the staff of RK Studios, Girish Karnad, Feroze Rangoonwalla, Ramesh Sippy, Rohan Sippy, and Sheena Sippy were extraordinarily forthcoming with their time and insights in Bombay, Chembur, Khar, and London.

Others, not involved with Hindi film, had the critical distance to ask clarifying questions and the patience to let me fumble over the answers: Ann Banfield, Ian Duncan, Jim English, Susan Stanford Friedman, Oliver Gaycken, Lewis Gordon, Peter Logan, Franco Moretti, Paul Saint-Amour, Ellen Scott, Todd Shepard, and Howard Spodek. Michael Rogin *got* my project before I did, and it's a shame I didn't finish it in time so he could help me make it better. A quarter century ago, two teachers at Columbia shaped much of my understanding of popular culture. Andreas Huyssen's trilogy on the Frankfurt School and Russell Berman's Freud seminar modeled the theoretical work I had no idea I would one day want to pursue. Here is the paper I probably still owe both of them.

At Columbia University Press, Jennifer Crewe's celebrated patience and loyalty to this book defy encomia. Her many kindnesses ushered this book and its author into print for which mute thanks. The anonymous readers for the Press provided helpful suggestions for revision and enthusiastic support when both were most needed. The Press's faculty board deserves special thanks for its loyal faith in the author. Kathryn Schell and Jordan Wannemacher cheerfully helped with the details of publishing that make most authors weep. Roy Thomas's editorial eyes were a precious gift that only an author in heaven's favor receives.

Versions of chapters 3 and 4 appeared, respectively, in considerably different forms in *South Asian Popular Culture* 8.3 (2010) and 10.1 (2012). Neither would have been possible without the kindness of the journal's founding editor, Rajinder Dudrah, who has been a model of professional courtesy to so many, including this author. His innumerable gifts have produced a debt that can only be paid forward.

Beyond the gifts of time and money is the gift of peace. And that, as every parent who is a writer knows, is the gift that comes from excellent childcare.

We were specially blessed with the magnificent Parent-Infant Center in West Philadelphia and Amanda Barkhorn. Endless thanks to both.

All the films I write about in this book were blockbusters because families went to watch them across generations, often together. Mine was no different, though the opportunities were sparsely doled out in our family during the 1970s. When a film was considered too violent or risqué, my mother Kusum Joshi's gift for storytelling narrated it in real time, so I knew *Sholay* well before I actually saw it, thanks to her. My sisters, Chaya Nanavati and Priti Joshi, embody middle-class responses to Bollywood in their total indifference and total immersion in it. (But when Chaya's playlist suddenly went from three songs to ten, we knew she was finally getting it.) My aunts in Delhi were unfailing resources with material often irretrievable from traditional archives. Kumud Pant's gift with translations is unmatched, and Mrinalini and Lalit Pande could recite forgotten lyrics on demand. Thanks to Rishabh Pande and Swetha Ramakrishnan for their frequent hospitality in Bombay.

They say virtue skips a generation, but that is not the case in the Nanavati household. My nephews, Akshay, Amal, and Anuj Nanavati, have been my closest collaborators in this project as we watched films and talked about them across the past decade. Amal Nanavati's authority, even as a 9-year-old, became legend in my Berkeley classroom. He has been a generous resource on contemporary Hindi film to whom I owe many of the insights of the Epilogue. Sameer Nanavati helped me get the 1970s right and keep it simple.

My own household has a different logic: the Scandogreeks in it have not been able to sit through a complete Hindi film though they generously allow me to do so in about 7-minute segments. One day . . . Nestor Fioretos's daring interpretive moves vanquished my timidity. His keen understanding of media frequently deepened my own. Monologues with him about my work were remarkably productive even when they took place with his fingers in his ears. Orfeo Fioretos set an example of analytical clarity that helped locate this book's core arguments and frame them. His ideas have become mine, and I've gratefully absorbed his brilliance and extraordinary work ethic. He kept our households and lives humming with joy when I disappeared for long stretches. And as Mentor, he did what his namesake in Ancient Greece once did: inspired me to go after the things that really matter.

I'd rather learn from one bird how to sing
than teach ten thousand stars how not to dance.

Thank you, my love. This book is for you, and if you'll share it, for Nestor and Amal as well.

PREFACE

E VERY NOW AND THEN, A film leaves the screen. Not once during its almost five-year first run did I watch the 1975 curry western, *Sholay*. It didn't seem to matter because the film was everywhere when I was growing up in India in the 1970s. We heard the songs on the radio, the dialogues were echoed in conversation, tailors speedily copied the film's fashions for every size and wallet, and thanks to my mother's formidable gift of narration, I felt I had seen the entire film with its larger-than-life characters shooting each other from steam locomotives and water towers.

A number of studies of this iconic film have grappled with what might be considered the *Sholay* effect, namely, the special status this blockbuster enjoys, often abstracted from its particulars, by "viewers" like me who might never have seen the film at the time. Returning to the primal scene as a scholar, my research affirms that *Sholay*'s outsize success was created in no small part by its formidable production that made it India's first 70mm film marshaling a multi-star cast with imported talent for shooting stunts and editing fight scenes. *Sholay*'s meticulous production transformed a four-line story to more than three hours of action-drama repeatedly reenacted by fans far from the large screen.

For some, the technical details of production and the institutional context of cinema in the 1970s remain the best approach for studying *Sholay*. For others such as myself, the film is best approached by studying its narrative strategies, their cultural contexts, and their combination in a mise-en-scène that exceeds the sum of its parts. The study of Hindi cinema has grown in the last decades to the point where both approaches can prosper productively without engaging in fratricidal warfare. The Thakur and Gabbar, arch enemies in *Sholay*, are both alive, although they don't live in the same village.

Bollywood's India analyzes the social work of popular Hindi cinema by focusing on the narratives of some of Bollywood's most iconic blockbusters. Tropes preoccupied with crime and punishment, family and individuality, vigilante and community, have persisted in the cinema across half a century despite dramatic changes in the industry's production and distribution practices. Attentive to the practices of the industry, I focus on analyzing the narrative content in the cinema and apply a range of interdisciplinary methods to understand Hindi blockbusters in the context of India's public culture. In this public culture, the stories *in* the cinemas, their shifting emphases, and their forms of attraction play a major role in capturing audiences. *Bollywood's India* focuses on these narratives of the cinema.

I analyze blockbusters produced during three tumultuous decades when the idea of modern India was made, unmade, and remade. During the 1950s, the 1970s and the 1990s, popular Hindi cinema played a major role in Indian public culture as it captured the diffuse aspirations of the nation as well as challenged them. Rather than being consonant with the interests of the state and a conduit in its production, popular Hindi film has served as a contact zone between the state and the nation. At times the block-busters of the cinema have corroborated and at other times contested the formation of both nation and state in the construction of an ever-shifting narrative of "India." These often contradictory narratives condense around certain aspirations that I call public fantasies. *Bollywood's India* analyzes the public fantasies captured in the blockbusters of Hindi popular cinema and studies the political work they undertake as they travel the globe.

Well before the study of popular Hindi cinema was formalized in the academy, scholars were writing about the cinema. The bibliography lists essays such as "Imran Khan, Sherlock Holmes, and Amitabh Bachchan" (Nandy 1987) that regard the appeal of Hindi cinema in India as a mania akin to that for cricket and detective fiction. In playful, sparkling prose, these essays develop a core claim: that popular cinema is popular because it "works" for its audiences and addresses their psychic lives. Written by scholars often trained in the social sciences who leaven their disciplinary methods with those borrowed from the humanities, these studies consider consumption broadly without being freighted by counting consumers; they "operationalize" narrative and its procedures using interpretive methods borrowed from psychoanalysis, history, anthropology, political theory, sociology, and literary analysis. Above all, their respect for popular film is propelled by an evident affection for it. Their work advances the study of popular Hindi cinema by inviting its diverse publics in. These studies have opened the party to all revelers for whom film is part of a vital public culture as it is in modern India.

As Hindi cinema has become an object of academic study with departments, peer-reviewed journals, scholarly book series, and conferences dedicated to it, the sparkle of its earlier analytical language and its intellectual accessibility have often been replaced by a specialist vocabulary and an occasionally strident insistence on the "proper" way to analyze the cinema. Scholars of Hindi cinema sometimes appear like Raj Kapoor after the release of *Mera Naam Joker* (My name is Joker, 1971). The cerebral, self-referential *Joker* virtually bankrupted Kapoor who had no idea that its language and treatment had isolated the film from its publics and cost him the magic that had hitherto been his at the box office. According to the biographer Bunny Reuben, Kapoor was only "faintly aware" of the changes around him, "sitting as [he was] in the ivory tower of Chembur."[1] It took an Archie comic and a plunge back into popular culture for Kapoor to leave the ivory tower and make a comeback with *Bobby* (1973).

Bollywood's India celebrates an area of study that has taken off because of scholarship by "outsiders" whose interdisciplinary approaches to cinema have placed it in broader contexts and ventilated the field in language accessible to the common reader and scholar alike. The study was inspired by the immense pleasures of the cinema and written to share them. Its methods are interdisciplinary and the language is straightforward. My intention is to celebrate popular Hindi cinema and welcome others to participate in its pleasures.

BOLLYWOOD'S INDIA

BOLLYWOOD'S INDIA

THE BLOCKBUSTERS OF HINDI CINEMA have played a prominent role in managing the euphoria and crises that confront the modern nation. In the decade following Independence and Partition, the period surrounding the Emergency, and the immediate aftermath of economic liberalization when the idea of India underwent considerable scrutiny, Bollywood's blockbusters vitally captured dispersed anxieties and aspirations about the nation that converged on the thing called "India." *Bollywood's India* names these aspirations public fantasies and analyzes the social work that popular cinema has done for the nation even as the cinema has challenged fundamental practices of the nation and the state during critical moments. It studies the ways in which the idea of India has been fabricated, critiqued, and revised in some of the most popular films of the post-Independence period.

During three notably turbulent decades, popular Hindi cinema played a major role in public culture as it undertook raw conversations with and as politics. The cinema's encounter with political culture is not new, nor is it confined to the periods of this study. It is, in fact, broadly constitutive of popular Hindi cinema and evident in a variety of ways in earlier and later decades. What differs across the historical periods is the kind of nation being envisioned in the cinema, the kinds of public fantasies to enhance and contain it, and the degree to which the nation constitutes the core fantasy of the cinema. What also differs across the historical periods are the narrative procedures by which the fantasies are deployed and the forms that convey them. Most prominently, what differs across the decades are the economics of film production and interpellation. The decline of studios, emerging financial instruments, alternately neglectful and interventionist state support, the arrival of new hardware for filming and screening, an expanding media ecology, and corporate partners with global marketing ambitions have all shaped popular Hindi cinema's practices and sometimes even its product. Each of these fundamental elements was reconstituted during the decades of this study, most vigorously during the 1970s when the very idea of "India" appeared to be in crisis, and the economic and political challenges confronting the state were magnified in an industry that was still not recognized as such.

The term *Bollywood* emerged during the 1970s in part to describe this unruly cultural site and its compact between popular and political culture that has been alternately embraced and rejected in the periods following. In using "Bollywood" in its title, the present study underscores the prominent role of the 1970s in constituting modern India. Beyond serving as a historical marker, "Bollywood" conveys a general tendency in the cinema toward social preoccupations and public fantasies. At its broadest, Bollywood conveys a cinema in which popular and mass, politics and pleasure are inextricably linked and are discernible far beyond, and even before, the moment of naming. The ruptures to the social contract that combusted the 1970s were not new. An analysis of the 1950s, for instance, reveals the decade's optimism and despair over the idea of India, rival sentiments that 1950's blockbusters nonetheless appear to have skillfully contained. Viewing the earlier decade from the perspective of the 1970s—when despair had fully trumped optimism, and containment was nowhere possible—reveals fissures and disappointments in the cinema of the 1950s that have been largely overlooked in extant accounts of the decade.

Bollywood's India uses the prism of the long 1970s to analyze the public fantasies of periods that lead up to and followed it into the present one. It is a study of popular blockbusters released during the 1950s, the 1970s, and the 1990s, three decades when the idea of modern India was made, remade, and unmade.

MAKING INDIA: NATION, STATE, AND PUBLIC FANTASY

The India that Hindi film addresses is no more real than the vagabond Raj or the dacoit Gabbar Singh. Yet, like the fictional characters from *Awara* (The vagabond, Raj Kapoor, 1951) and *Sholay* (Embers, Ramesh Sippy, 1975), Bollywood's India is a creature of fantasy and fiction that gestures toward that special version of reality that all fantasy and fiction simultaneously mask and reveal. To speak about India through Bollywood is akin to speaking about London through Dickens. Recognizable by physical locations, topical events, and perhaps even language, Dickens' London of Newgate and Lincoln's Inn conjures the metropolis through a set of preoccupations closer to—and perhaps more indicative of—Dickens than they might be of London or perhaps even the age. Yet one learns of *a* London and *a* Dickens in the process, each throwing the other in relief even as both remain partially shrouded. The promise of relief overcomes the reluctance at shadows and underwrites the study of an age through its cultural products. *Bollywood's India* develops a similar promise: it examines the cultural product alongside the nation of which it is part.

Within months of the Lumière brothers' invention, the cinematograph arrived in India in 1896, and the country began a love affair with film that continues to this day. The arrival and development of the medium coincided with the articulation and consolidation of the new nation. Held at arm's length by some early nationalists such as M. K. Gandhi of whom it was noted by an aide that "[as] for the Cinema Industry he has the least interest in it and one may not expect a word of appreciation from him," early film enjoyed the admiration of many others such as Prime Minister Jawaharlal Nehru, who actively inspired and cultivated the film world in numerous ways.[1] Recalling the early years of the nation, Raj Kapoor (1924–1988), one of Bombay's most popular and commercially successful filmmakers, observed of the 1940s and 1950s:

It was the post-Independence era. There were a lot of factors that influenced young minds, and they influenced me. Pandit-ji [Nehru] said that he wanted every Indian in this country to do something for the nation, to build it up into the beautiful dream that he had. He was a visionary and I tried to follow him, to do my best, whatever I could, through films. Despite all problems, despite all obstacles, you go ahead towards the horizon which you have seen. It is there in your eyes and in many other eyes. Very many people want to reach that horizon — and if I can help them through my work, I think I have done something for humanity.[2]

Kapoor's characterization of the nation as Nehru's "beautiful dream" was more than a poetic flight. In 1947, "India" was a horizon and a dream in many eyes, enacted into statehood by caveat on August 15. Standing before the Constituent Assembly, Nehru delivered the 500-odd word oration that remains one of the most quoted in modern Indian history:

Long years ago we made a tryst with destiny, and now the time comes when we shall redeem our pledge, not wholly or in full measure, but very substantially. At the stroke of the midnight hour, when the world sleeps, India will awake to life and freedom. A moment comes, which comes but rarely in history, when we step from the old to the new, when an age ends, and when the soul of a nation, long suppressed, finds utterance.[3]

As a speech, Nehru's was both celebration and caution of the work that remained in building a nation even as it was being torn apart by Partition. "That future is not one of ease or resting but of incessant striving so that we may fulfill the pledges we have so often taken and the one we shall take today. . . . And so we have to labour and to work, and work hard, *to give reality to our dreams*," he warned the millions of newly made citizens of independent India (Nehru 2, emphasis added). The specific task that Nehru outlined was presented in language that combined a Protestant ethic ("incessant striving," "labour," and "work") wrapped in Freudian terms ("to give reality to our dreams").

Freud's terms were necessary because so much of what constituted the Indian nation for Nehru and his audience was the stuff of fantasies and dreams, and not just the collective dream of a large polity, but the inchoate and unarticulated fantasies of millions of very different and differently motivated people that had to be shaped, named, and comprehended within a single and unifying "reality." Unlike popular nationalisms in Europe and the New World that imagined the community before it became a nation, quite the opposite was the case with India. Independence created a state in 1947 after which it had to be imagined as a nation in the hearts and minds of its citizens. "Giving reality to our dreams" was, therefore, not just a matter of building dams and developing foreign currency reserves. It was equally a matter of managing the dispersed and intangible desires for the nation that incorporated, and exceeded, its institutions, customs, cultures, and ideals. Nehru was asking for an act of public fantasy.

But nation and state were comprised of very different desires. One was a cultural fantasy with social aspirations (an "imagined community" with the emphasis on "imagined");[4] the other was a political fantasy with economic and judicial aspirations. Ideally, both kinds would converge on the entity called India. Yet, as it turns out, nation and state embarked on very different destinies, at times inimical to each other despite their shared investment in the "dreams" that Nehru invoked. It could be argued that the nation prospered exactly when—and perhaps because— the state descended into crisis, as it did before and during the 1975–1977 Emergency. During this period, popular cinema persistently pursued the cultural work of recalling the nation and retrieving its ideals. In retrospect, through the many crises confronting India, the blockbusters of Hindi cinema have remained one of the key places where the dueling desires fueling the nation's collective fantasies are indexed, shaped, and challenged. These blockbusters speak to and about the nation, for and against the state, and they serve as a space where the logic behind both is captured and contemplated in a language accessible to a large majority. These blockbusters constitute the core of *Bollywood's India*.

A number of scholars have posited popular Hindi cinema as a site that produces and reinforces the ideology of the state, a point developed in an influential study by Madhava Prasad, who regards popular Hindi cinema "a site for the ideological production . . . as the (re)production of the state form." A host of books with "nation" in their titles or subtitles make similar claims that regard popular cinema as a space consonant with the interests of the state and unproblematically a conduit in its production. Like Prasad, these studies sometimes appear to condense all possible "Indias" under the term *nation*. The cinema is read as "impersonating" the nation in Sumita Chakravarty's term, suggesting the nation and state as homogeneous entities indistinct from each other.[5]

In contrast to studies that regard the nation as singular and largely interchangeable with the state, *Bollywood's India* distinguishes between two formations that it regards as fundamentally different and even at times divergent. The state refers to those political and administrative components of modern polity that have the power and authority to govern.[6] The nation, in contrast, is the set of imaginative constructions that, ideally, are congruent with the enterprise of the state and underwrite its governance, but more often contest and correct the practices of the state. The nation, in this formulation, is both more and less than the state. It is the repository of ideals and ambitions—all far from homogeneous—that precede the formation of the state. The nation can create the state, but it also contests it, or coalesces into it on some issues and diverges from it over others. The nation thus embodies a broad set of desires. It is the "soul" that Nehru proclaimed at Independence to which the state is the answer, however incomplete. "We have to labour and to work, and work hard, to give reality to our dreams," urged Nehru, clarifying the difference between the two concepts at stake. The state marks a "reality" that is often compromised; the nation, its "dreams" that are also possibly its nightmares.

In this act of collective dreaming, popular cinema plays a role that is both a revision of reality and a restoration of its originary impulses. Its social work is not to maintain the state but to contain it and, where possible, to regulate it by writing the social contract in language that inspires broad assent. Popular cinema neither fully represents the state nor the nation. It is a contact zone *between* the two entities. It provides a space for engagement, enchantment, and possibly reenchantment if not with the nation itself then with the stories that undergird all acts of collective fantasy of which the nation is but one example. At best, it is a third space that fabricates and filters the experiences of politics and modernity for its viewers.[7]

Psychoanalysis, with its focus on interpreting desire and narration, provides a powerful apparatus for investigating the public fantasies embedded within popular cinema. In Freud's analyses, desire and the conflicts it spawns are related to narration in two ways. Subjects fabricate narratives in order to render the world amenable to their desires. Analysis sifts through these narratives, retrieving the subject's desires and conflicts which it returns to consciousness through another narrative. The analyst's task of "transforming hysterical misery to common unhappiness" in Freud's memorable phrase is accomplished by interpreting the double roles that stories play in simultaneously masking and revealing desires.[8]

Freud's basic framework for analyzing narratives has so shaped interpretive practices far outside the clinic that psychoanalysis has been called "the most influential and elaborate interpretive system of recent times . . . whose model and terms drawn from it are to be found strewn at great distance from their original source."[9] Disciplines such as folklore, literature, history, philosophy, politics, religion, film studies, and sociology use the general framework even when their focus may not be the subject but culture, or what the theorist Fredric Jameson termed its political unconscious. Concepts such as fantasy and the family romance initially developed in psychoanalysis to understand individual behavior have proved insightful in uncovering cultural and historical processes that might have remained invisible otherwise.[10] Many of *Bollywood's India*'s core terms such as public fantasy as well as its exposition of latent meanings behind a narrative's manifest content come from the interpretive framework developed in psychoanalysis and long at the center of narrative analysis in film and other media.

REMAKING INDIA I: THE 1970S

The social work of imagining India remains ongoing (a "daily plebiscite," as the philosopher Ernst Renan anticipated),[11] occurring in numerous places, not just in film. In the 1970s, as in the two decades immediately following Independence, political life dominated public culture and was the organizing topos for approaching much that occurred in India. Taking a cue from the political theorist Sudipta Kaviraj, this study conceives of the 1970s beyond the Emergency as the decade of Indira Gandhi. In this reading, the 1970s "begins" in 1966 with Mrs. Gandhi's appointment as prime minister and concludes in 1984 with her assassination. The political and economic context of a long 1970s exposes the waning of Nehruvian ideals, Mrs. Gandhi's centrist consolidation of power with its skillful division of the working poor and the middle classes, and the eventual fracture of Nehru's unifying vision. The Emergency so defines the decade that it remains the core point of orientation, though as chapter 2 elaborates, many of the long decade's convulsions were already apparent as early as the 1950s.

During the 1970s, when the very idea of India seemed to disintegrate, popular cinema more than any other form engaged the political unconscious of India in vital ways. Blockbusters from earlier decades such as the 1940s and 1950s also directly engaged in this project, but in these pre-crisis decades, public fantasies appeared largely consistent with the public and its conscious aspirations.[12] Observing India through these moments of optimism is one thing: grappling with it during a period of crisis is quite another. The India of the 1970s fundamentally transformed the future, but also, paradoxically, its past. After midnight, nothing looked the same again, neither the day that followed nor the one that preceded. The cinema of the 1950s could never again be regarded as it had been before, and one of the unintended legacies of the 1970s is that it changed utterly how the past was read.

"India" today is a product of conflicts and compromises between nation and state that occurred in the formative 1970s, underscoring just how profoundly the decade *made* India. Each chapter of the study anchors its core questions from the perspective of the 1970s. Each rethinks other decades from that vantage, as ways of understanding their future, but also as prologue to an inevitable if unforeseen crisis. Thus, chapter 2 on Nehru's presence in a triptych of films by Raj Kapoor is as much about the elation following Independence as about the anxieties bordering that elation that only become evident if read through eyes that lived through and insist on remembering the 1970s.

Despite the Emergency's dominance over the 1970s, silence about it—initially originating in official circles—has produced an elaborate mythology of the period but not much scholarly analysis.[13] In studying the decade, as the anthropologist Emma Tarlo discovered: "too recent to be of interest to historians yet too distant to have attracted the attention of other social scientists, it has somehow slipped through the net of academic disciplines."[14] *Bollywood's India* returns the decade to academic scrutiny in several ways. First, the book regards the decade's anxieties and aspirations—its public fantasies—as expressed in a number of popular blockbusters and exposes how fundamentally the decade created the terms that have come to define the idea of "India." Second, much of what followed the 1970s in political, social, and even economic culture is evidently an effort either to repress the decade altogether or to rewrite it. If the 1970s was a period of "India Falling" and "Garibi Hatao" ("Abolish poverty"), the 2000s and beyond are known for India Rising and India Shining, referencing election slogans that have been deployed at different post-liberalization political moments. If the cinema of the 1970s is dominated by images and preoccupations of the poor and indigent, the sunshine cinema (as Anupama Chopra ironically called it) of the nineties and noughties diegetically erases those figures altogether. The fasts in *Jai Santoshi Maa* (Hail, Goddess Santoshi, Vijay Sharma, 1975) have given way to *karwa chauth* feasts in *Dilwale Dulhaniya Le Jayenge* (aka, *DDLJ*, The man with the heart gets the bride, Aditya Chopra, 1995), and the poor and indigent are completely excised from the glittering cinema that purveyed India Shining to itself and the world (see chapter 4). The BJP's (Bharatiya Janata Party) 2004 electoral defeat surrounding its India Shining campaign was no surprise to a generation that had lived through the 1970s and still lived there in spirit if not in flesh. "Shining" for whom was the riposte, as working voters recoiled from the orgy of self-congratulation that ignored and eliminated them altogether.

Third, the 1970s saw a cleavage in the Nehruvian contract uniting middle with lower classes. Up to this point, there was a broad consensus among the classes to stand behind the idea of the nation promulgated at the center. But with two wars following Nehru's death in 1964 (with China in 1965 and Pakistan in 1971), a global oil crisis, 1 percent growth, widespread shortages of staple foods, runaway inflation, and trouble meeting debt payments, the consensus frayed. In blockbusters throughout the 1970s, the villain was always rich, Teflon-coated from prosecution, and often had some contact with the West. In short, he was everything the middle classes wanted to be in the dire decade. The poor, on the other hand, were everything the middle classes wished to disavow, by rejection, demonization, and eventually by betrayal. With a skillful sleight, Indira Gandhi's 1971 political slogan to exterminate poverty ("Garibi Hatao") became a practice to exterminate the poor ("Garib Hatao"). If the screen villain was the rich, the everyday problem was projected on the poor, and the real challenge was not a matter of "Garibi Hatao" but possibly "Garib Hatao." When the poor would not move, they would *be* moved as they were through slum relocations and forced sterilizations. Absent the protections of a constitution, these exterminations took place in plain view during the Emergency where they were conducted with the tacit consent of a middle class observing its own security and future evaporate in the desperate economic climate that surrounded the Emergency.[15]

The cinema of the 1970s was the last moment when the compact between the classes is still evident, though its rupture is equally evident in the period as blockbusters such as *Sholay* amplify (chapter 2).[16] This was still a decade when a middle-class policeman and a homeless knife sharpener could unite in common cause against a local crime boss (*Zanjeer* [Chains], Prakash Mehra, 1973) or when the slumdwellers of Bombay unhesitatingly donate blood to a genteel woman injured in an accident (*Amar Akbar Anthony*, Manmohan Desai, 1977). The cinema, like the society, gentrified shortly thereafter. Both became suffused with the preoccupations of the middle and aspiring middle classes with the poor almost entirely disappearing from mainstream screen attention.[17] "Much of India's upper-middle class," wrote the social theorist, Ashis Nandy, "is simply a lower-middle class with more money."[18] Through the 1970s, when money was in short supply, the social compact across the classes was still visible in the cinema as a set of shared cultural, social, and political solidarities. In the decade following economic liberalization in 1991, as chapter 4 elaborates, the "slum solidarity" that Nandy rhapsodizes gives way to a cinema screened far outside India's urban slums in suburban "malltiplexes" that disowned the poor as less amenable images of themselves and of India's modernity.[19] In this later cinema that I dub "Bollylite" (chapter 4), the angry hero of the 1970s becomes the affluent hero quite literally as Amitabh Bachchan is seamlessly refashioned from a renegade youth intent on destroying the social order (chapters 2 and 3) to a reactionary elder intent on upholding it (chapter 4).

REMAKING INDIA II: BOLLYWOOD

The tensions over class and class aspiration get condensed in a new term that came into being during the Emergency. Like the unruly economic and political order of the decade, the culture industry was remarkably unruly as well, though in contrast to the former, the film industry's turbulence was accompanied by a renaissance evident throughout India's cinemas. Observing the superficial chaos of this informal "industry," the British crime novelist H. R. F. Keating (who had never to the point visited the Subcontinent) coined the term "Bollywood" in an Inspector Ghote detective novel, and it started being used in the domestic Anglophone film press.[20] Other genealogies for the term have more recently been proffered, including one crediting a U.S. journalist and another an Indian for it.[21] The term was received with immediate opprobrium by figures within the Hindi film industry because it seemed to condemn the industry for being derivative. However, as the term got used more and more into the 1980s, the cinema itself increasingly became the object of condemnation by India's urban elites, without a sustained analysis of its popularity or social work.[22] Had Hindi cinema died the death augured in this condemnation, the term would likely have died as well. But with the influx of new capital and talent following economic liberalization in the 1990s, popular Hindi cinema was renewed, and the term "Bollywood" was revived as well. It now became used to designate not just the popular cinema of Bombay from the 1970s with its signature commitment to social and cultural politics, but any cinematic product associated with India. Writers using the term today have to remind readers of its reference to Bombay's Hindi cinema and not to "Indian" cinema more generally. Yet the slippage between the two is revealing, and "Bollywood" is often misunderstood to designate not a regional product but a national one. As the scholar Ashish Rajadhyaksha observes, a lot went into "nationalizing" this term—in having it represent India's global aspirations, but also having a singular cinema from Bombay stand in for a far larger and diverse set of cultural products that were never intended in the term.[23]

Today the term "Bollywood" has mutated considerably from its origins, as has the industry that gave rise to it. In the new millennium, the term "Bollywood" has risen alongside post-liberalization Hindi cinema both in its widespread usage as well as in the designation for an industry with renewed financing, energetic distribution, and global ambitions. Its current usage no longer refers to signature elements from the cinema of the 1970s such as a passionate commitment to pleasure and politics. Where current usage largely references form, *Bollywood's India* uses "Bollywood" to underscore content. It recalls the term's origin in the 1970s when the concepts of nation, class, and social solidarity were still widely shared, and the compact between them was still evident. "Bollywood" in this study refers to the tendency toward social responsiveness embedded in public culture. The term is not just limited to a historical phase as the scholar Sangita Gopal suggests in her taxonomy.[24] Rather, "Bollywood" includes both the popular cinema that predated its arrival in the lexicon and that succeeded it when those cinemas share its social tendencies. Chapter 4 elaborates on *why* Bollywood matters, and what happens when its social and political commitments are sheared from it. The term, thus, is as much about the formal qualities associated with the cinema as well as the political ambitions and public fantasies that these elements convey.

UNMAKING "INDIA"

Under Western eyes, Nehru and the early nationalists had seemingly few tools at hand for the task of publically imagining India. Print, which had been so powerful in shaping European nationalisms in the eighteenth and nineteenth centuries, seemed relatively irrelevant for India where literacy rates ranged between 3.5 percent in 1881 and 16.5 percent in 1947, a period of roughly seven decades that coincided with the most important phases of the nationalist movement. This is not to say that the newspaper and the novel, *pace* Benedict Anderson, were not important for imagining India's new national community. Rather, the literacy rates allow one to emphasize how unimportant print may have been to large parts of the Indian electorate. Despite this, India's large illiterate and semiliterate population has been and continues to be an avid participant in the nationalist project as it exercises its right to vote in far larger numbers than elsewhere in the democratic world.[25] Bracketing print, this book is about a more widely accessible cultural system that coincided with Indian nationalism, out of which as well as against which it came into being.

At no point can one claim that popular Hindi cinema created the nation. Rather, the blockbusters of the age are testament to some of the public fantasies that accompanied the national project. Their omissions and commissions occasionally converge upon broad public questions of the day; at other times, they diverge spectacularly from and even appear to reject the national imaginary. *Bollywood's India* examines India through film and film through the notion of "India."

"India" in particular bears some scrutiny. The impulse to fabricate a homogeneous entity has inevitably characterized its nationalist narratives and has persisted for good reason as the political theorist Sudipta Kaviraj elucidates:

> By its nature, this [early] conception of nationalism had to be homogenizing: what I mean by this inelegant term is that although these scholars were often conscious that people opposed the British with ideas that were differently inflected, grounded, expressed, coloured, stylized, motivated, the major purpose of the concept of nationalism was to point to their level of historical similarity. This does not necessarily deny the presence of other strata in these ideas or other possible and appropriate descriptions. But, clearly, what got emphasized (and not unwittingly, because this point was written into the historiographical programme) were the points of similarity, the sense in which all these Indians were doing the same thing with these ideas.[26]

Kaviraj's scholarship cautions against regarding the nation as a common destination to which all modern actors, regardless of origin, proceed with a common agenda, a prefabricated set of tools, and unvarying historical conformity. His insights help recall the many, often chaotic, strands that comprise "India" and its national narratives and also help clarify the discontinuities that persist in the fabrication of a national culture after the putative "triumph" of Independence. Not only are there varieties of India, much as there are varieties of capitalism or modernity or globalization, these varieties persist both geographically as well as historically within India.

The geographical variation—the internal distinctions between north, south, east, west, and center toward the nation—is tellingly thematized in Mani Ratnam's 1998 film, *Dil Se* (From the heart), in which Amar (*literally*, eternal), a New Delhi reporter for the state-sponsored All India Radio, interviews a separatist leader in an unnamed Northeastern state during the fiftieth anniversary of India's Independence. (Italicized text indicates words spoken in English during the exchange.)

> AMAR: What do you think of the last fifty years of India's freedom?
>
> LEADER: What freedom? We have no freedom.
>
> AMAR: Has free India made any progress?
>
> LEADER: No. The central government threatens us and keeps us cowed down. Atrocities are inflicted on the poor and the innocent. And you say we are free! Is this what freedom means?
>
> AMAR: What's your aim?
>
> LEADER: Freedom. *Independence.*
>
> AMAR: From whom?
>
> LEADER: Your government. Hindustan.
>
> AMAR: Why?
>
> LEADER: Fifty years ago, when India became independent, many promises were made to us. Not one was kept. We have been oppressed. You think Delhi is India. The states in the far-flung areas have no meaning for you. Because they are small not big. The center is concerned with big vote banks.
>
> AMAR: *Terrorism* . . .
>
> LEADER: We are not terrorists. We are revolutionaries.[27]

The leader's insistence that each term Amar uses has an entirely different meaning for his people comes through powerfully in the exchange. *Freedom, Independence, liberation,* even *terror,* occupy vastly different registers in the gulf separating the man from the center who thinks "Delhi is India" and the man from the Northeast who holds Delhi responsible for the oppression of his people. Much later in the film, Amar has the point condensed even further when the revolutionary with whom he has fallen in love retorts, "it's your nation, not mine," as she heads off to blow up the president during Delhi's Republic Day parade.

Geography, in the separatist's world, creates the chasm between a nation that can broadcast itself as "All India" and a state far removed from it. Geography for him creates not just spatial distance from the nation, but a linguistic and ideological one as well, a distance that renders unintelligible the fantasies put out by the state. Ironically, the national fantasies put out by the state, and even their pre-Independence acts of resistance, are reborn in Mani Ratnam's version of the Northeast conflict. Even as the leader disputes Amar's use of terms, they are some of the very ones he embraces for his cause.

> LEADER: We have no freedom . . . Is this what freedom means?
> AMAR: What's your aim?
> LEADER: Freedom. *Independence.*

Ratnam's film, perhaps more sharply than most, plays out the varieties of nationalism conveyed in the term "India." Not all nationalisms converge, nor do they all convey the same fantasies. Some, such as the one from this exchange, seek out alternatives to the geographical entity current around the state.

Beyond the variations in space, there are the variations of "India" played out across time. The exchange from *Dil Se* focuses on two historical strands: the radio reporter sees the Independence jubilee as a celebration of accomplishments visible today while the leader recalls the present as evidence of betrayals from the past. His "today" is shaped by what did not take place in the fifty years of Independence; the reporter's "today" by what did. Like the blind man's elephant, the "India" one sees both in film and in discourse changes shape and identity depending on where and when and who touches it. The discontinuities often coexist, and the cinema captures them.

By the 1970s, the India one encounters in popular Hindi cinema is largely preoccupied with problems internal to it such as labor unrest, poverty, urban decay, economic stagnation, and political corruption. By the 1990s, another "present" arrives with irrational exuberance, initiated by economic liberalization and the return of a muscular Hinduism. The West is not only no longer an object of oppression or fear as it was in the long 1970s (*Around the World in Eight Dollars*, S. Pachhi, 1967, captures this trepidation in its title). It is now a source of renewed economic wealth and ideological certitude supporting both economic and religious ideologies of the post-liberalization state.

A more recent present might be "India Now," the banner announcing the country as a global economic powerhouse at the 2006 World Economic

Forum in Davos that launched an "India Everywhere" campaign to draw attention to the country as a destination for foreign investment.[28] The new millennium has seen India's economic muscle evident in an unmistakably public way with multinational corporations such as Reliance Media bailing fabled Hollywood icons such as Steven Spielberg's DreamWorks and MGM, and the Tata Group acquiring British marquee brands such as Jaguar. If predictions by Goldman Sachs and the *Financial Times* prove accurate, India's growth is poised to rank it with elite G6 producers by 2025.[29]

Alongside the creation of multiple Indias off disparate temporal strands is inevitably the presence of different attitudes toward the past. Hindi film with its insistently "modern" technologies of production symbolically elicits and projects different modernities of content at different moments. Watching hits from the 1950s such as Raj Kapoor's *Awara* (1951) and *Shree 420* (The gentleman cheat, 1955), or Guru Dutt's *Mr. and Mrs. 1955*, the Indian "modern" is revealed as a confidently cosmopolitan and sophisticated figure, at ease with Western-style nightclubs and clothing, automobiles, and forms of address. The coexistence of "India" with a West, however fictional, is neither a problem nor a source of tension. By the 1970s, cosmopolitanism may have become acceptable but the West had not, and most screen villains from the period were figures recently returned from the West or headed to it. To be "modern" was to be largely suspect by the small-town core bent on capturing the metropolis itself. By the 1990s, however, cosmopolitanism gets refashioned as does the West. Neither is quite rejected though both are considerably indigenized. The West by this point exists as a space conquered by the diasporic Indian who confidently commands its economic resources in the form of brand-name material acquisitions. In a faintly ironic form of reverse colonization, "foreign" in these modes is largely a scenic backdrop, almost exclusively populated by Indians all in tune with a homogeneous homeland and its elaborate dance steps.[30] India in this narrative fantasy provides unblemished "values," and the non-resident Indian (or NRI) returns "home" frequently to imbibe from this well, usually by wedding an all-too-willing beauty among Punjab's abundant mustard fields, a theme played out most prominently in Aditya Chopra's *DDLJ*. In this iteration, to be "modern" is to assimilate "traditional" social values seamlessly alongside "contemporary" values of economic accumulation and conspicuous consumption.

In the very brief sketches of some "presents" that have come to constitute India's "pasts," two matters become evident. First, different histories constitute "India." At different junctures India constitutes itself by eliciting and projecting different notions of its modernity that themselves braid different attitudes toward the past and future. In this chutney of representations developed both internally and externally across and within time and space, it becomes abundantly clear that no monolithic dream can capture "India." Nehru's insistence on the plural—"to give reality to our dreams"—attests in a small but revealing way to his recognition of the complexity of the process. Bollywood's blockbusters viewed in the dark by over twelve million Indians a day purvey not a single dream but multiple ones, and some of the thematic clusters around which they constellate are the subject of this book.

THE BOOK IN HAND

This is a book about Bollywood's India. Its main preoccupation is with the iconographies of the nation embedded in the cinema's blockbusters. It does not argue that Bollywood created the political entity that is India. Rather, its focus is on Bollywood's *commentary* on the entity that is India, a commentary on an India both fictional and real, mythic and palpable whose contours resemble those of a political and social entity recognizable to social scientists and historians. No story of India could begin better than the nation-state's. Created by pen on August 15, 1947, it is a myth that the novelist Salman Rushdie describes as "a fable rivaled only by the two other mighty fantasies: money and God."[31] The blockbusters of this study engage with some of India's public fantasies. Many others (such as sexuality, terror, and devotion, to name a few) find only passing mention in the chapters. This silence is not meant to signal that these issues are insignificant but simply that they are parts of conversations occurring elsewhere.

The pages that follow acknowledge that making, unmaking, and remaking the idea of India echo similar currents occurring in the Bombay film industry as well. Thus, the 1950s were not just a period of Nehruvian adoration. The decade also observed the post-studio era of independent producers and the arrival of rogue capital. Meanwhile, any account of the 1970s as a decade of political crisis would need to acknowledge that this degraded political moment occurred alongside an extraordinary revitalization in India's cinemas with the consolidation of a state-supported alternative cinema; an energetic middle-cinema that flourished alongside the commercial industry; the arrival of graduates from the Film and Television Institute of India (founded in 1960) who brought new talent in acting, directing, cinematography, and writing to all India's cinemas; and the arrival of television, to name some major currents.[32] In the aftermath of economic liberalization, the 1990s were characterized by the state's recognition of cinema as an industry in 1998; the influx of corporate capital; new forms of digital filmmaking and editing; the incursion of the multiplex in 1997 and its rapid expansion into large and medium cities; a burst of new media platforms and formats that revolutionized funding, production, and distribution; and global marketing strategies that interpellated overseas viewers through narrative content and language. Recent scholarship on Hindi cinema that researches industry practices—notably, labor, hardware, distribution, and financing—supports the core arguments of this book, but the present study is not fundamentally about the workings of the industry.[33]

Bollywood's India focuses instead on the narratives embedded in popular Hindi cinema. With their dense and layered mise-en-scènes, the stories *are* the cinema, even as new cameras, locations, editing, and financing enable core "stories" to be shot, edited, distributed, and screened differently in the present moment than they were half a century or more ago. The genres of these stories, the modes in which they are narrated, the performance of song and the substance of their lyrics convey layers of meaning that this study's interpretive practices analyze. The multiple texts that constitute this cinema are read closely alongside the material conditions that accompanied their production and consumption. The focus at all times is on the narrative structures within the cinema and on procedures and cues inscribed in these structures. A number of well-studied films such as *Awara* and *Deewaar* (The wall, Yash Chopra, 1975) are paired alongside those less frequently analyzed such as *Ab Dilli Dur Nahin* (Delhi is not far now, Amar Kumar, 1957) and *Shakti* (Power, Ramesh Sippy, 1982).

Chapter 2, "Cinema and Public Fantasy," explores the shifting grammar of public fantasies captured in attitudes toward crime and punishment in a triptych of Raj Kapoor's films spanning the period of Nehru's administration till his death in 1964, and *Sholay* (1975), one of Hindi cinema's biggest grossers at the box office. In the representation of crime and its punishment, the new nation most visibly revealed its ideals and its idealism. In selecting and depicting a particular kind of crime, in fashioning and eventually reforming a particular kind of criminal, post-Independence Hindi film did much in articulating the fantasies of a newly created citizenry over a social contract still under review.

In chapter 3, "Cinema as Family Romance," the biological family and the symbolic nation-as-family become sites of mutual threat in 1970s Hindi cinema, each destabilizing the other in cinema's representation of the period. The chapter analyzes *Deewaar*'s (1975) tensions at narrating and containing an incendiary critique of the decade, and it exposes the revisions to this film's master plot as they were rescripted in *Trishul* (Trident, Yash Chopra, 1978) and *Shakti* (1982). Through a reading of these blockbusters, the chapter explores the extent to which the traumas of the decade were displaced on the family and the crisis in political culture was recast in so-cial terms as a Family Romance in popular Hindi film. In this inversion, the oppositional culture of political life is represented as infecting private life as well, and both are rendered combustible. Freud's concept of Family Romance allows one to probe the work that particularly popular narratives do in a specific cultural moment and to ask what traumas they mask, what "reality" they seek liberation from, and what kinds of fantasies a culture develops in the process. Above all, the scrutiny of Family Romance in a society enables one to uncover the structure and function of narratives that were particularly popular and to ask what kinds of unconscious they convey and conceal.

Chapter 4, "Bollywood, Bollylite," reckons with Hindi cinema's global ambitions and analyzes what gets lost when Bollywood's politics are sheared from it in anticipation of its travels worstward. It begins by asking if *Slumdog Millionaire*'s (Danny Boyle, 2008) commercial and critical suc-cess in the U.S. market might have created a wider appetite for the Oscar winner's "ancestors" from Bollywood. In an effort to address the question of Bombay cinema's penetration into the U.S. mainstream, the chapter ar-gues that the germane issue is not the influx of Bombay cinema *en masse* onto America's screens but rather the *specific* forms from Bombay that have been able to capture the interest of mainstream audiences in the United States. This form is such a major departure from the internal conventions of Bollywood that it is more properly understood as a separate concept I identify as "Bollywood Lite," or Bollylite. Bollylite, I argue, is a relatively re-cent fabrication that heavily pillages formal characteristics from the Bolly-wood cinema that *Slumdog Millionaire* honors while shearing much of that cinema's fabled social substance and political edge. Thus lightened, Bolly-lite travels—though, in contrast to Bollywood—with a remarkably limited commercial and critical half-life. Observing Bollylite's fortunes and the ma-terial conditions that produce it allows one to capture the stubbornness of Bollywood's cultural product. The chapter contrasts the narrative logics separating Bollywood from Bollylite and offers remarks about their respec-tive futures, recognizing that Bollylite is a commercial as well as industrial phenomenon tied to forms of financing and distribution that are undergo-ing considerable transformation both in India and globally.

"Epilogue: Anthem for a New India" outlines the extent to which the book's core arguments continue to resonate with the industry as it is de-veloping. It sketches current trends in the cinema and acknowledges some of the challenges of speaking about "Bollywood" and "public fantasy" when both are ongoing phenomena. Notwithstanding the mutations in cinema enabled by twenty-first-century technologies, Bollywood cinema's core impulse toward social responsiveness remains. As in the previous half century, today as well certain films easily penetrate the firewalls of a carefully niched marketplace to reach viewers. Bollywood blockbusters in the new millennium rescript the social purpose of popular cinema through unexpected means, including the unlikely figure of M. K. Gandhi. As an illustration, Rajkumar Hirani's blockbusters, *Lage Raho Munnabhai* (Keep at it, Munnabhai, 2006) and *3 Idiots* (2009), depict an India characterized by land-grabs and global corporate ambition run amok. The cinema selectively retrieves past Gandhian practices against the colonial state in order to articulate alternatives to the ongoing vortex of social and economic neoliberalism. Abstracted from history, both Nehru, who frames the body of this study, and Gandhi, in the "Epilogue," serve as devices for the cinema to address a "New" India that both resembles and restores the "Old."

2

CINEMA AS PUBLIC FANTASY

THERE IS A FAMOUS PHOTOGRAPH of Jawaharlal Nehru taken in 1963 with three of Bombay cinema's most legendary figures: the actor, producer, and director, Raj Kapoor; and the period's two other reigning screen idols, Dilip Kumar and Dev Anand (fig. 2.1). The stars were attending a fundraiser organized by the National Defence Committee in New Delhi at which Nehru was present. As was typical of the man whose movie-star good looks and personal style rivaled any leading man's, Nehru had a special affinity for the Bombay industry, and lore is that he invited the matinee idols to his official residence at Teen Murti Bhavan where the photo was taken. Not long thereafter, on May 27, 1964, Nehru died. His legacy, though, was secure in the hands of these men. As Raj Kapoor affirmed in a reminiscence of Nehru: "Pandit-ji said that he wanted every Indian in this country to do something for the nation, to build it up into the beautiful dream that he had. He was a visionary and I tried to follow him, to do my best, whatever I could, through films" (as recorded in Kak 1987; also quoted in Nanda 1991:74).

Kapoor was not the only bearer of Nehru's dream, though he may have been one of its most influential. Film was his medium, and he reached millions in the blockbusters he wrote, directed, acted in, and produced. However, notwithstanding the filmmaker's personal admiration for Nehru and his family's close ties with the prime minister, Kapoor's work can hardly be characterized as singularly focused on "building . . . the beautiful dream [Nehru] had." In fact, as this chapter shows, Kapoor's cinema intersected only briefly with what might be called the Nehruvian dream. Equally quickly, it diverged from it to expose the many social fissures and political corruptions that rendered that "dream" a figment of midnight, largely unavailable in the clear light of day.

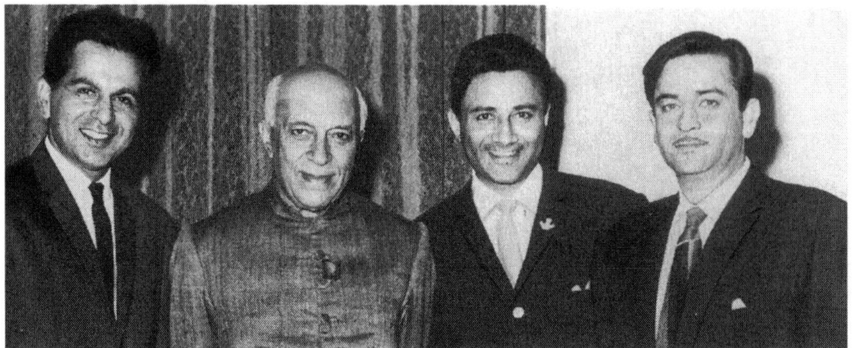

FIGURE 2.1 *Left to right:* Dilip Kumar, Jawaharlal Nehru, Dev Anand, and Raj Kapoor (January 1963).

Kapoor's respect for the first Prime Minister aside, his cinema had its own mission. "I want my pictures," he explained in a 1956 interview, "to portray faithfully the life and times in which we live."[1] Hindi cinema likewise insisted upon its independence from New Delhi, and at no point did the obstreperous industry serve as a blind propaganda machine for the center.[2] Yet Kapoor's remarks on Nehru's charisma remind one that from an early and formative stage the Indian film industry aligned—if not allied—itself with the nation ("to invite [the spectator's] attention to problems which have contemporary relevance" insisted Kapoor).[3] Cinema's arrival and development in India coincided with the emergence of Indian nationalism and the birth of the nation. To those who could not read or did not understand Nehru's cinematically evocative "tryst with destiny" speech in 1947, Hindi film provided its own dreamscape of India. In a series of wildly popular blockbusters, the cinema imagined the social geography of India, tackled its problems, and addressed their solutions. As the political theorist Sunil Khilnani observes, "such films dramatized in a diffuse but evocative way a democratic outward-looking and secular nationalist sentiment."[4] While Kapoor identifies the nation as Nehru's dream ("the dream that *he* had"), this chapter makes clear that Kapoor's most popular films—and others made in Bombay generally—at different moments commented, critiqued, and even revised those dreams in significant ways. Nehru may have been the visionary that Kapoor set out to extol, but his fellow citizens also had their own visions that the cinema captured. At their broadest, the blockbusters of Bombay reveal the many nations to be conjured by "India." They explain both the ideals of the nation as well as its anxieties. Rather than representing a unity, these blockbusters provide a plurality, clarifying but also confounding the world of which cinema remains part.

This chapter explores a very specific aspect of these larger questions of nation-building and social cohesion. It analyzes dramatic changes in attitudes toward crime and punishment in the most popular Hindi films that were made in two crucial moments in the nation's development: those from the so-called Golden Fifties, that immediate post-Independence moment when the victories of the liberation struggle were unblemished by subsequent betrayals; and a blockbuster released during the 1975 Emergency when the myth of the nation seemed to have evaporated along with due process, civil liberties, and adherence to constitutional law.

In the representation of crime and its punishment, the new nation most visibly revealed its ideals and its idealism. Memories of the large-scale violence of Partition undoubtedly underwrote the desire for a social order that could guarantee civic tranquility. Hindi film collaborated in this project, creating villains and heroes in an apparently endless confection that seemed to provide some form of entertainment and edification for all its different audiences. In selecting and depicting a particular kind of crime, in fashioning and eventually reforming a particular kind of criminal, post-Independence Hindi blockbusters did much in articulating the fantasies of a newly created citizenry for what constituted acceptable social behavior and asserting the mechanisms that would reproduce the good and reform the criminal.

For many, it is a cinema characterized by three things: musicals, dancicals, and fightsicals.[5] "We don't make talkies," Girish Karnad dismissed in a 2003 interview with the author. "We make singies." Until relatively recently, most observers evaluated this cultural product accordingly, dismissing it as a saccharine cocktail of elements that characterize escape and fantasy. Taking a cue from Gramsci that all popular forms provide fantasy and illusions, this chapter probes the particular public fantasies embedded in Hindi cinema.[6] Like the private fantasies of individuals, the public fantasies of a collective can be conscious (i.e., willed by the collective just as daydreams are by the individual), or unconscious (requiring interpretation to uncover), or they can be somewhere in between. Fantasies might express a desire for wish fulfillment ("to build up the nation" as Nehru expressed) or a defense against an unpleasant reality (by offering an "escape" from it). They might provide real solutions to imaginary problems, or imaginary solutions to real ones. And they might render reality palatable either by exposing it, or by covering it up.

Fantasies, in short, are a device for managing desire. They vary by *what* they seek (namely, their purpose: cover-up or exposure), in *how* they seek it (namely, their function: conscious or unconscious), and *when* they seek it (namely, at what specific time). Fantasies might conceal, reveal, revise, or renew desires, sometimes all at the same time. They have a logic that is consistent if not always coherent, and a mise-en-scène designed to dramatize desire and resolution. To understand fantasies requires the tools of analysis and interpretation. Properly used, these tools provide a way to unearth desires and to understand them better without reducing their complexity or coherence.

The Hindi film blockbusters that this chapter studies with their enduring popularity convey a set of conscious and unconscious public fantasies that condense on the idea of India. These public fantasies throw into broad relief the psychic geography of Indian nationalism at its apex in the 1950s and its nadir during the Emergency in the 1970s, two moments when the idea of India was under particular scrutiny. A reading of these blockbusters provides a way to analyze some of the public fantasies conveyed during notably fraught moments of national self-definition.

The chapter proceeds in three parts. The first elaborates on attitudes toward crime and punishment depicted in a triptych of Raj Kapoor's blockbusters spanning the period of Nehru's administration in the 1950s till his death in 1964, addressing a massively popular filmmaker's engagement and disengagement with Nehru's beautiful dream. The second part explores popular cinema's depiction of crime and justice during the Emergency captured in Ramesh Sippy's blockbuster, *Sholay* (1975). Finally, the conclusion analyzes the ways in which Hindi popular cinema exposes public fantasies and revises the notion of "India" across the first quarter century following Independence.

"TWO DYNASTIES THAT RULE THE NATION'S POPULAR IMAGINATION"

Raj Kapoor built a film empire in Bombay from his family's modest origins in Peshawar. Fair-skinned, blue-eyed, dashing and cosmopolitan, with impeccable diction in Hindi and English and a perfect ear and eye for beauty, Kapoor wrote, directed, acted in, and produced films that played before enthusiastic audiences in most parts of the world. He has been called the great showman with a reputation unrivaled in Indian cinema and "the monarch of Indian cinema's royal family."[7] To speak of the Golden Fifties is to speak first of Raj Kapoor before contemporaries such as Guru Dutt or Bimal Roy, both of whom were publicly respected but never popularly revered to the extent Kapoor continues to be today. Even Kapoor's critics grudgingly acknowledge his Midas touch for creating entertaining and purposeful films for half a century.

Of the three most successful films at the box office from the 1950s, two were Raj Kapoor's: *Awara* (The vagabond, 1951) and *Shree 420* (The gentleman cheat, 1955).[8] Both films played in packed movie houses and continue to circulate among audiences in India and overseas (notably the former Soviet Union, the Middle East, East and southern Africa, parts of Latin America, East and Southeast Asia). A 2002 Andrew Lloyd Weber musical, *Bombay Dreams*, paid homage to Kapoor's blockbusters: Weber's heroine too pulls the protagonist back to Bombay in a scene borrowed from the ending of *Shree 420*, and the play is rife with dialogue from *Awara*, including the signature line, "it's not you; it's my face." More recently, a 2011 retrospective during the Toronto International Film Festival claimed Kapoor "the biggest superstar in Indian cinema," and the neighboring city of Brampton named a street after him.[9]

As a young filmmaker, Raj Kapoor's respect for Nehru was both intellectual and personal. His father Prithviraj was a close friend of the Prime Minister's who saw in the renowned stage actor an ally and a cultural envoy whom he deputed for cultural missions and later nominated as a Member of Parliament to the Rajya Sabha. The connections between the families, both symbolic and real, continued for several generations and had one biographer observe that "the Nehru-Gandhis and the Kapoors are two dynasties that rule the nation's popular imagination."[10] In a sense, both Nehru and Kapoor might be credited with publicly imagining powerful fantasies for India in the post-Independence period, fantasies that resonated with a broad public if not always with each other. In an *oeuvre* spanning half a century and over seventy productions that is equal parts entertainment and edification, melodrama and melancholy, Kapoor created a powerful mythography of India that was—and remains—simultaneously an elaboration of and an alternative to the prevailing myth of the nation promulgated by Nehru.

Called a "romantic nationalist" by one biographer (Madhu Jain 92), Kapoor's work falls into three main phases in which the "nation" was always a presence however romanticized, even when it was spectral at best. In the 1940s, *Aag* (Fire, 1948), Kapoor's breakthrough hit, barely addressed Partition even as trainloads of mutilated bodies were crossing an incomprehensible new border and survivors were making their way to his family's Matunga flat. Youth and romance defined this early body of work that included Kapoor's disquisition on love and the artist in *Barsaat* (Rain, 1949), his first major box office success. The 1950s brought new themes into focus: *Awara* (1951) and *Shree 420* (1955) comprise his most direct paeans to Nehru's "dream." The tenth anniversary of Independence saw films like *Ab Dilli Dur Nahin* (Delhi is not far now, Amar Kumar, produced by Kapoor, 1957) that, along with *Pyaasa* (The thirsty one, Guru Dutt, 1957) and

Mother India (Mehboob Khan, 1957), were direct invocations of Nehru (who is scripted as a character in *Dilli*) even as they were beginning to catalog the corrupt social and political system that even Nehru could not fix. By the time color entered Kapoor's *oeuvre* with *Sangam* (Union, 1964), so did spectacle, and the third phase of his work replaces a national vision with social commentary alongside eye-popping visuals and button-popping bosoms.[11]

In key ways, the man described as "mostly apolitical"[12] and "no great ideologue" was nevertheless not "allergic to ideas" as Kapoor's collaborator, the Communist writer K. A. Abbas, noted of him.[13] In Kapoor's public mythography of India in the 1950s, two central ideas circulate: the nature of crime and efforts to reform it; and the predicament of the "little man" caught in a hostile social world. Kapoor neither owned these themes nor was he their sole exemplar. He was, however, their most popular explicator. Kapoor so defined the issue of crime and punishment in the 1950s, especially with *Awara* and *Shree 420*, that every treatment since is noted either as a departure from his vision (*Sholay*) or an elaboration of it (*Satya* [Truth, Ram Gopal Verma, 1998]). A triptych of Kapoor's works from the 1950s captures the alternating fantasies of a society seeking social and legal justice as well as its anxieties of betrayal. In its expression of conscious desires and unconscious fears, the triptych conveys both Nehru's "beautiful dream" and the increasing limits of the dream as the euphoria from Independence receded before the challenges of building a just society. The triptych inevitably conveys optimism and disenchantment. More crucially, it also conveys ways of *managing* optimism and disenchantment as fantasies so critically do.

SHREE 420

Shree 420 centrally addresses the presence of crime and the many avenues of containing it. The film takes its title from an article in the Indian Penal Code under which cheats and frauds are prosecuted. In Hindi today as in the 1950s, the number 420 is used both as a verb and a noun to designate behavior just on the other side of the law. The film opens with a penniless protagonist, Raj, who will shortly turn into a 420, walking from Allahabad to Bombay hoping to hitch a ride. Frustrated because no one will stop for him, he pretends to faint on the roadside. Within seconds, he is offered refuge in the car of a wealthy Bombay businessman and real estate developer, Sonachand Dharmanand (the name literally means "Gold and Silver, Happy Religion"), and the family wonders what caused Raj's state.

Dharmanand thinks Raj must have collapsed on the roadside because of starvation. His daughter breathlessly mourns that Raj must be love-struck.

Mrs. Dharmanand ripostes that Raj is probably a thug (*uthai-gira*), best left by the roadside where he belongs. These three responses to the unknown Raj reveal the range of middle-class attitudes in recently decolonized India toward the anonymous migrant, the working underclass, and the starving. Dharmanand's conviction of Raj's poverty is an astute one borne of exploitative capital. In recognizing Raj's hunger, Dharmanand perceives in Raj one more laborer who will work for subsistence pay in his booming real estate business. The daughter's fantasy of Raj as lovesick speaks of a world of postcolonial youth engulfed in romantic fantasies. Mrs. Dharmanand's suspicions and severity mark the complacence of a class that criminalizes the migrant and the poor with scant concern. Her attitude toward Raj stands in for that part of the social order that the film implicitly seeks to reform.

In the course of the film, Raj travels to fulfill these three fantasies of his social destiny: the starving, the lovesick, and the criminal. He desperately searches for and fails to find an honest job. He falls in love with a beautiful schoolteacher, Vidya (played by Kapoor's then-lover, Nargis), and hopes to have a home with her. He becomes a hustler in high-end card games at Bombay's Taj Hotel, then a con artist in a complex stock fraud in a precious gold mining company (fig. 2.2), then the marketer of a fraudulent housing-scheme to the very street people who had once housed him on the sidewalk when he had nowhere to go (fig. 2.3).

However, Raj Kapoor redeems his character from his criminal pursuits at the end. In a marvelous inversion predictable from the early scene of misrecognition in the car, Raj and Sonachand Dharmanand change places. In the tense shoot-out at the end of the film in which he is first killed then reborn, Raj reveals the businessman's villainy in devising scheme after scheme to defraud his investors and the poor alike in which Raj is himself trapped against his wishes. If Raj is a 420, he comes nowhere near Dharmanand's order of criminality augured early in the film in the businessman's car's license, 840 (figs. 2.4 and 2.5).

The dénouement occurs when the police and the poor together storm Dharmanand's mansion and take him and his corrupt cronies off in handcuffs. Raj abandons Dharmanand's get-rich-quick seductions and delivers a moving speech to the homeless masses whom he had almost swindled out of their life's savings. The film adumbrates the message that solidarity and honesty will prevail over the ways of unscrupulous and exploitative capitalism.

In reinstating Raj's essentially socialist and humanist solutions to the problems spawned by urbanization, unemployment, migrancy, and homelessness, *Shree 420* articulates a discomfort with capitalist modernity and its economic structures (banks, real estate developments, gold speculation,

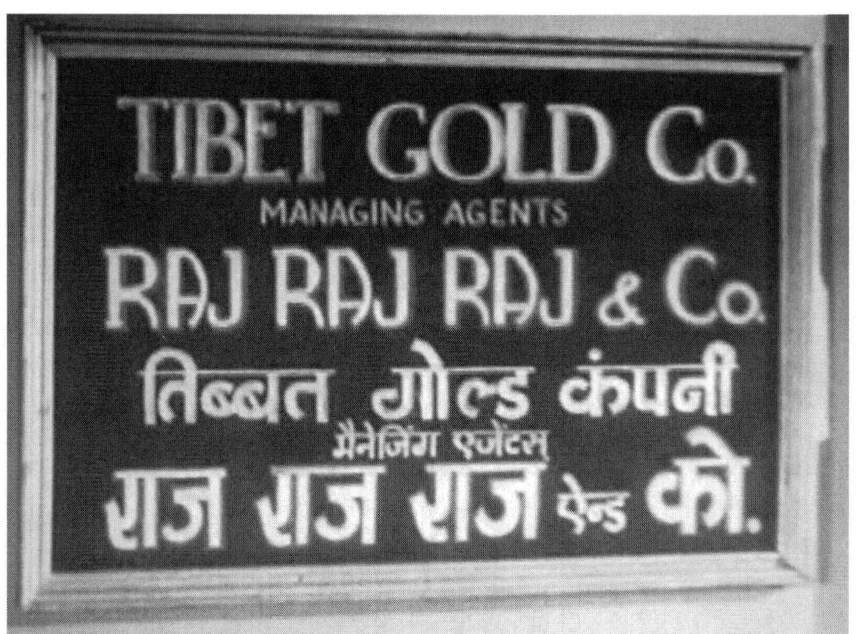

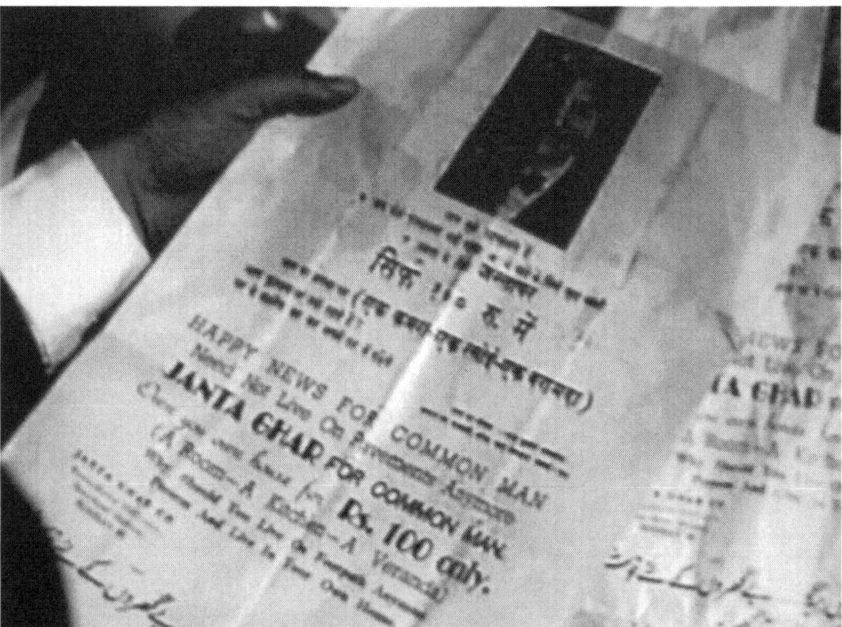

FIGURES 2.2 AND 2.3 Raj's criminal enterprises in *Shree 420* (1955) include a stock scam in a gold mining concern and a fraudulent housing scheme ("Janta Ghar") that defrauds his fellow footpath dwellers.

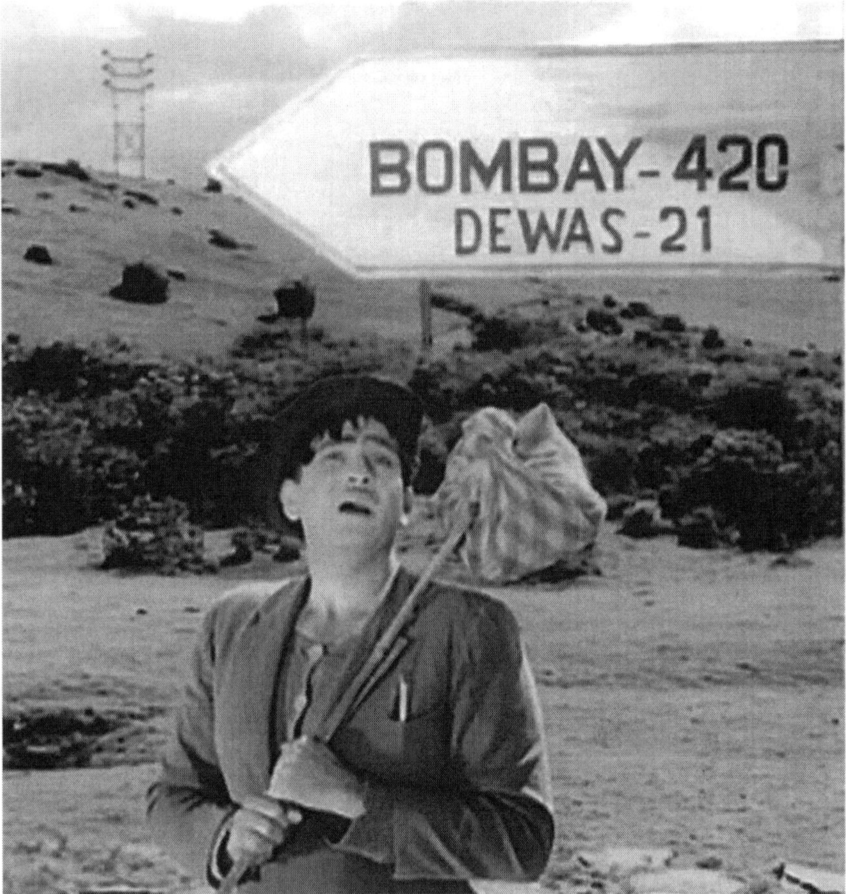

FIGURE 2.4 Raj Kapoor under the "Bombay 420" marker in *Shree 420*.

(COURTESY YASH RAJ FILMS)

venture capital). Its resolution reinstates premodern, pro-socialist solutions and values (solidarity, collective ownership, community, honesty) into what is represented as an increasingly alienating economic landscape. In the film's resolution, Sonachand Dharmanand is the real villain not just because he defrauds innocent people (Raj does this as well). Dharmanand is the villain because he manipulates capitalism's manifold technologies first to perpetuate, then to mask widespread treachery and fraud ("it's your signature on the stock certificates, not mine," Dharmanand slyly warns Raj when the latter tries to exit his schemes).

In displacing crime from the fraud alluded to in the 420 of the title to capitalist modernity, the film gives voice and name to its audience's

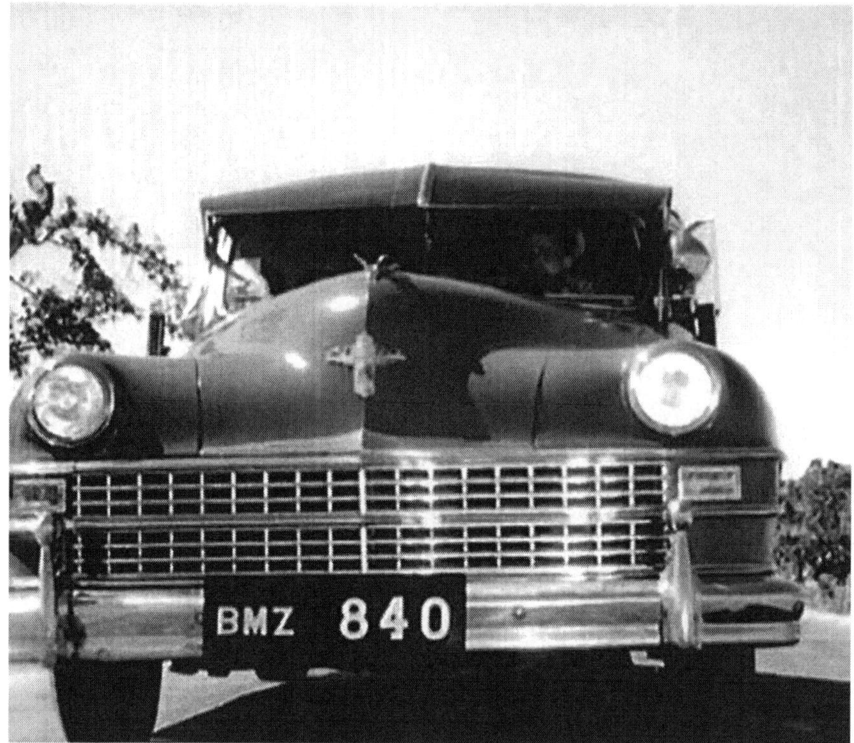

FIGURE 2.5 Sonachand Dharmanand's automobile (BMZ 840) in *Shree 420*.

(COURTESY YASH RAJ FILMS)

unnamed apprehensions, projects them on screen, and dissolves them through the compensatory satisfaction of seeing Dharmanand led out of court in handcuffs, presumably to serve time in prison. Meanwhile, *Shree 420* restores Raj to its audience's affections. He redeems the honesty-medal (*imandari ka enam*) that he had pawned shortly after arriving in Bombay, and he wonders whether he should stay in the city with Vidya or return to his hometown, Allahabad.

Raj's origins in Allahabad are hardly accidental, nor is Allahabad referenced as a stand-in for a generic anytown (as E. M. Forster, for example, intended with the fictional Chandrapore in *A Passage to India*). Allahabad was Nehru's birthplace, a city deeply associated with him and with his particular vision of harmony among difference. Situated by the confluence of three major rivers (Ganga, Yamuna, and Saraswati), Allahabad is known for the view of this coming together (or *sangam*), which became a major aspect of Nehru's—and Kapoor's—vision for modern India as a place of coexistence amongst different faiths, ideologies, and practices. Kapoor honored the concept of *sangam* in a blockbuster of the same name (*Sangam*, 1964) with its hit single "Bol, Radha, bol . . . sangam hoga ki nahin" (say Radha, will a union happen or not?), riffing on the union between two very different lovers whom the song compares to Ganga and Yamuna.

In other Hindi films, characters associated with Nehru's vision of tolerance and *sangam* get similarly marked, such as the poet, Akbar Allahabadi, played by Kapoor's son, Rishi, in *Amar Akbar Anthony* (Manmohan Desai, 1977). In that blockbuster, the poet's name recalls both a late-nineteenth-century nationalist poet as well as the sixteenth-century Mughal emperor Akbar, who built a major fort in Allahabad and whose political legacies include due process and access to legal recourse, much as Nehru would insist for modern India. In Manmohan Desai's version, Nehru's political and social vision has its origins in Emperor Akbar's legacy. Desai's character Akbar Allahabadi effortlessly combines religions in worship, uses poetry for persuasion rather than his fists, and is frequently seen wearing a Nehru jacket with a red rose (fig. 2.6), much like the Prime Minister in popular iconography.[14]

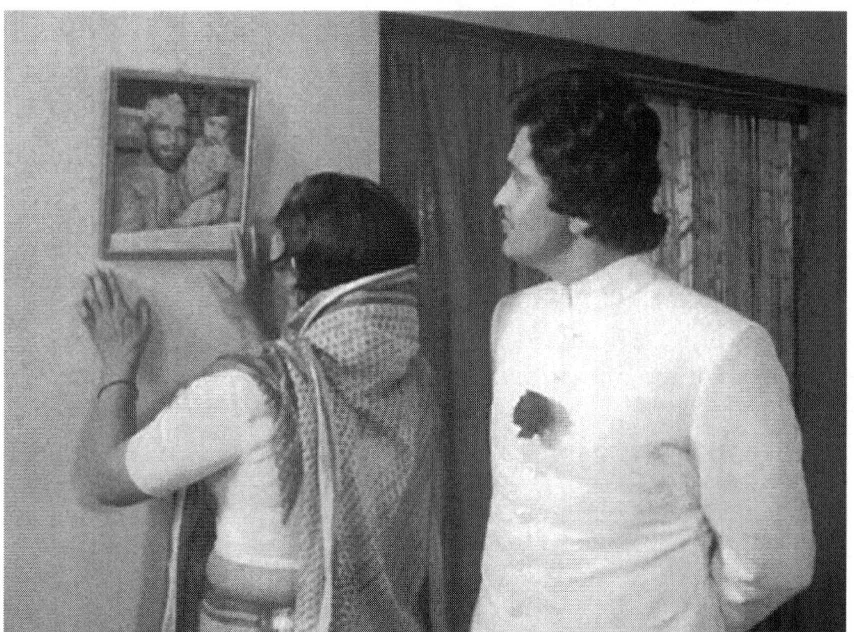

FIGURE 2.6 Rishi Kapoor in white Nehru jacket and red rose as Akbar Allahabadi in *Amar Akbar Anthony* (1977).

(COURTESY DEI ENTERTAINMENT)

Thus, for Raj in *Shree 420* to "return" to Allahabad or to stay in Bombay is not just a choice between past and future, origin and destination. It is also a political and philosophical conundrum: whether and how to carry one's origins into a new, modern future—and how that markedly different future might harmoniously blend with a markedly different past, much as Allahabad's rivers seem to in their *sangam*.

Shree 420 ends with this dilemma—a serious one under any circumstance, providing the once-penniless migrant with the luxury of choice. And the rhetoric of choice is exactly what the films of the Golden Fifties purveyed: the right to choose the kind of nation India was to be and to choose its means of achieving this national destiny. One choice *Shree 420* poses is between Dharmanand's exploitative capitalism or Raj's soft socialism coded as 840 vs. 420. It was a rhetoric that underwrote a narrative of empowerment that Hindi film as public fantasy extended to every strata in Indian society, even to those forced to live below or outside its borders.

In Kapoor's earlier blockbuster, *Awara* (1951), a petty criminal, again named Raj, is saved from the gallows by the passionate appeal of his lawyer and lover, played by Nargis, who places half the blame for Raj's attempt at murder on the father who long ago abandoned his wife and unborn son. Instead, Raj is sentenced to three years in prison. As he bids farewell to his lawyer-lover, Raj rejects his earlier life of crime and embraces his sentence for the choices it provides:

RAJ: I need this punishment. I'll deserve you [Nargis] only once I've served my time in prison. I'll be good. People will respect me. I'll read. Study. As my mother dreamed, first I'll become a lawyer, then a magistrate. Then a judge.

It is not just Raj's belief in the criminal justice system that is striking (the sense that prison can fully reform him) but rather the particular fantasy *Awara* so effortlessly deploys. Not content to reform the criminal and reintegrate him into society, the film's fantasy insists that only by becoming his exact opposite in the social spectrum can the criminal be fully redeemed. Not content to be good and read and study, Raj has to choose to become a judge in order to win society's respect—and presumably to reform other 420s like himself.

For this project of reform, to an extent never screened before or since, *Awara* places complete faith in the newly formed institutions of civil society. It depicts these institutions as blind to the claims of caste and privilege, capable of delivering justice within laws that are both fair and just. The court scenes in *Awara* are amongst its most inspiring and optimistic

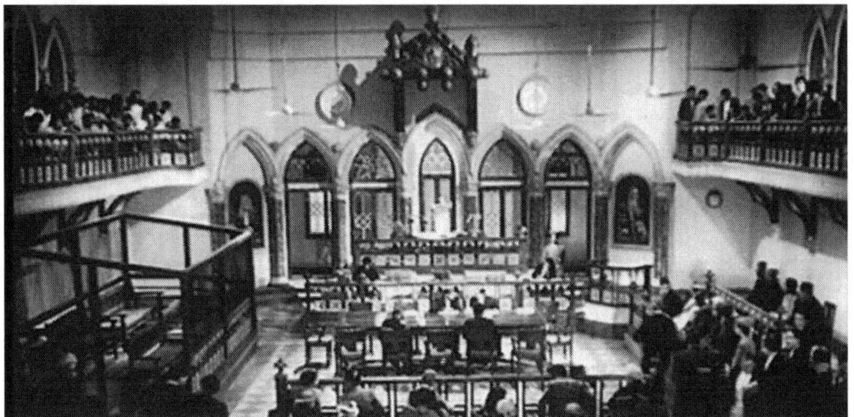

FIGURE 2.7 The court scene in *Awara* (1951).

(fig. 2.7):[15] a rookie lawyer on her first case makes an appeal in a death penalty case. Both she and the defendant offer passionate speeches before the bench that outline the social causes of crime and the court's duty to locate just punishment on *all* culprits. "You have to commit a crime to get the chance to be heard as seriously like this," Raj observes in his speech before the judge and jury. He is pardoned from the gallows.

Unlike *Shree 420*'s complex approach to crime—it is not what you do but what you are made to do; it is not what the individual does but what society does to him—*Awara* purveys a fairy-tale attitude toward crime. The ease with which Raj places his faith in the justice system to reform him from his life of crime recalls the melodramatic code that virtue and corruption are superficial qualities that can be transformed as long as the individual's heart is in it. Such faith in the redemptive power of a criminal justice system that can effectively isolate crime, decisively mete punishment proportional to it, and reform the criminal was a crucial article of faith in a newly decolonized India.[16] Not for long. Neither crime nor punishment would continue to have such reassuring faces in film or in public life for much longer in the 1950s. Despite also addressing itself to criminality as the earlier *Awara* did, *Shree 420* never shows its criminals in court, nor does it demonstrate the kind of justice that due process or a court trial might deliver. The later film places reform largely on the social network (on the schoolteacher, or the well-intentioned fruitseller) and not on legal institutions. What can be described as *Awara*'s innocence has given way to *Shree 420*'s experience in which the crime at stake is beyond the reach of the justice system.

As if to alert the audience of this transformed world without entirely souring their faith in the nation of which it is part, *Shree 420* sutures an extended tutorial on the rapidly decaying political order of post-Independence India. In this pivotal early scene, Dharmanand stands at a podium in Chowpatty Beach dressed in a politician's signature khadi (homespun), making a slick speech before potential voters. "Look at me: I'm dressed in Swadeshi from head to toe. I'm an Indian, here to serve you," he begins. "And look at me," interrupts Raj's voice: "I'm wearing Japanese shoes, English pants, a Russian hat, but my heart: it's completely Indian!" Raj is back, and in the exchange that follows, he and Dharmanand vie for the crowd's attention. In the end Raj wins because he more effectively taps into the desires gnawing at his audience. He promises that the Jai Hind (Hail India) toothpowder he is peddling is a cure-all for the underlying canker of the nation. "Without teeth, how can we eat? And if we can't eat, how can we be strong? And without being strong, we'll be colonized all over again," he exhorts. As the crowd swells to purchase his toothpowder, Dharmanand's cronies expose Raj's fraud. What is in the jars is not toothpowder but sand and crushed bones. The crowd turns on Raj, who is severely beaten.

Despite his university education and a gold medal for honesty, neither Raj's intelligence nor honesty is evident in his sales pitch for fake toothpowder. What is visible is the ease with which political rhetoric and public spectacle obscure both virtues. Once a marker of integrity and idealism during the anticolonial struggle, Swadeshi apparel such as khadi on Dharmanand invokes those ideals without occupying them. The crowd flocks to Dharmanand because of what he wears, unable to detect his hypocrisy; it flocks to Raj because of what he speaks, unable to detect his duplicity. It is *their* honesty and intelligence that this scene exposes. The real tutorial is that neither clothes nor words deliver: both are corrupted in this tarnished moment, and the public has to exercise a degree of wariness against both that was previously unnecessary. And that, in the end, is *Shree 420's* larger message: it is not clothes that make the man (neither Swadeshi nor Japanese shoes are indicative), but the heart (*dil*) that lies obscured behind them. To understand *dil* requires the audience's keenness and intelligence. The scene serves as caution of the perils of innocence as well as an exposition on experience that confront the citizen of the new state.

The tutorial on innocence and experience soon passes. Larger questions on choice and political destiny ebb as well, reappearing at the very last minutes of *Shree 420* when much of its audience was already departing the theater. The love affair with India becomes one between Raj and Vidya, and an agreeable romance displaces disagreeable politics through much of *Shree 420*, earning it the reputation as "easily one of [Kapoor's] most delightful and socially significant comedies" in the words of a prominent documentarian (Kak 1987).

AB DILLI DUR NAHIN

Shree 420 marked a break from the *oeuvre* that succeeded it. Delight and social significance parted ways in Kapoor's 1957 production, *Ab Dilli Dur Nahin*, a film ostensibly made to celebrate the tenth anniversary of Independence. Like Guru Dutt's *Pyaasa* and Mehboob Khan's *Mother India* that were released the same year, *Dilli* comments on the elusiveness of the earlier national fantasy and the demons intrinsic in it. In different ways, all three landmark 1957 films expose the mounting political and social corruptions of the day, even while ascribing very different causes to them. *Mother India* displaces long-standing social corruption on individual sacrifice: the revolutionary who promises to avenge his mother's rape is killed in order to preserve their village's harmony. As if anticipating objections to his murder, his mother accepts her lifetime of suffering, insisting "even if life is poison, we have to swallow it; once we're born, we simply have to live" (duniya main hum aaye hain to jeena hi parega; jeevan hai agar zahar to peena hi parega).[17] Walking the nighttime streets of Calcutta amongst beggars and brothels, Guru Dutt's protagonist, more directly than others, asks, "zara mulk ke rahbaro ko bulao . . . jin he naaz hai Hind par, vo kahan hai?" (call the nation's residents [and show them these streets] . . . where are those who are proud of India?). The question forms the refrain of a lengthy poem by Sahir Ludhianvi that is picturized more as social documentary than song in the feature film. That both these critiques of India in *Pyaasa* and *Mother India* appear as song is no accident. The powerful lyrics and musical scores simultaneously contain the disruptive message even while establishing it in the auditor's memory. The songs allow critique a space in the films, but also contain it as an "interruption" to the plot.[18]

In Kapoor's *Dilli*, critique is handled differently and more directly. The issues are not just social (such as poverty and class exploitation) as they were with Guru Dutt's or Mehboob Khan's films of the year, but political as well. In contrast to the earlier *Awara* and *Shree 420*, *Dilli* focuses less on crime than on justice and the little man's access to it. In further contrast to Raj in *Awara* or *Shree 420*, *Dilli*'s little man is literally little. A 10-year-old sees his father sentenced to death based on circumstantial evidence. When a friendly pickpocket has evidence to exonerate the father, the boy walks 200 miles to Delhi to deliver it to Prime Minister Nehru and ask for his clemency. Nehru appears as a spectral presence in the film, in speedy motorcades, posters, photos, and as a speaker at distant rallies (figs. 2.8–2.10).

Apparently persuaded by Kapoor that "the film would put his government on a high pedestal and bring the desired credibility," Nehru initially agreed to appear in the last shot of the film when the boy finally meets him, though he later declined, and, as Rishi Kapoor recalls, "the film fell flat. Obviously no one could empathise with it."[19]

The anecdote about Nehru's appearance in the film says much about the close ties between the two mythographers. More significantly, it also reveals the Prime Minister's limits and the filmmaker's reach. By India's tenth anniversary, it was not just achieving industrial and agricultural targets that were at stake for the new nation. The very fabric of the social had to be remade, and cinema was a crucial participant in the project. When Kapoor

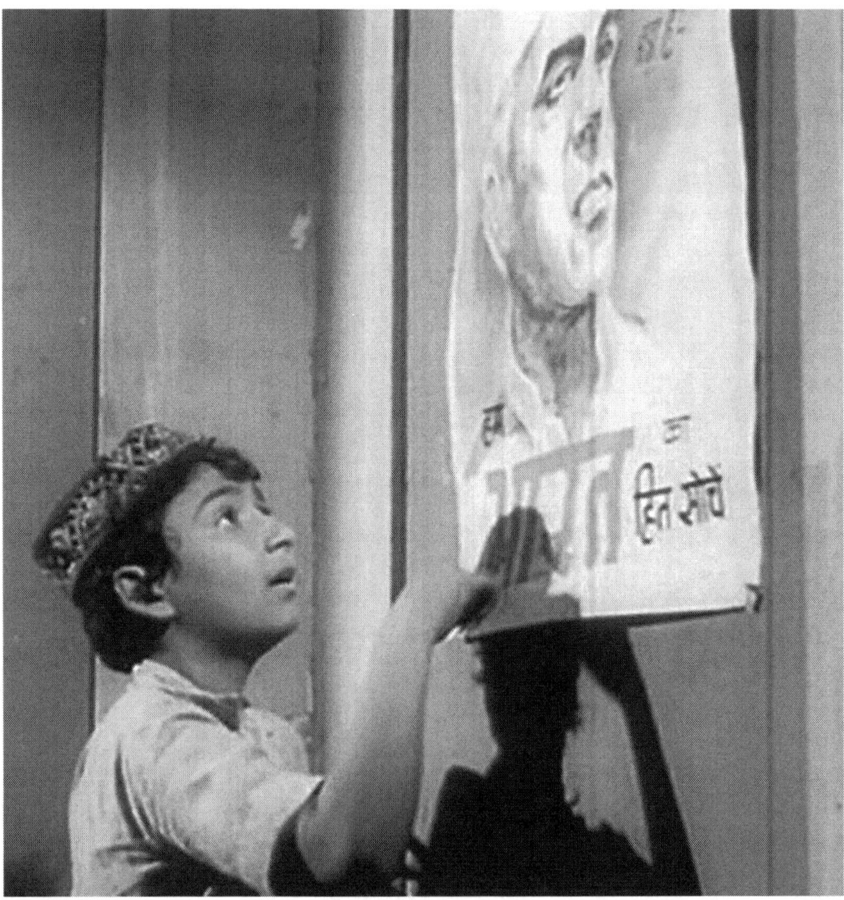

FIGURES 2.8–2.10 Nehru as image and specter in *Ab Dilli Dur Nahin* (1957).

(COURTESY SHEMAROO)

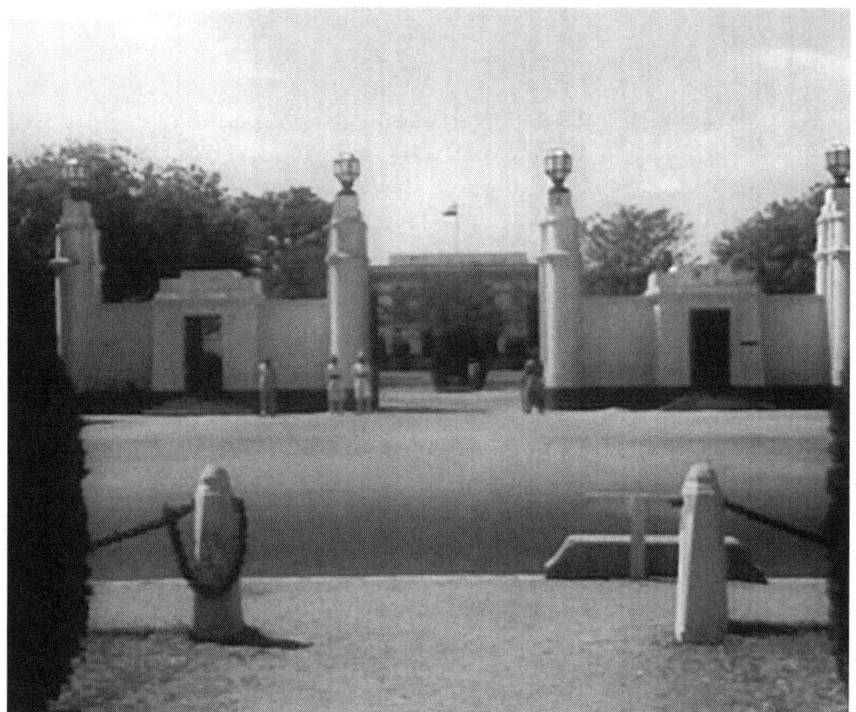

FIGURE 2.9

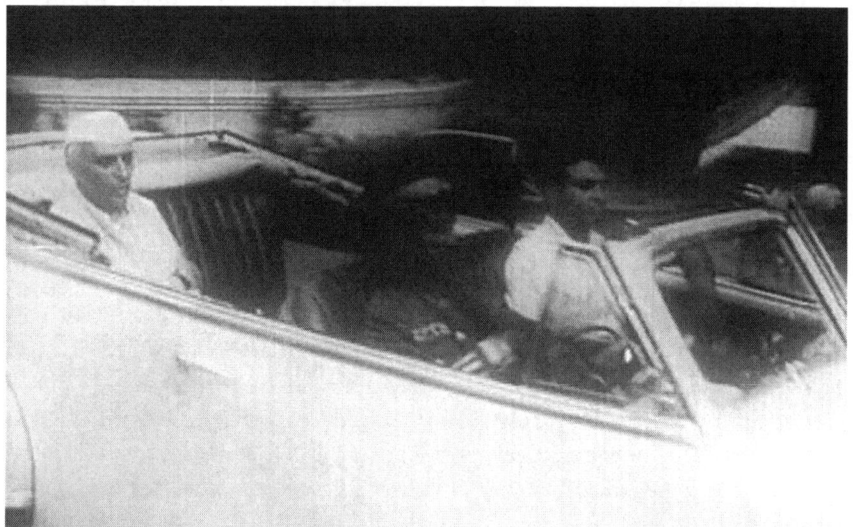

FIGURE 2.10

and others tried to do whatever they could through film to build up Nehru's beautiful dream, they quickly discovered its sordid underbelly. Nehru's cosmopolitan, urban vision was one in which the individual could arrive in the city, reform it and himself there, and provide some sort of a happy ending as happens in both *Awara* and *Shree 420* among others. But the other reality of India where its majority lived and that Gandhi had labeled its destination was the village, and here the abominable injustices of caste and usury were unreformed and rampant. The little man was caught in a permanent cycle of poverty in the hands of an upper-caste moneylender who took possession of his land (his capital) and his labor (his means of production). To reform *this* India required a conjurer, not the courts that *Awara* provided, and a conjurer is precisely what Nehru got in Kapoor when he produced *Dilli*.

It became apparent quickly, though, that even the magician could not conjure Nehru's fantasy to include rural India. The entire justice system in it was crooked. Not only does it prey on the little man in *Dilli*, it incarcerates him when he objects as the father did in threatening the unscrupulous moneylender who had ruined him and the entire village. Kapoor's signature optimism dissipates quickly in *Dilli*'s village scenes and returns only when the young protagonist finds himself in Delhi in the company of other runaways like him. In this alternative urban community, everyone is equal, a meager meal of rotis is shared by all, an upper-caste landowner is sent packing, and the entire community of children vows to seek Nehru for their friend and get justice.

At the end of *Dilli*, Kapoor provides the happy ending that the film required, but years later his son Rishi is not wrong to insist that "it fell flat." No amount of urban mythography could dispel the horrors that awaited *Dilli*'s protagonist on his return to the village, and none could quite distract from the social canker beyond the urban surface. In a film most directly invested in giving Nehru's dream its desired credibility, *Dilli* instead paradoxically exposed the many disruptions to the idea of India.

Nehru's embrace of political modernity on August 15, 1947, ushered a hierarchical, caste-ridden society into democracy; his Fabian socialism exposed the real attractions embedded both in capitalist *and* socialist modernity; and his cosmopolitan urban vision was an inevitable contrast to M. K. Gandhi's insistence that the real India—and the only one—was in the village. In short, the political, social, and economic modernity Nehru sought disrupted another, older, premodern India to the core. *Dilli* exposed the intractable nature of a conflict to which no *sangam* seemed possible, a conflict according to which the vast majority were not fully allowed—or prepared—to participate in the bounty of the modern state. Kapoor's salute to Nehru in *Awara* and *Shree 420* embraces his idol's cosmopolitan vision and largely ignores the other side of it. Nehru repeatedly appears in these films as a benevolent visual backdrop to Raj's foreground (figs. 2.11–2.13).

Raj's origins in Allahabad in *Shree 420* gesture to Nehru's own, and Kapoor's sartorial smorgasbord in these blockbusters combining Chaplin, Visconti, and James Dean (figs. 2.14–2.16) echoed well with the Prime Minister's own hybrid style with its bespoke Swadeshi jackets and an English tea rose in his buttonhole (see fig. 2.6).

Awara and *Shree 420* are frequently regarded Kapoor's landmark social films and his contribution to the contract between modernity and nation spelled out in Nehru's beautiful dream. *Dilli*'s rural realism, on the other hand, has relegated it from Kapoor's canon (it is seldom screened in retrospectives both during Kapoor's lifetime and since). However, considering *Dilli* as constitutive of Kapoor's 1950s *oeuvre* allows a study of the three films as a triptych that marks the journey from innocence to experience. The triptych's evolving responses to the common problem of criminality and justice in post-Independence India reveal an increasing wariness toward the ability

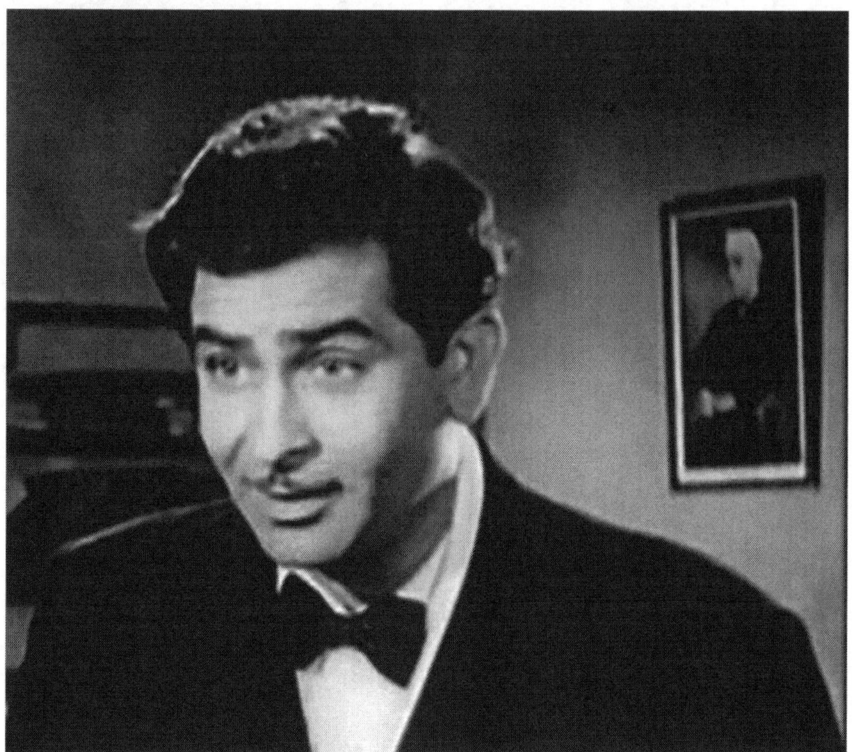

FIGURE 2.11 Nehru as backdrop to Raj in *Shree 420*.

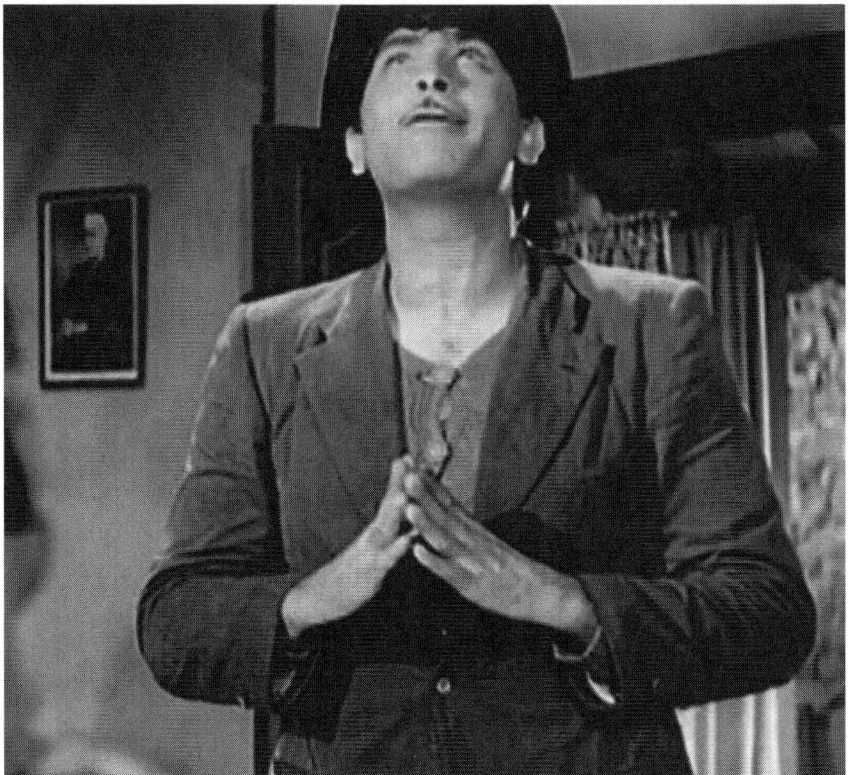

FIGURE 2.12 Nehru as backdrop in *Shree 420.*

of civic institutions to address social problems. *Awara*'s inescapable optimism about crime and punishment was balanced by *Shree 420*'s nuanced compromise, with its focus on social solidarity to solve problems that civic institutions could not. Together, the two films provide ways of managing the extraordinary expectations that Independence inevitably ushered. Rather than deflating public fantasies for justice that *Awara* celebrates, *Shree 420* displaces them upon the community, which is charged with delivering what the state's institutions cannot. In contrast, *Dilli* dispatches with both optimism and compromise and retreats from civic institutions altogether. If there is an arbiter of justice left available, it is the mythic Prime Minister himself, but the figure is spectral at best, fleetingly glimpsed but impossible to access (fig. 2.10). As the scholar Nandini Chandra avers in her reading of *Dilli*'s children: "Nehru does nothing for them."[20] The little man is on his own here, severed from community when he searches for justice.

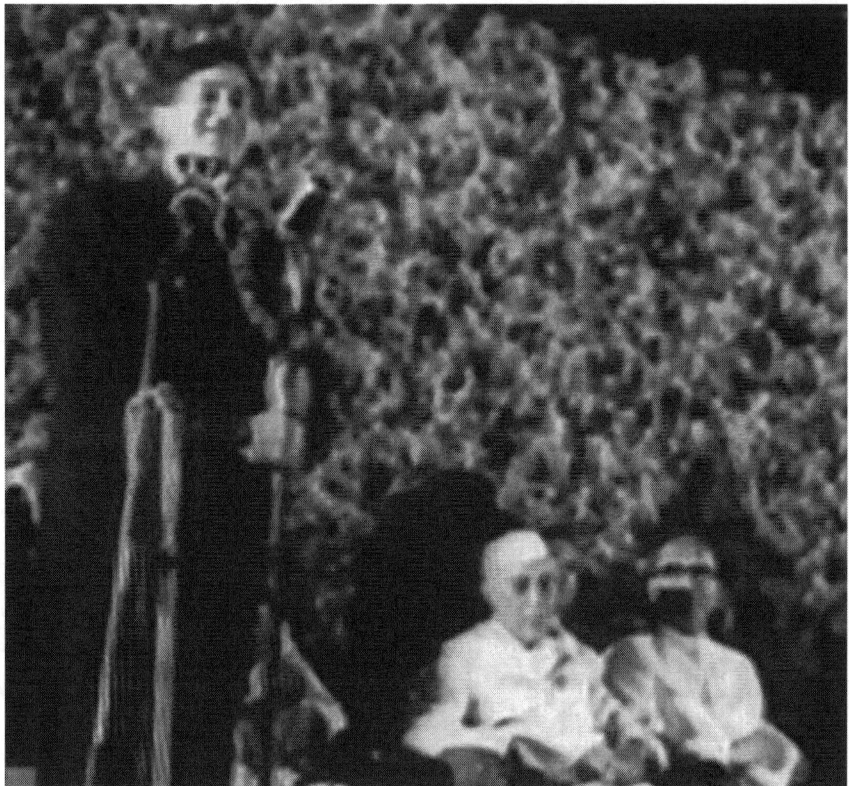

FIGURE 2.13 Raj Kapoor on stage with Nehru at the National Defence Committee fundraiser in New Delhi (January 1963).

In *Dilli*, Kapoor exposed an India that could not (yet) be incorporated fully in the dream before him. Inimical both to colonial modernity and the Nehruvian version elaborated during Independence, this India is represented as the source of "crime" in *Dilli*, a crime that the judicial system can neither reach nor reform. Since social revolution was never Kapoor's interest, he left it aside and developed the cosmopolitan version of modernity and its attendant crimes in films following *Dilli* such as *Bobby* (1973) and *Ram Teri Ganga Maili* (Ram, your Ganges is dirty, 1985), where the emphasis falls on class, not caste, and the disruptions to social stability that romantic love exposes.[21]

By the 1970s, however, the easy separation between the Nehruvian social vision and what is somewhat crudely named the Gandhian was not so easy to maintain. For one, the little man was no longer a figure easily contained

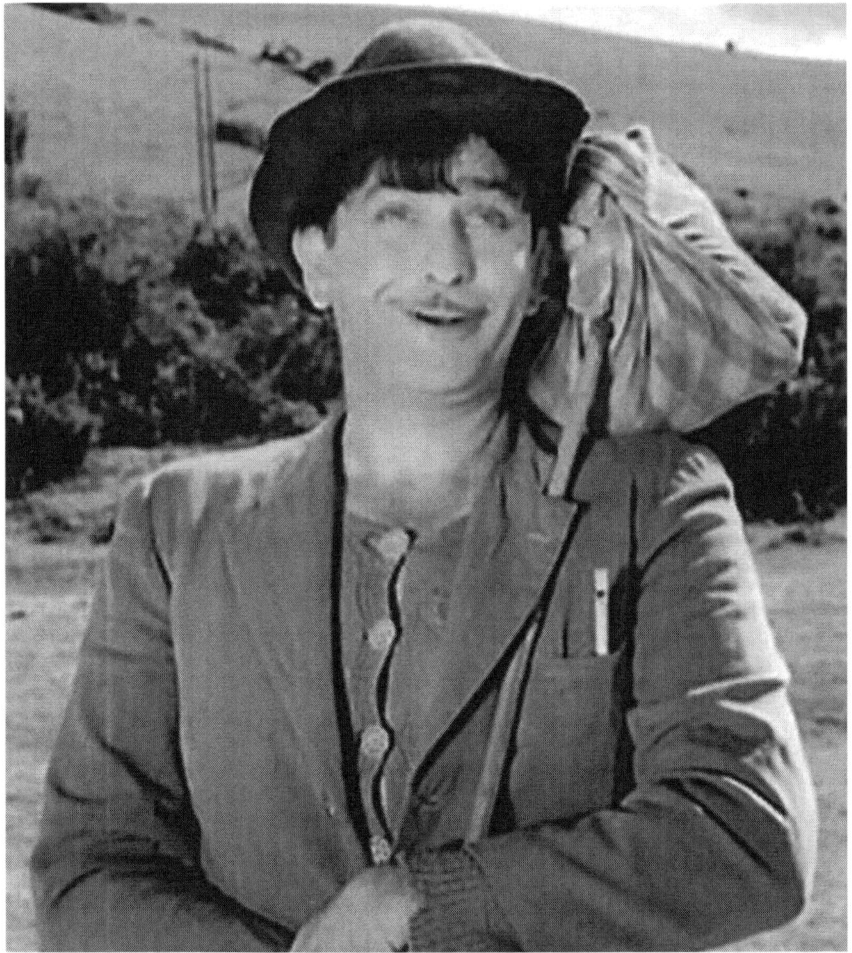

FIGURES 2.14–2.16 Raj Kapoor as Chaplin in *Shree 420* (*above*) and (*next page*) recalling Visconti and James Dean in *Awara* (1951).

by region or class, nor was he easily identified by his origins or even his destination. The nation that Nehru dreamed died with him in 1964, and a new one had come to the fore that Kapoor's mythography had yet to address. As his publicist and later biographer Bunny Reuben alerted Kapoor in a published open letter:

Between 1964 and 1970, many changes took place in the country and in the entertainment world, changes which I submit you were only faintly aware of, and of which you took little or no cognizance, sitting as you were in the ivory tower of Chembur. . . . The "little man" has said his say. Over the past decade or so,

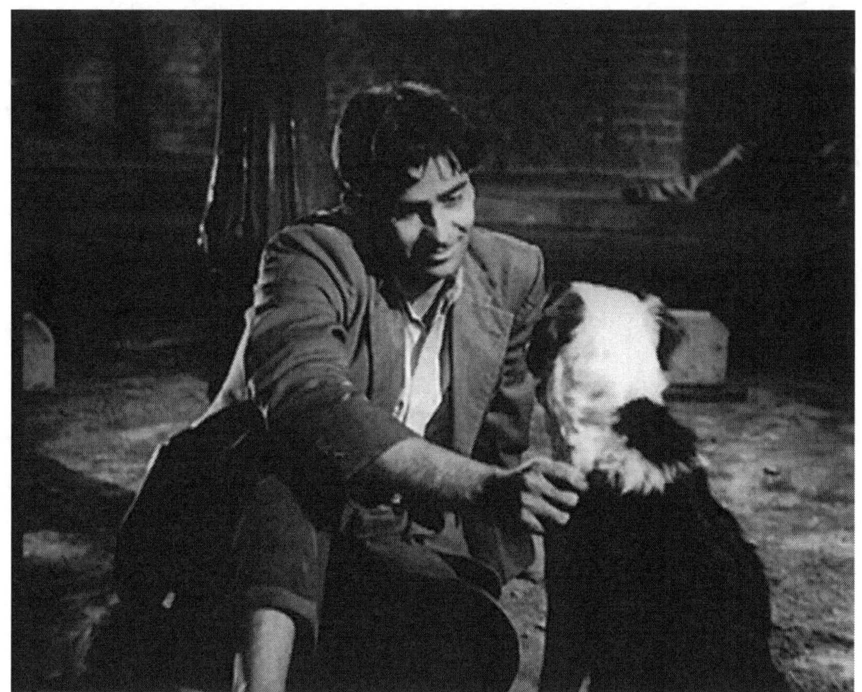

FIGURE 2.15

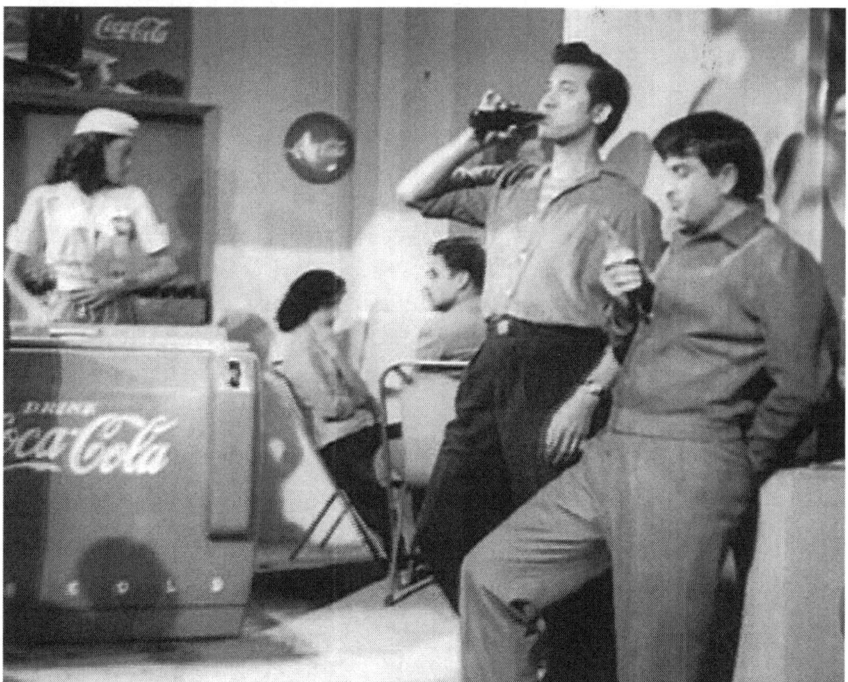

FIGURE 2.16

the entire strata of India's middle class, instead of being able to rise to a higher economic status, has been reduced to the penury of the "little man" due to steady inflation, the spiraling cost of living, and growing corruption at all levels of social and national life in our country. We have all been reduced by bad government to the economic status of "little men" and we do not want to be reminded of it in the movies we pay to see. . . . Witness therefore the colossal box-office success these days of purely escapist films.[22]

Reuben's allegation of Kapoor's isolation notwithstanding, the film-maker was hardly removed from the changes that 1964 ushered. Indeed, Nehru had died, the era of the red rose had ended, India embarked on two wars (in 1965 and 1971), and Nehru's daughter, Indira Gandhi, was elected prime minister in 1966.[23] Nehru was deemed so sacred in political life that no prime minister following him has moved into his official residence. Teen Murti Bhavan was, quite literally, rendered a secular shrine to him and exists as the country's premier historical repository, entombing the glorious revolutionary struggle and its many public fantasies. Indira Gandhi's election in 1966 removed her to a different residence, much as her political vision was characterized by a marked departure from—even a displacement of—her father, Nehru's.

Kapoor was not so much ignorant of the changed world, as he chose to ignore many parts of it. His own fantasies of India were not encumbered by Nehru's. Kapoor's little man sometimes became a big man (as he did in *Sangam* where he plays a fighter pilot wounded in an unnamed conflict), and at other times a young cosmopolite, as Raja in *Bobby* (1973). His *oeuvre* continued to explore the exploitation of this figure and his desire for respect. But Kapoor had given up the notion that the respect was forthcoming from the institutions of the state. In every work since *Shree 420*, the sources of degradation and violence remain social (such as rich landlords, industrialists, ambitious parents, businessmen, the dowry system), and the solutions increasingly borrowed from melodrama and its code of individual reform.

But Bunny Reuben is correct in one crucial regard: if audiences of the 1970s did not wish to be reminded of their degradation in the films they saw, they still sought some respite from it. And for this, the cinema continued to play a role in managing desire, even if Raj Kapoor was not always the man to provide it.[24]

POLICE AND THIEVES

On June 26, 1975, Indira Gandhi declared a state of Emergency in India that was to last for twenty-one months into 1977. Two months later, on

August 15, 1975, the anniversary of Independence, the filmmaker Ramesh Sippy released *Sholay* (Embers) upon audiences starved and humiliated within a blatantly corrupt and increasingly unscrupulous political system. The journalist, Anupama Chopra, captures the period as follows:

> The early seventies were a time of social and political upheaval. The post-Independence optimism of the fifties and sixties was slowly giving way to a deepening disillusionment with authority. The legacy of selflessness and integrity left by the politicians of the freedom struggle had been replaced with widespread corruption, and the use of violence for criminal and political ends was on the rise. The common citizen felt that law and order had broken down. The mood in the country was one of hopelessness and frustration, even anger, and a new morality was taking shape, typified by Jayaprakash Narayan's socialist movement.[25]

Critics panned *Sholay* almost immediately, faulting it most prominently for its violence. *The Illustrated Weekly of India* named 1975 "The Year of Violence and Sex in Films."[26] "You realize that a story built on *negative* emotions like hatred and violence can have no lasting impression on the mind," wrote Raju Bharatan,[27] notwithstanding which *Sholay* played for over five years (267 weeks) at Bombay's first-run Minerva Cinema.[28] "Where the film fails is in its music," Bharatan continued (ibid.): yet R. D. Burman's song, "Mehbooba, Mehbooba" (Beloved, Beloved), was still being played in discos twenty years later and "Yeh Dosti" (This Friendship), the "male bonding anthem" (Chopra 13), found new meaning in Bombay's emerging gay subculture of the early 1990s.

Shortly after its release and throughout the decade, many superlatives accrued to *Sholay* and its lore circulated: the first 70mm film made in India; the most expensive film made to date; the first production to hire American action directors for stunt sequences; an early multi-starrer, casting Bombay's most fabled stars; and, above all, the film that remains the all-time biggest grosser at the box office for Hindi cinema.[29] *Sholay* was bigger, bolder, and more daring than any Hindi film made to date. And audiences loved it to a degree hitherto unseen in Hindi cinema.[30] Yet the critics did not get it at all. Anupama Chopra records the major reviews panning it during the first week for a "gravely flawed attempt" (*India Today*), its "unsuccessful transplantation attempt . . . an imitation Western" (*Filmfare*), with "no reason for a repeat show" (*Film Information*).[31]

In an *India Today* essay condemning *Sholay*'s violence entitled "Kiss Kiss, Bang Bang," the journalist Bindu Batra prevailed upon reason to make an argument about the film's portrayal of "intoxicating action, brutal sensationalism, and barbaric fights." "There is no need to end violence in the cinema," she placated her counterparts who insisted otherwise in the uniform outcry that followed *Sholay*'s popularity. "On the contrary, there is a need to encourage its portrayal with the injunction that it must be shown in *realistic* terms [as an undesirable way of life]."[32]

Batra's criticism of *Sholay* unwittingly identifies the film's sustained appeal among its immediate audiences. *Sholay*'s familiar plot and setting derive extensively from Sergio Leone's spaghetti westerns, earning the film the epithet, "a curry western."[33] Like the Western tradition that inspired it, *Sholay* depicted a lawless world in which even the sheriff turns to the vigilante for justice. The temptation to claim the film as just another "story" is strong, but it is worth recalling, as its coscriptwriter Javed Akhtar did, that *Sholay*'s story captured the zeitgeist of the 1970s in a particularly resonant way:

> If you considered the political mood of the country [in the 1970s], you'd find a lot of frustration. Social protest had begun. That was the time when Jayaprakash Narayan's socialist movement had begun. Hindi films are most widely seen in the Hindi belt and in that area, law and order was gradually breaking down. So the common man was experiencing upheaval. There was disillusionment with all the institutions, colleges, the police force. People were disillusioned with the government. So it wasn't surprising that the morality of the day said that if you want justice, you have to fight for it yourself. No one will fight on your behalf. And if you didn't fight, you'll be crushed and finished off. . . . You can see that the hero who has developed between 1973–75—the Emergency was declared in India in 1975—reflected those times.[34]

Akhtar's remarks, published almost twenty-five years after *Sholay* was released, recall the range of institutions that had "broken down" in the 1970s, including the government, the judiciary, and even the educational apparatus. Other films of the period such as *Deewaar* (The wall, Yash Chopra, 1975; see chapter 3) and *Roti Kapda aur Makaan* (Food clothing and housing, Manoj Kumar, 1974) amplify the special pressures of a "broken" educational system as college graduates confronted one of the worst employment conditions in memory, and large-scale social unrest threatened to erupt at any moment. The industrialist, J. R. D. Tata, on the other side of the political spectrum from Akhtar, lamented of the period: "You can't imagine what we had been through here—strikes, boycotts, demonstrations. Why, there were days when I couldn't walk out of my office on to the street. The parliamentary system is not suited to our needs."[35]

In *Sholay*, two modern, jeans-clad city boys named Jai and Veeru are obliged to seek work in a remote village without automobiles or telephones. The dissonance between their urban world and the one they are called upon to protect vividly underscores the persistence of a rural India coexisting alongside one of strikes, boycotts, and demonstrations. Rather than being an arcadia, however, the village of Ramgarh closely resembles the lawless cities Jai and Veeru have left. Neither world seems to be able to deliver justice or order, and both seem prey to forces that threaten to disrupt them without a moment's notice. Both worlds, in short, require the labor of underclass migrants to preserve and to protect them, even as they criminalize migrants and deny them basic civic protections. If *Sholay*'s release date links it to a political order associated with Nehru's daughter, Indira Gandhi, other cues clarify just how elusive Nehru's dreams for a just society have become in the Age of Indira.

A few minutes into the film, two revealing conversations take place that capture the dramatic shift in social attitudes toward crime between the 1950s and the Emergency era. In the first conversation, an armless ex-police inspector now a civilian asks a jailer to help him locate two men named Jai and Veeru. "But they're absolute crooks," the jailer expostulates. "Total thieves. They're no good at all those two." The Thakur prevails with the logic that a good heart redeems even the criminal when he argues: "For all their vices, they have virtues too." "A fake coin is fake on both sides," the jailer insists in a statement that recalls Mrs. Dharmanand's dismissal of unknown youth in *Shree 420*. The contrast between the punitive righteousness of power (in this case, the law) and the moral right of the powerless (here deemed "thieves" and "crooks") collides head-on in this exchange. *Sholay* proceeds to thematize their intractable conflict and to reconfigure a latent economy in which "crooks" nevertheless deliver justice.

In a flashback that immediately follows, the Thakur recalls a conversation he had while he was still a police inspector with the alleged crooks who audaciously insist they are just like him. "We work for money just like you do. We too play with danger in our jobs. And like your job, ours too requires bravery." The Thakur tries to separate himself from Jai and Veeru by claiming he works within the law, they against it. But Jai dismisses this logic immediately: the similarities prevail over the differences since both jobs require bravery. The real distinction between the two groups is contained in a throwaway line the Thakur offers when justifying his line of work. "I don't need to work for money as such," he tells Jai and Veeru. "My ancestral lands provide me with sufficient income to live quite well."

Herein lies the difference between these two uneasy allies. The Thakur represents the leisured order of landed property, unified with state power (the police), while Jai and Veeru are the landless *needing* to work where they can find it. They may be criminals under the old order that the jailer reminds the Thakur of in the first conversation, but in the new world of the Emergency, these two are *as good as the police*. In fact, they are better, because when the Thakur's lands need protection, he does not go to the police but to Jai and Veeru and the particular code of "justice," bravery, and violence that they represent. On a manifest level, *Sholay* is the most reactionary of films, invoking not *noblesse oblige* but a kind of underclass-*oblige*, calling upon those most oppressed by the feudal order to protect that very oppressive order. The murder of the Thakur's entire family displaces the audience's attention from any other kind of suffering (i.e., that perpetrated by him and his class upon the villagers), and the film becomes a narrative of upper-class suffering at the very moment in post-Independence history when that class had extracted and was enjoying its greatest privileges. That subaltern group of rootless, indigent laborers most dis-armed and dis-membered by social "progress" is called upon to restore the authority and "dismembered" prestige of an upper class that has oppressed it in the first place. Despite this reactionary content, *Sholay* was a huge success among lower-class and rural audiences.[36] Why?

A large part of the reason lies in the film's depiction of violence. Despite critics who decried it, the problem with *Sholay*'s violence was not that it

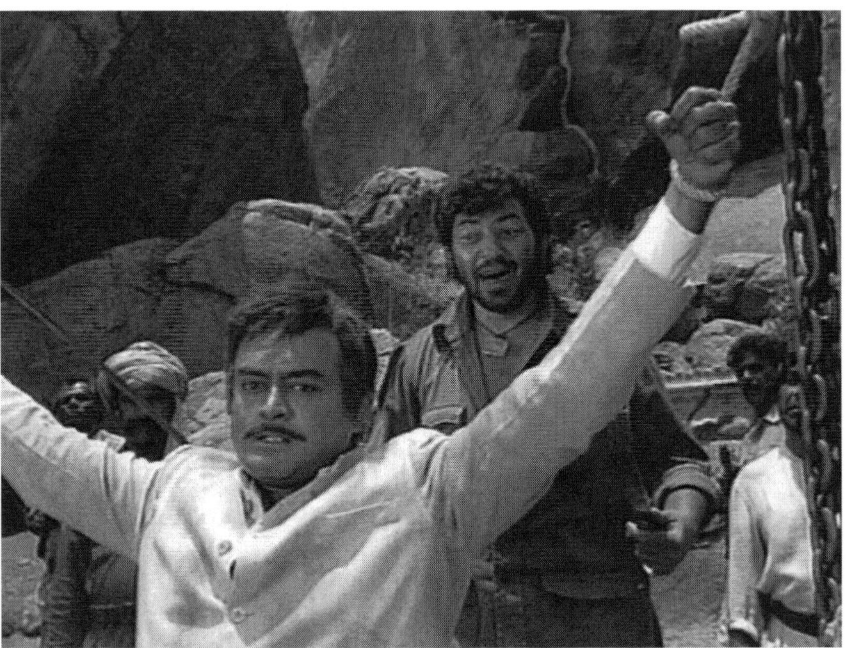

FIGURES 2.17–2.19 Gabbar delivering his punishment of choice to the Thakur (*above*), and Veeru (fig. 2.18). Jai and Veeru to the rescue with their weapons of choice (fig. 2.19) in *Sholay* (1975).

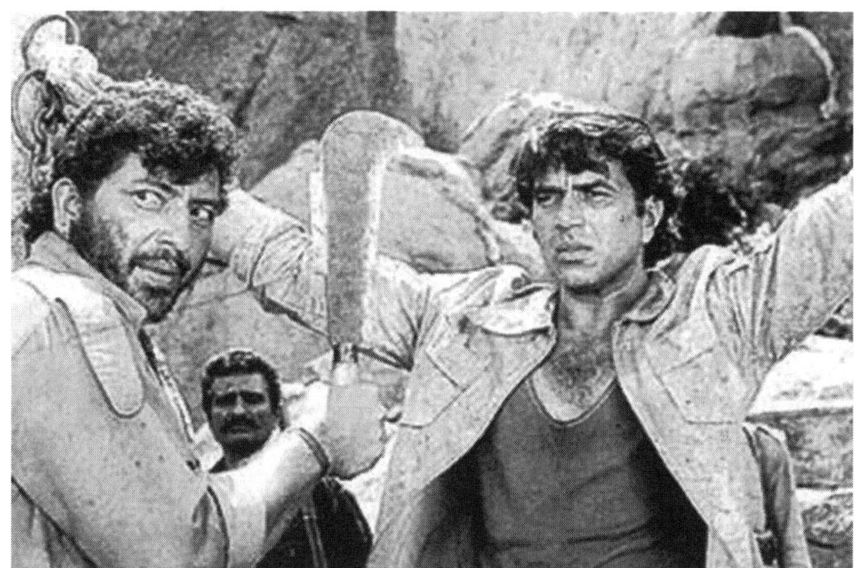

FIGURE 2.18

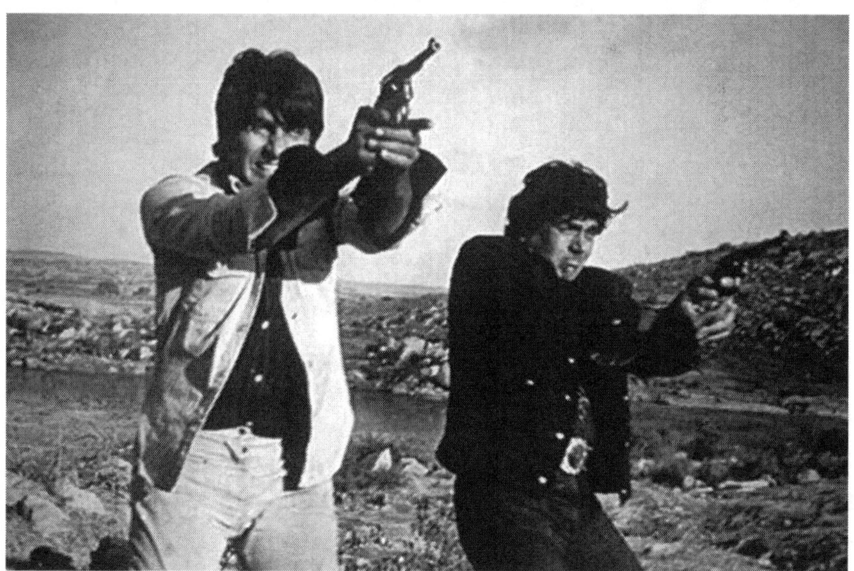

FIGURE 2.19

was inordinate or particularly brutal, but rather that its brutality and savagery (the chopping of arms, the extermination of an entire clan) were so resonant with a moment when whole neighborhoods of the working poor were being exterminated by government bulldozers, and men of all ages among the lower classes were being forcibly sterilized under government-sponsored programs to control population growth.

Sholay's appeal lay in affirming the logic that violence and brutality can only be redressed by more violence and brutality; that modern civic institutions such as the state and the police are complete failures in protecting the people.[37] The film's unabashed dismissal of civic institutions and the implicit critique of their governability and corruption make Jai and Veeru more than copies of Leone's inverted cowboy-heroes in the Western tradition. As vigilantes called to restore peace to the Thakur's villages, the Jai-Veeru duo amplify a desperate solution to a modern problem, though it comes with some caveats.

Hindi cinema has always been reluctant to accept the vigilante fully or to allow him unambiguous sanction. In landmark films such as *Mother India* (1957), the lone vigilante, Birju, is first beaten, then expelled, and finally killed after he takes on a usurious moneylender whom he threatens to bring to court for his crimes against an entire village. Even though *Mother India* endlessly exposes the moneylender's atrocities upon the village's most vulnerable population of widows and fatherless children, it still manifestly casts Birju as the problem for the disruptions his acts instigate, implicitly preferring to await a solution from above rather than endorsing one from within or below. When Birju as vigilante is the self-appointed arbiter of justice in his village, he is promptly ejected from it for his attempt to replace the old order with a new one. (It merits mention that Birju in *Mother India* is already a considerably more outspoken figure than the Puckish original as scripted in Mehboob Khan's *Aurat* [Woman, 1940]. In the earlier film, Birju goes "bad," and his mother dies of heartbreak. In the 1957 remake, Birju's pursuit of social justice permeates the film's ending, and his mother's efforts at containing him seem as futile as the filmmaker's.)[38]

Likewise, in *Sholay* Jai and Veeru are initially hailed for their courage in standing up against the dacoit who has terrorized the Thakur's village. However, their efforts are rapidly contained. Their instructions from the Thakur are to bring him Gabbar: "zinda!" (alive). After Jai dies in a shootout with Gabbar's men, Veeru storms Gabbar's hideout and has him in a noose when the Thakur appears. "Remember your promise; Gabbar is mine now," the Thakur insists, and Veeru hands him over. It is a critical transaction that underscores Veeru's vassalage to the Thakur. Veeru's visual glamour and masculine bravado notwithstanding, his vigilantism is subordinate to his employer's authority, which denies him even the honor of avenging a friend's death.

Sholay's "vigilantes" are a far cry from the typical figures who "maintain justice and order in an imperfect society" (*OED*), nor are they figures who protest an existing order as Birju did. At best, they are paid enforcers in a desperate law-and-order situation who protect the status quo (i.e., the Thakur's class), which is being threatened.[39] Unlike the typical vigilante who maintains order or delivers justice because of the belief that it is not otherwise available (Birju in *Mother India* is a key example), Jai and Veeru work for money, not for ideals.[40] Their many attractions aside (including the star power that Amitabh Bachchan and Dharmendra brought to the roles), Jai and Veeru remain subalterns to the ruling class, and their contract with it commits them to restoring that class to its power. Any disruptions by Jai or Veeru to this class's sense of stability are rapidly contained. Jai is killed when he threatens the baronial marriage plot (first for attempting to marry the Thakur's widowed daughter-in-law, Radha, and then for thwarting Veeru's marriage to Basanti, the belle of the Thakur's village).

Jai's death is symbolic—and necessary—in other ways. As the repository of history ("I always forget these stories: you're the one who remembers them and has to tell them to my kids," insists Veeru), Jai represents the persistence of past memories that need to die in the new present of the Emergency. His subaltern position notwithstanding, Jai vigorously challenges the Thakur's logic on class and criminality ("we're just like you," he reminds the policeman in the early exchange in a remark dripping with irony). His presence in the film thus symbolizes both the past (history), and past ideals (*read* Nehru) that once connected the state with the citizen in a shared social contract. The Emergency renders both kinds of past and its social contract null, and both are made to die in Jai's gory and prolonged death sequence.

Like the fictional Raj in *Shree 420*, the biographical Amitabh Bachchan who plays Jai also hails from Allahabad, Nehru's birthplace, and his end in *Sholay* symbolically underscores the necessary demise of the national icon during the Emergency.[41] If Jai's death is symbolically necessary so that the ideals he represents can be laid to rest, it is also a death redolent with exposure: weeping over his dead friend, Veeru finds the counterfeit coin that Jai had used to win every important coin toss. It is a small form of subterfuge that Jai used to good ends, but it underscores that even noble ideals sometimes have dubious origins.

In contrast to Raj Kapoor's fantasy that criminality can be identified, neutralized, and eventually redeemed by benign and just social institutions such as the courts and the penitentiary, *Sholay* unquestioningly introduces Jai and

Veeru as the only solutions to a corrupt and irredeemable institutional crisis. Neither the court nor the penitentiary can contain them, or Gabbar for that matter, who boasts that a jail to hold him has yet to be built. The issue of reforming Jai and Veeru never appears for they are essentially good sorts, while Gabbar is irredeemably evil and corrupt—just like the state and its institutions that are incapable of holding him. Rather than the criminal embodying society's worst fears of antisocial elements that must be reformed or neutralized, as Kapoor depicts him in his films from the 1950s, *Sholay*'s power lay in insisting that the real criminal elements lay beyond society's reach, insulated by their absolute evil, sheer power, and total corruption. The violence that *these* criminals practice upon their victims is amplified by Gabbar's gratuitous and sadistic violence, which renders the Thakur's brutality in attempting to crush Gabbar to death all the more thrilling.

What *Sholay*'s public fantasy achieved is two things. In locating the nature of criminality beyond the individual and on social and political institutions, it helped articulate a growing public unease with a political and social system gone horribly wrong in the Emergency. In redressing criminality not through liberal-humanist beliefs or institutions but by the economy of violence (an eye-for-an-eye, an arm-for-an-arm), *Sholay* offered an alternative narrative to help cope with the demise of a utopian nationalism gone bad. The film's putative satisfaction lay not in the order that follows it, for none does. (Jai dies; Radha rots in lonely widowhood; the Thakur has lost his family and his arms for a very belated revenge; and Veeru rather than settling in Ramgarh leaves it with Basanti, though it is not clear to where or for what.) The film worked among audiences not by addressing their fantasies, but by helping exorcise their fears. Rather than providing prescriptions, it provided depictions of a grim everyday that had not been projected on screen before.

CAREER OPPORTUNITIES

Despite the generally gloomy reading of a manifestly reactionary film, *Sholay*'s popularity was unabated. Indian audiences claim to have seen it ten and twenty and forty times, revealing an entirely new calculus of consumption in popular Hindi cinema.[42] *Sholay*'s songs and dialogues were played and purveyed endlessly on radio and cassettes that formed part of its extraordinary appeal.[43] Gabbar, more than any other figure from *Sholay*, enjoyed a special popularity. He got the best dialogue, with lines such as "kitne aadmi they?" (How many men were there?) entering oral legend. His military fatigues and swagger became the standard of masculine aspiration among youth, and Brittania's Glucose D biscuits sold millions among little children following an ad campaign calling the biscuits "Gabbar ki asli pasand" (Gabbar's real favorite).

In Gabbar, *Sholay* presented a villain so immune from justice and so insulated from the reach of the law that he became a new kind of hero. "Everybody wanted to be Gabbar, not Jai or Veeru, in their own theatres of the bedroom," recounted Ramesh Sippy in an interview.[44]

"The audience loves the villain because he can do things they can't," explained the actor Gulshan Grover, who made a career playing screen villains in the 1980s.[45] In giving face and flesh to some of the audience's worst fears of civil society gone awry and social justice corrupted, *Sholay* served not to promote or satisfy public fantasies, but to identify and magnify its worst fears. In this regard, it became a corroboratory narrative of what many in India were going through before and during the Emergency. The film touched upon the violence and criminality simmering below the surface of what one critic has called "a people eulogized for their tolerance" (Batra 31), in an era punctuated by the Emergency that came to mark the destruction of the myth of civic harmony so crucial to Indian nationalism. Rather than fulfilling deeply held though inchoate wishes, as Kapoor's films of the 1950s did, *Sholay* functioned by exorcising deeply ingrained and very specific demons. Its appeal lay exactly in this inversion. It was cathartic in the classically tragic tradition that provided its audience pleasure not by projecting fantasy but by arousing fear. It simultaneously reassured its audience by the ethos that absolute evil requires absolutely evil solutions (violence stops violence) and the satisfaction that the film could share and exorcise its audience's deepest demons.

As the next chapter elaborates, *Sholay* was very much part of the cinema of the 1970s, in kind if not degree. In characterizing this cinema, the scholar Madhava Prasad notes a key feature that he calls its "aesthetic of mobilization," described as strategies by which the "hero" becomes a figure of what Prasad names "national reconciliation and social reform" (Prasad 1998:141). According to the argument, the hero affirms the prevailing national story and mobilizes a predominantly middle-class majority to validate it as well. Prasad locates the source of that mobilization in the figures of Jai and Veeru in whom, he argues, criminality is "deployed as a metaphor for all forms of rebellion and disaffection."[46] A reading of *Sholay*'s manifest plot would fully support this. The film's mise-en-scène with its admiring, even adoring, gaze lavished over Jai and Veeru's towering forms and the extended camera sequences of their camaraderie is in stark contrast to the almost perfunctory attention the camera gives to the figures of Basanti (played by Hindi cinema's "dream girl," Hema Malini) or the semiclad Helen in a sultry item number. A lot of the camera's attention went into creating the Jai–Veeru "aesthetic" and its attractions (figs. 2.20 and 2.21).

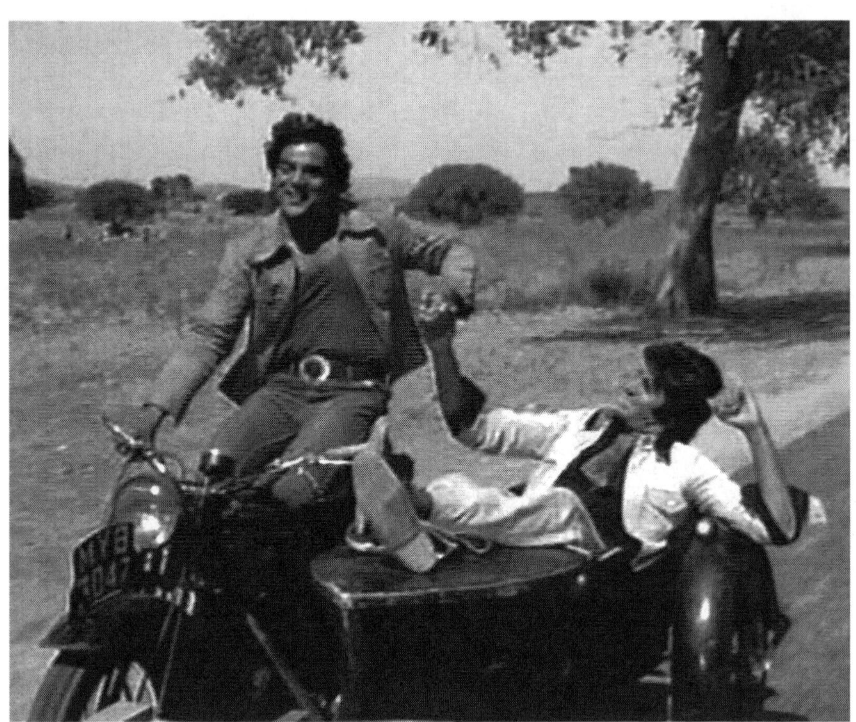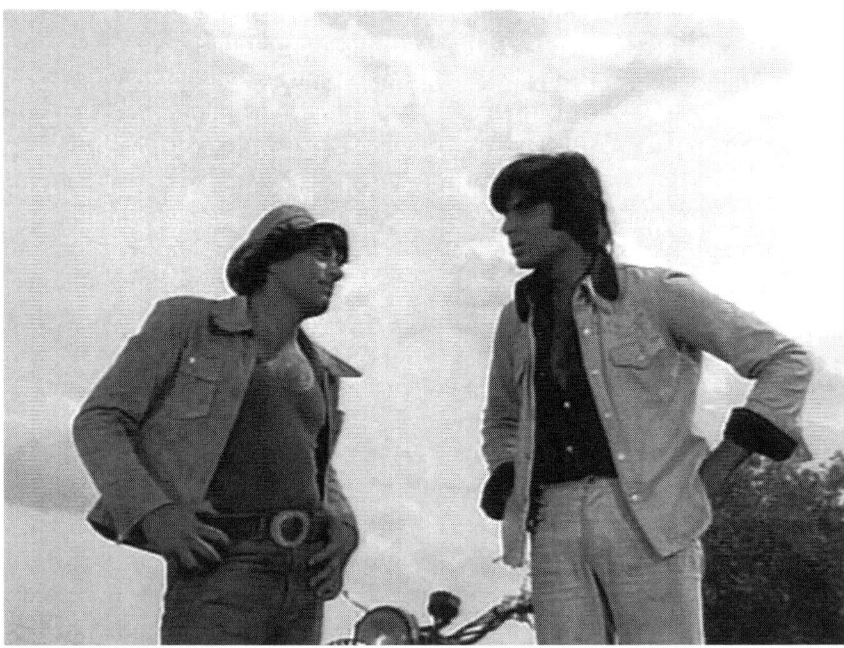

FIGURES 2.20 AND 2.21 The Jai–Veeru glamour in *Sholay*.

But Gabbar's immediate and long-standing popularity among audiences suggests another kind of "mobilization" at work, resonating with an entirely different—and perhaps more powerful—register of rebellion and disaffection that validates a profoundly counter-hegemonic narrative embedded as *Sholay*'s latent plot. This inverted narrative does not affirm the national story, but exposes it. The focal audience of this latent narrative is not the middle classes, as Prasad urges, but the lower classes who stand to lose everything from the "reconciliation" work undertaken by the middle classes in the manifest plot. In Gabbar, one finds a villain "doing things [the audience] can't," as the actor Gulshan Grover observed. But unlike Jai and Veeru (who also do things the audience can't), Gabbar *gets away* doing things while Jai and Veeru do not. Jai dies after challenging the Thakur and daring to claim equal status with him ("we're just like you"); Veeru is forced into exile far from Ramgarh when he snares a domesticity that has been snatched from the Thakur. Their "rebellions" are short-lived in a plot that provides them no happy ending. In contrast, when the Thakur strangles Gabbar, Gabbar chops off the Thakur's arms; when Gabbar is jailed, he escapes; and in the version that circulated for a quarter century and consolidated *Sholay*'s fame, Gabbar survives the Thakur's efforts at apprehension to likely escape, for he has already shown that no jail can hold him.

Focusing on Gabbar as the film's "hero" exposes *Sholay*'s latent plot, one that effectively challenges the authority of the feudal order and its complicity with the state. Whereas the manifest plot celebrates Jai and Veeru, it also affirms the hegemonic status quo that they are hired to serve, in however unorthodox a fashion, even as they expose its weaknesses. In this regard, Jai and Veeru confirm what the writer Fareed Kazmi calls *Sholay*'s "conservative, status-quoist, even regressive" elements that do not frontally combat the agents of social and political oppression.[47] That challenge *does* exist in the film, but it comes from Gabbar, on whom the camera lavishes equal if not similar attention. He is heard *about* before he is seen, in lore before language, possessing his own haunting background score that plays each time the camera nears him. His possessions appear before his presence in a much-heralded sequence that reveals first Gabbar's bullet-studded belt then his spurs, then his boots before his face, or his full form (figs. 2.22–2.24).

In contrast to the glamorous jeans-clad Jai and Veeru, Gabbar's appearance is sinister and counter-heroic. Paunchy, unshaven, dressed in military fatigues, chewing paan, he speaks with a strong lisp and a regional accent in crude, nonstandard Hindi that had seldom been performed on large-screen before.

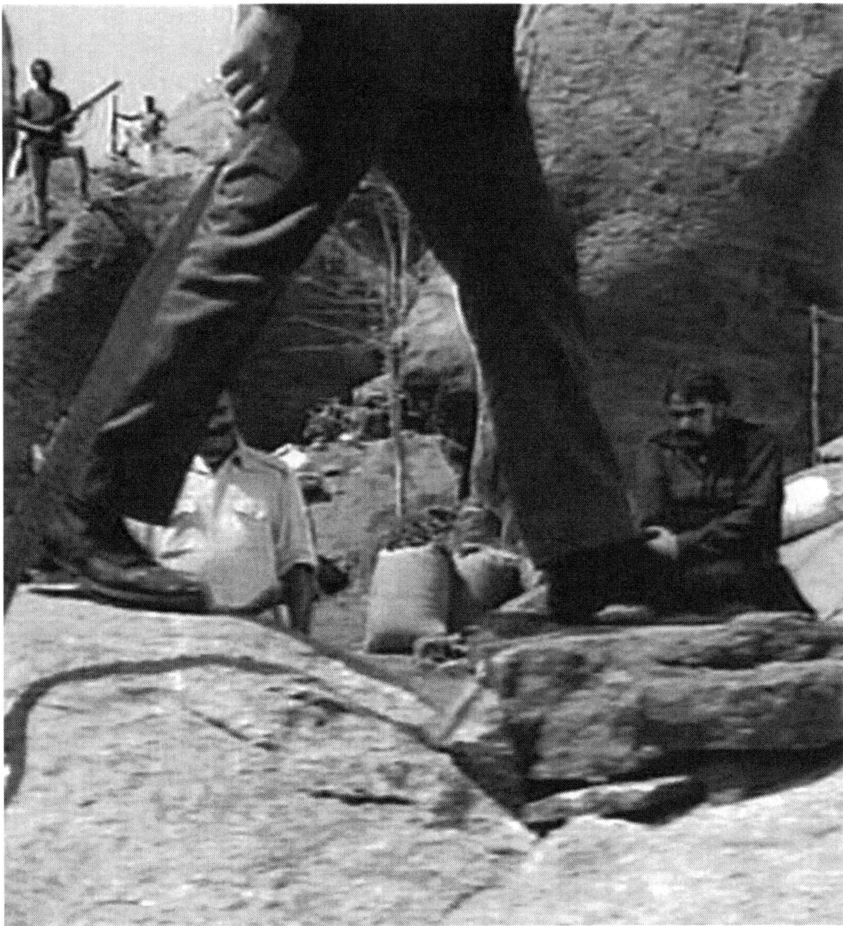

FIGURES 2.22-2.24 Gabbar Singh's first appearance in *Sholay* (boots, belt, legs, before face, before whole body).

Any overt sympathy for Gabbar dies in the manifest plot when he returns the mutilated body of young Ahmed to the village as a warning to the Thakur. But the scene equally decisively abolishes the Thakur's claims to sympathy as the villagers mutiny against his demands and blame their plight on him.

DINANATH [*pointing to Ahmed's body*]: Look at what you've done to us, Thakur. It's all your fault.
THAKUR: To live an honorable life, you have to pay a price, Dinanath.

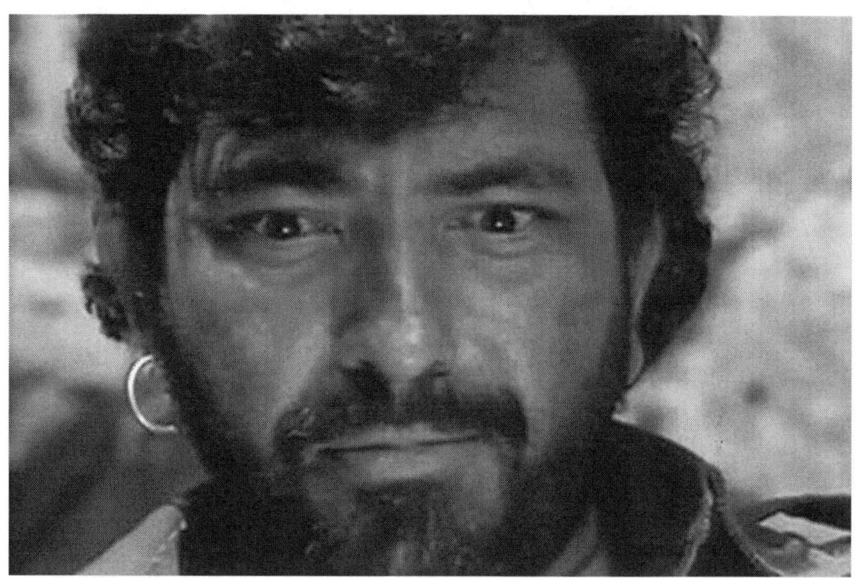

FIGURE 2.23

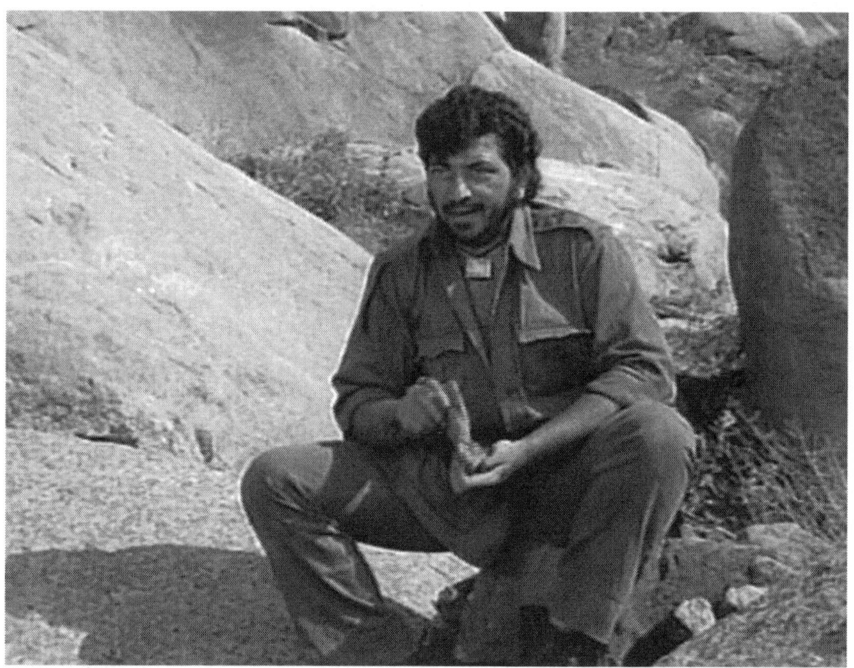

FIGURE 2.24

SHANKER: We are farmers not soldiers. We can pay with grain, but not with our children's lives.

THAKUR: Yes, Shanker. We're farmers. This country has been a country of farmers for many ages. But when an oppressor [*zalim*] attacked us, it was farmers who melted their ploughs into swords. The blood of cowards does not flow in our veins.

CHACHA: But how is this violence and bloodshed going to help? Nonviolence [*ahimsa*] has its place too.

THAKUR: I believe in *ahimsa* too, Chacha. But to bow before an oppressor [*zalim*] isn't *ahimsa*: it's cowardice.

KASHIRAM: Those who don't bend, break, Thakur.

THAKUR: The Thakur will neither bend nor break, Kashiram. The Thakur can only die. But as long as I live, I'll live with my head held high.

It is an unusually frank exchange between slave and master that to a degree hitherto unseen in Hindi cinema exposes the ignobility of the class that continues to demand the blood of its slaves to prop up its position. The heated exchange over Ahmed's body is remarkable. The villagers emerge as courageous pragmatists, preferring to bend rather than break, to pay Gabbar's tax in grain not blood. The tax-exempt Thakur emerges as increasingly unhinged. His invocation of hallowed nationalist rhetoric (*zalims*, attacks by oppressors, ploughs into swords) paradoxically aligns him with the bombast of unscrupulous politicians rather than the burnish of nationalist saints whom he eschews when he rejects the Gandhian practice of *ahimsa*. In response to each of the villager's challenges, the Thakur's voice and rhetoric get more impassioned, suspended from both logic and community as he clenches his teeth and delivers his replies with repeated vocatives. He invokes ideals like honor; they see the price in their children's blood. He invokes oppressors (*zalims*), missing entirely his own oppression over the subsistence farmers from whom he demands both labor and blood for the prosperity of his class. The scene dissipates quickly into peroration from an unexpected quarter when Ahmed's father, the blind Imam, tonelessly observes: "It's time for my namaaz. Today I'm going to ask God why he didn't give me two or three more sons to martyr for this village." Unable, once again, to provide or to protect, the Thakur has the most wounded in the village rescue him. In this case the blind and bereaved father is called to provide the peroration for the Thakur's faltering logic.

In retrospect, the exchange laments the death not just of Ahmed, but of the nation as well. If the Imam has no more sons to offer, the nation has no more heroes either. The *zalims* have gone from being outsiders (foreigners) to being insiders (the Thakur). If the villagers are not fully successful in standing up to the Thakur, Gabbar is, which is one of the reasons that he mobilizes *Sholay*'s unprecedented popular appeal, not Jai and Veeru, as scholars such as Prasad have suggested.[48]

Sholay's manifest narrative, urging the preservation of the feudal order at all costs, gets rewritten in the new economy of consumption inaugurated by the Emergency. Two things happen in this rewriting that illuminate the film's powerful latent counter-narrative. Gabbar emerges as the unexpected hero with a popular appeal dramatizing the plight of a class for whom the "national reconciliation narrative" proposed by critics such as Prasad is not paramount. It is this class that suffers, more directly than others, the violence of feudal and state overlords. Gabbar helps draw attention to an India that the state has forgotten or wishes to forget, providing an urgent reminder of those living below or outside middle-class purview. His person and presence counter the Jai-Veeru appeal addressed to the middle classes and their aspirations, and his counter-hegemonic stance addresses a subaltern culture to which it extends the bounty of voice and the hope of political inclusion.

Along with Gabbar, the figure of the Thakur also gets reconfigured in the film's latent narrative. Rather than rejecting the Thakur outright, *Sholay*'s viewers seemed to identify with him. If his suffering is melodramatic and unrealistic, theirs is not. While the Thakur loses his entire family to Gabbar's bullets in the film, the subalterns lose theirs to Sanjay Gandhi's bulldozers and his aggressive sterilization campaigns in everyday life. In exaggerating the sufferings of a ruling class, the film paradoxically ended up providing a believable portrait of India's underclass, one that viewers voraciously absorbed in their consumption and discovery of *Sholay*'s latent content. *Sholay*'s revenge plot allows a coexistence (or *sangam*) between latent and manifest content, absorbing the aspirations of multiply-motivated viewers and simultaneously allowing for the coexistence of profoundly contradictory ideologies and identifications.

CONCLUSION

Despite differences in compulsion and composition, Kapoor's triptych and *Sholay* both align with post-Independence India's underclasses and articulate their attractions to and disenchantments from the social contract. Like *Awara* and *Shree 420*, which were both committed to the "little man," *Sholay*'s latent plot in which Gabbar appears also speaks to that figure and brings his needs and preoccupations to the center of the screen. Like the Rajs in Kapoor's films, Gabbar too represents public fantasies. He too addresses a fractured civil society and a national dream irretrievably shattered. His use of violence and confrontation dramatizes the form of public control exercised *on* the subalterns, but it is not to be mistaken as an endorsement of action *by* them. Gabbar provides a potent tutorial (not dissimilar to Raj's on Chowpatty Beach in *Shree 420*) on the urgency of retrieving and recalibrating a national fantasy to include the little man and his concerns. The figure of Amjad Khan, the actor who played Gabbar, provides a small but powerful biographical detail connecting him to Kapoor's social vision beyond the logic of a role: Amjad Khan made his screen debut in 1957 playing Lachchu in Kapoor's *Ab Dilli Dur Nahin*.

Though Sippy's film shares much with Kapoor's, it also diverges from the earlier *oeuvre* in key points. The two appear almost a quarter century apart. Much changed in the four years between *Shree 420* and *Ab Dilli Dur Nahin*, and even more between *Dilli* and *Sholay*. It is not just that the era of the red rose had come to an end with the death of Nehru. It is also that Nehru's wide class base was fractured in the Age of Indira. The center of gravity from the 1950s' *oeuvre*, with its slum dwellers, sidewalk sleepers, and urban migrants as the focal point of screen and narrative, has given way in *Sholay* to a narrative dominated by the concerns of an aspiring middle class. Kapoor's soft-focus critique of that class is edgier and more direct in *Sholay*. If Raj in the earlier films can display national icons as backdrops to his ideology (fig. 2.25), *Sholay* exposes the narcissism of 1970s' ruling elites, who surround themselves with self-portraits to promote their claims to social ascendancy, as the Thakur does in his somber office (fig. 2.26).

Yet the heterogeneous subjects in these different bodies of work separated by a quarter century share one thing—a passionate, even persistent sense of what could have been but is not. Both sets of work provide ways of managing desires for that beautiful dream as well as regret over its demise. They both provide ways to contain, displace, and conceal large-scale public desires. They provide tutorials and critiques and embed melancholy and memory for the many fantasies that Nehru tried to combine into the idea of India. Raj Kapoor's ideal and idealized social solutions satisfied the fantasies of a post-Independence public keen to believe in political and institutional solutions to social problems. With *Sholay*, audiences discovered their nightmares projected on screen in films that outlined the inner lives and fears of viewers. If Raj Kapoor's films from the 1950s talked to Nehru's utopian nationalism, *Sholay* talked (and talked back to) his daughter, Indira's. In *Sholay*'s public fantasy, audiences had their fears both acknowledged and played out, and in this regard *Sholay* did much to "give reality to our dreams" as Nehru had urged in the "tryst with destiny" speech from 1947.

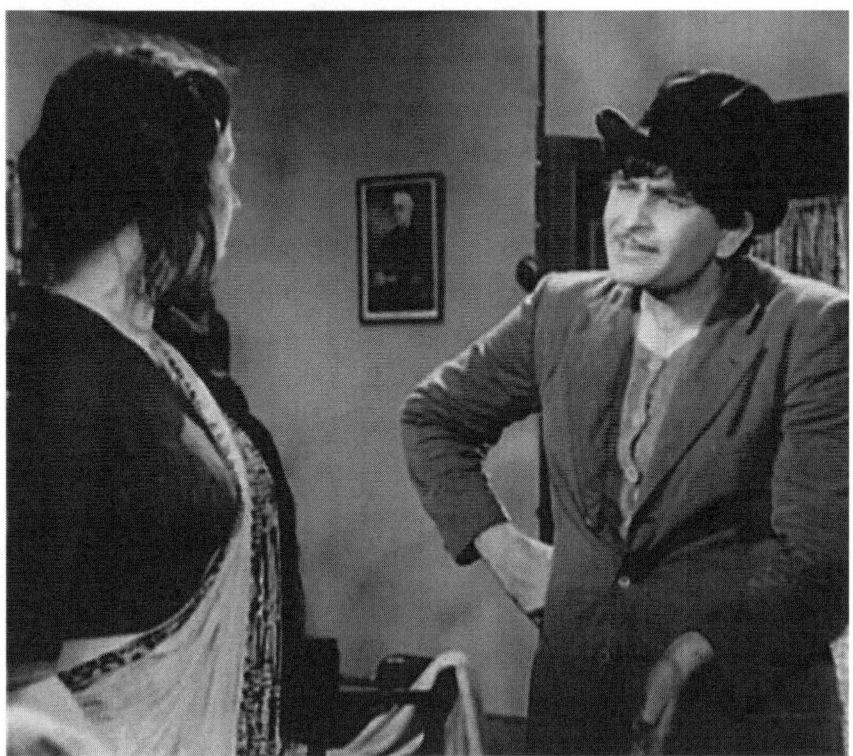

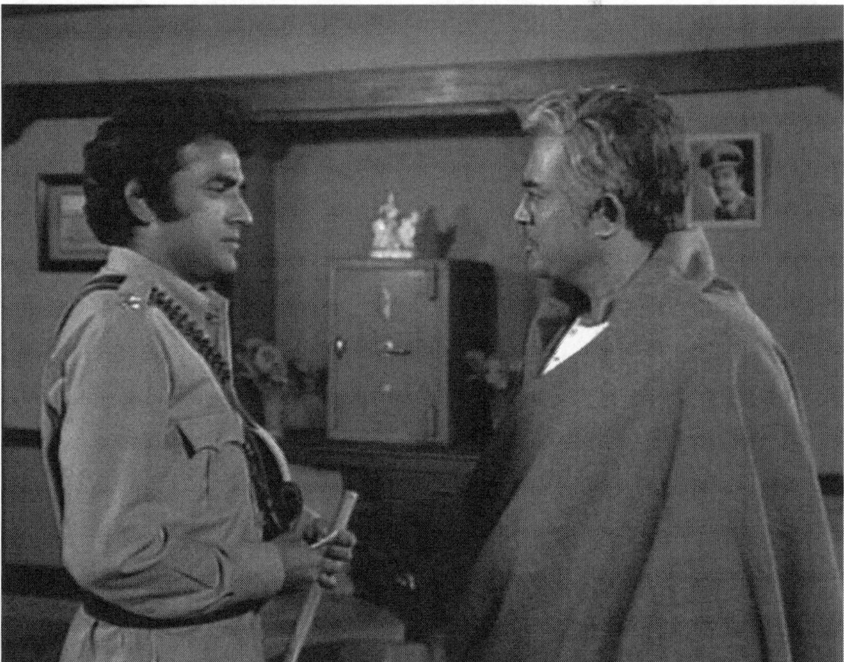

FIGURES 2.25 AND 2.26 Raj with Rita and Nehru's picture in background (*Shree 420*). (Courtesy Yash Raj Films) / The Thakur (*right*) and jailer with pictures of the Thakur and his class at the Police Academy in background (*Sholay*).

It is this process of talking and talking back that marks *Sholay* as distinct from the body of revenge films, frequently starring Amitabh Bachchan, that it spawned and with which it is frequently associated. In contrast to that cinema of immediate reaction, *Sholay*'s narrative and visual density made demands on its audience to contemplate, absorb, and reflect on images and desires projected for the first time on a 70mm screen. The result was, initially, stunned silence. "There was no reaction. . . . As on the premiere night, there was only silence," records the writer Anupama Chopra of the film's opening night (Chopra 2001:163). A week later, the theaters started filling up, and one owner informed Ramesh Sippy that his film was a hit, "because the sales of my soft drinks and ice creams are going down. . . . By the interval, the audience is so stunned that they are not coming out of the theatre," he explained (Chopra 2001:169). As viewers began to *get* the film, or parts of it, they returned for more, and kept returning for the multiple viewings that catapulted *Sholay*'s enduring success.

The encounter with *Sholay* was not short-lived. It required and requited a dialogue, both as noun, and as verb. One was *in* dialogue with *Sholay*, with its manifest and latent plots, with their contradictions and opportunities, a dialogue that began in the silence of absorption that marked *Sholay*'s first public screenings. Its latent plot inverted the manifest. Gabbar, paradoxically, contained Jai and the propulsive star power that Amitabh Bachchan had accrued by 1975 with *Zanjeer* (Chains, Prakash Mehra, 1973), *Deewaar* (The wall, Yash Chopra, released earlier the same year; see chapter 3), and now *Sholay*. In contrast to these Bachchan starrers that created and eventually destroyed an industry, *Sholay* had one crucial element none of the Bachchan revenge films of the later 1970s and 1980s had: Gabbar. *Sholay*'s complex latent plot required reflection not (re)action. Gabbar's actions were so outrageous that they halted imitation. Jai's on the other hand had a logic that was familiar and even rational. He would spawn imitators, and had to be eradicated. It is no accident that he has to die in *Sholay*.

However, in the cinema that followed without Gabbar's cautionary presence, Bachchan's characters proceeded unchecked in films such as *Andha Kanoon* (Blind justice, T. Rama Rao, 1983), *Inquilab* (Revolution, T. Rama Rao, 1984), and *Aaj ka Arjun* (Today's Arjun, K. C. Bokadia, 1990). Unrestrained by a Gabbar figure, Bachchan's avenging characters think nothing of gunning down brothers, friends, and even all of Parliament before disappearing in smoke themselves (as Bachchan's character did in *Inquilab*). If audiences could not *like* Gabbar, they would not imitate him. With Bachchan's characters, on the other hand, there was much to like and so less to restrain imitation. With these films, regrets the scholar Ziauddin Sardar, "society disappeared into a nebulous background blur, social justice was replaced with implausible, ridiculous scenarios of avenging personal wrongs," a depiction that aptly captures one of the darkest periods in Hindi cinema (Sardar 49–50). The diegetic violence associated with Bachchan's angry films underscores the gulf between this cinema and the 1950s, a decade "when culture, decency, and idealism prevailed. Those were the times of Jawaharlal Nehru," lamented Javed Akhtar, who scripted most of Bachchan's angry films.[49] Bachchan's *oeuvre* reveals two legacies that originate in his birthplace, Allahabad. One legacy is associated with Nehru and the other with his daughter, Indira; one with the rule of law and the other with the outlaw; one with unity, the other with rupture. After Bachchan (or Indira), *sangam* was no longer possible.

But before that decade arrived, and even alongside it, there appeared a corpus of films that pursued public nightmares not personal desires, social problems not ideals, criminals not solutions. In that corpus, which the following chapter analyzes, popular Hindi cinema seemed to have found a way to manage public fantasies and to *be* them when necessary.

3

CINEMA AS FAMILY ROMANCE

Hindi films can be regarded as contemporary folklore. And a folk hero, in any period, in any decade, is a personification of the moral values of that decade; he reflects the collective fantasies of the time.
—JAVED AKHTAR (RECORDED IN KABIR 1999:72)

THE 1975 EMERGENCY WAS A cataclysmic blow to modern India. The suspension of the Constitution and the termination of civil rights evaporated illusions of a democratic open society. The press was censored, opposition parties banned, and opponents of Prime Minister Indira Gandhi jailed and tortured. The nightmare ended with elections in 1977 that routed Mrs. Gandhi. Democracy returned, battered but emboldened. Most Indians around at the time recall the 1970s as a decade marked by grinding poverty, shortages in just about every essential commodity, and widespread labor unrest. Were they to try to study the period, though, they would find scant material to guide them, for a relative silence still surrounds much of the decade.

India's cinemas, however, did not let the political crisis pass unremarked. The year 1977 saw a burst of films in regional languages denouncing the Emergency, including *Mukti Chai* (a Bengali documentary, Cry for freedom, Utpalendu Chakraborty), *Ram Ram Gangaram* (in Marathi; Dada Kondke), and *Kissa Kursi Ka* (in Hindi; The story of a chair, Amrit Nahata), although these productions appeared to regional audiences and often for very short runs. Because the list does not include feature productions from Bollywood, it would be tempting to conclude that the cinema ignored the Emergency, or, if lore is correct, was effectively silenced by it.

To the contrary. If Bollywood did not directly pillory Mrs. Gandhi and the labia-lipped Sanjay (as novelists such as Salman Rushdie and others have done in memorable epithets), its blockbusters actively archived the culture of the period. In stark, often photographic, fidelity, its hits captured the everyday desperations that erupted in the protests that Mrs. Gandhi described as the "climate of violence and hatred" in her Emergency broadcast of June 27, 1975.[1] Unlike Rushdie, who was protected by his residence abroad and a foreign passport (despite which Mrs. Gandhi filed suit for his description of her in *Midnight's Children* that she won in a London court), Hindi popular cinema had no such protection.[2] It had to tread carefully if it wished to avoid the fate of *Kissa Kursi Ka*, the film allegedly buried under a Maruti car factory for its critical representation of an unpopular prime minister.[3] Bollywood's commentary on the 1970s, much as its commentary on other moments, is widely present, though it emerges indirectly through the use of highly elaborate symbols that displace the nation's political crisis and its public fantasies elsewhere.

Popular cinema from the 1970s is very much a cinema *of* the 1970s. The fashions in the cinema with their exuberant bell bottoms, runway-width collars, shaggy sideburns, and platter-size sunglasses conjure the abandon of the decade. But the faces and features on screen also tell another story, albeit a darker one. In a blockbuster such as *Deewaar* (The wall, Yash Chopra, 1975), for instance, the face of the dockworker who refuses a payday shakedown is the face of the Naxalite activist from Bengal with his distinct features, complexion, and accent. Likewise, the labor organizer who must be taken down by a corrupt mine owner is shown at a demonstration before a red banner, its color, the honorific after his name (Anand*babu*), and his industry (coal) all recalling the violent standoffs between labor and management in Bengal during the 1970s. The details are part of *Deewaar*'s referential illusion: small, almost insignificant signs that gesture toward a familiar reality without fully substantiating it. Other more explicit cues, including plot topoi such as the dearth of jobs for college graduates, are more direct signifiers of the period's tensions. Sedimented together they reference aspects of the decade and its complexities. Thus, while *Deewaar* is putatively the story of two brothers in Bombay, cues such as these—some visual, some aural—insert layers of meanings that dramatically expand the narrative canvas, making it also the story of India at a particular moment.

This chapter analyzes the narratives and iconographies of India embedded in a trilogy of blockbuster Hindi films from the 1970s: *Deewaar*, *Trishul* (Trident, Yash Chopra, 1978), and *Shakti* (Power, Ramesh Sippy, 1982). All three were scripted by Salim Khan and Javed Akhtar; all three cast Amitabh Bachchan as a character named Vijay; and all three mobilize the family as a topos around which the nation's imaginary is structured and on which its most pressing anxieties are projected. *Deewaar* and *Trishul* were blockbusters; *Shakti* is regarded as a film to rival Sippy's *Sholay* (1975), though it never quite achieved the latter film's outsize achievement at the box office where *Sholay* (Embers, Ramesh Sippy, 1975) remains the #1 all-time top grosser adjusted for inflation (see ibos.network.com). These films represent some of the decade's aspirations as well as its repressions that together I call its public fantasies. Through a reading of these blockbusters, this chapter explores the extent to which the traumas of the decade were displaced onto the family and the crisis in political culture was recast in *social* terms as a Family Romance in popular Hindi film. For reasons that will become evident shortly, two dominant myths collide in these blockbuster narratives: the nation as mother and the family as nation. Films such as *Deewaar* invert the nation's central political conflicts in terms of the family and reframe it around its most cherished social belief, namely, the sanctity of motherhood.[4] In this inversion, the oppositional culture of political life is represented as infecting private life as well, and both are rendered unstable, even combustible. Rather than resolving conflict, the mother is placed as the source of it both in political life (where she is symbol of the nation) and in private life (where she is represented, often in highly sentimental terms, as the center of the family).

The biological family and the symbolic nation-as-family become sites of mutual threat in 1970s Hindi cinema, each destabilizing the other in cinema's representation of the period. These narratives of popular cinema provide access to the political unconscious of modern India in striking ways, revealing what the political theorist Michael Rogin, in the context of Cold War U.S. cinema, identifies as the "register of anxiety" that pervaded the public culture of the decade.[5] The nation's political unconscious, like that of human subjects, communicates in symbols in order to evade the strenuous repression of the nation's conscious. Cinema's use of formal symbolism renders it a medium eminently capable of expressing and evading the apparatus of repression especially characteristic of the decade of the Emergency.

In a series of wildly popular blockbusters such as Salim-Javed's *Deewaar–Trishul–Shakti* trilogy, popular Hindi cinema imagined the social geography of India, addressed its problems, idealized their solutions, and—to borrow a phrase from Laura Mulvey—generally became the primal scene of many of independent India's modern mythologies.[6] Appearing a few months before the Emergency when the myth of the nation appeared to have devoured its young, *Deewaar*'s manifest content initially appears conciliatory if not downright celebratory of the state. It is, after all, the story of a boy who is unjustly rendered homeless, arrives penniless in the metropolis, and makes a home and a fortune for himself. When it is discovered that his wealth is the result of smuggling operations, the state comes down hard, and the man is shot by a policeman who is also his righteous younger brother. Both subject and state get their moments of triumph, though in the end it is the collective, in the form of the state, that prevails over the individual who is punished.

However, rather than restoring the nation's myth of opportunity and justice, *Deewaar* exposes its collapse and uncovers a form of violence so grotesque that it is displaced onto the family. Here, the latent narrative is one of a mother who desires her son, commissions his murder when her desire is brought to light, and a state that rewards her for it. In short, the film rescripts the Oedipal drama from Jocasta's point of view, with her desires and agency at the center. In this script, the victim is criminalized and the criminal rendered the victim. The ironies of such a displacement are cued throughout the film. *Deewaar*'s family violence on the child is widely understood to symbolize the state's upon its citizens, and both are rendered culpable in this inversion. Uncovering some of these acts of displacement in *Deewaar* and their revisions in *Trishul* and *Shakti* exposes both the social work that the cinema did *in* India and the social work it did *for* the nation.

Amitabh Bachchan's reprise of the role of Vijay, pioneered in *Zanjeer* (Chains, Prakash Mehra, 1973) as the man who would break the law to restore justice, assured *Deewaar* immediate success. Its box office returns placed it #2 for the year, following *Sholay*.[7] Scholars such as Jyotika Virdi, Vijay Mishra, and Ranjani Mazumdar among others regard Bachchan's role in *Deewaar* as shaping not just the decade but his entire star persona to the extent that the star, somewhat paradoxically, began to reframe his outsize status in Hindi cinema to what Virdi calls a "story of victimization against which he fought each time with resilience and grit, uncannily matching the characters he played on screen."[8] In readings such as this, *Deewaar* provides a transformative master plot that reframes both star and audience within an intoxicatingly self-referential narrative.

Attentive to these accounts, this chapter pursues a different text to "read" alongside *Deewaar*'s. Rather than the actor as a parallel text to the film, as Vijay Mishra named him (V. Mishra 2002:125ff.), I read the film alongside the public fantasies of the nation, which serve as its parallel text. In this approach, *Deewaar* exposes fissures in the national narrative that might not otherwise be apprehensible. It also reveals efforts at dissolving, if not resolving, differences between public and national fantasies that diverged so spectacularly in the decade.

The chapter proceeds in three parts. It analyzes the dominance of the trope of the family to represent anxieties of the period, explores *Deewaar*'s tensions at narrating and containing an incendiary critique of the decade, and develops the "revisions" to this film's master plot as they were re-scripted in *Trishul* and *Shakti*. The chapter concludes with proposing the social function of cinema as Family Romance.

FILM, FAMILY, AND FAMILY ROMANCE

The persistent use of the family as source and symbol of national tension is not new to *Deewaar*.[9] What is remarkable in *Deewaar* is how the national traumas of the 1970s are displaced almost wholesale upon the family, which in turn is rendered patently dysfunctional in the film. The hitherto mythologized mother is a murderer; the crime she commits is infanticide; and the state participates in the cover-up. Rather than the family providing solace *from* the state, it provides solace *for* the state, which escapes culpability for its crimes through the act of displacement.

Deewaar's dystopian account of both family and nation had a rawness hitherto unseen in a commercially successful popular film. The story was too intense with its exposure of too many wrongs for its ending to be fully satisfying. And so the scriptwriters Javed Akhtar and Salim Khan rewrote the story and kept rewriting it till they got it right.[10] This chapter analyzes *Deewaar*, its first revision *Trishul* (1978), which easily outpaced *Deewaar* at the box office for the decade and in retrospect,[11] and *Shakti* (1982), the second effort to rewrite *Deewaar* from a different directorial perspective. The rewrites are a structuralist's dream. The essential elements remain the same: nation allegorized in the family, conflict between parent and child, youth as a problem, the identity of criminality, and the diegetic use of death to accentuate—or to solve—problems. What changes across the films, however, is the role each element plays in creating and solving problems. Thus, in *Deewaar* the state creates a problem that the family solves; in *Trishul*, a parent creates the problem that the child solves; and in *Shakti*, a criminal outside the social order creates a problem for both the state and the family that the two together solve.[12] The migration of criminality across the three films from state to a caricatured smuggler external to the social order serves to contain problems and even to render them innocuous by the time they are staged in *Shakti* where the drama of national conflict has devolved into a family melodrama. In each new script, youth goes from indicating a prob-lem *(Deewaar)* to being the problem *(Shakti)*. The death of the protagonist halts the future in *Deewaar*; in *Shakti*, it enables it.

The three films together form a Salim-Javed trilogy that functions as a Family Romance, and the term deserves elaboration. It was fleetingly outlined by Freud in 1909 as a coping mechanism by which a subject, almost always male, authors fantasies about his origins that are more amenable to him than his real family. Freud postulated that the child's ability to create an alternate "reality" through storytelling generally involved "getting free from the parents of whom he now has a low opinion and of replacing them by others who, as a rule, are of a higher social standing."[13] In short, the Family Romance is a liberation narrative that enables the child to master a world in which he is otherwise powerless. The *gesture* of narrating and telling a story is a way of liberating the subject from his subjection. In Freud's account, the power of the family is typically inverted in the Family Romance, and its taboos, notably the Oedipal complex, are evaded by the subject's acts of fantasy and storytelling. Replacing the biological father with a fantasy one allows the child to evade the consequences of Oedipal desire. The romance allows the child to believe that the man he abhors is not really his father, which makes patricide and the guilt associated with desiring it unnecessary.

The Family Romance explains two main functions of narrative. It provides a frame for reflecting on the *structure* of stories and also for postulating their *function,* and it is in these contexts that it has such resonance in domains beyond the couch. Despite its apparent manifest violence to the parents, the Family Romance is above all a conciliation narrative. In enabling the subject to fabricate an alternative history to the one he inhabits, the Family Romance enables him to manage and eventually to accept "reality," even as it liberates him from it. Its biographical fantasy is crucially linked to a sense-making function, allowing the subject to displace perceived traumas of the family onto the realm of fantasy where they can be archived if not fully resolved. In this, the Family Romance is an epistemological project: its act of narration is also one of interpretation that explicates even as it narrates. What matters is not the actual story itself but the *act* of ordering and telling stories that the Family Romance captures. It is thus both a form of exposure (of the subject's deepest desires and his "reality") as well as of subterfuge (in which one reality is covered by another more desirable one).

Applied beyond the individual to culture more widely, the concept of Family Romance probes the work that particularly popular narratives do in a specific cultural moment. It allows one to ask what traumas these narratives mask, what "reality" they seek liberation from, and to explore the kinds of fantasies a culture develops in the process. The application of Family Romance from individual to society enables one to uncover the structure and function of narratives that were particularly popular and to ask what kinds of unconscious they convey and conceal.[14]

DEEWAAR, THE MANIFEST NARRATIVE

Released on January 24, 1975, *Deewaar*'s story has a singular preoccupation with provision that captures above all the shortages of the decade. Every character in the film and every conflict is driven by the desire to provide materially for others, or to withhold provision from others. Workers ask management for a share of the profits from their labor to provide for their families; parents sacrifice to provide for their children; children do the same for their parents and siblings; the state proves unable to provide basic amenities such as housing and food; and criminals step in at the breach. The film opens with a labor organizer standing before a red banner: "Hum majdooron ki ek hi mang: roti, kapda, aur makaan" [We workers have only one demand: food, clothing, and housing], a manifesto emphasizing the shortage of fundamental goods during the decade (fig. 3.1).

The slogan "roti, kapda, aur makaan" echoes a widespread cry of the period made famous in a 1974 film of the same name that celebrated its golden jubilee (50-week run) the week of *Deewaar*'s release and that went

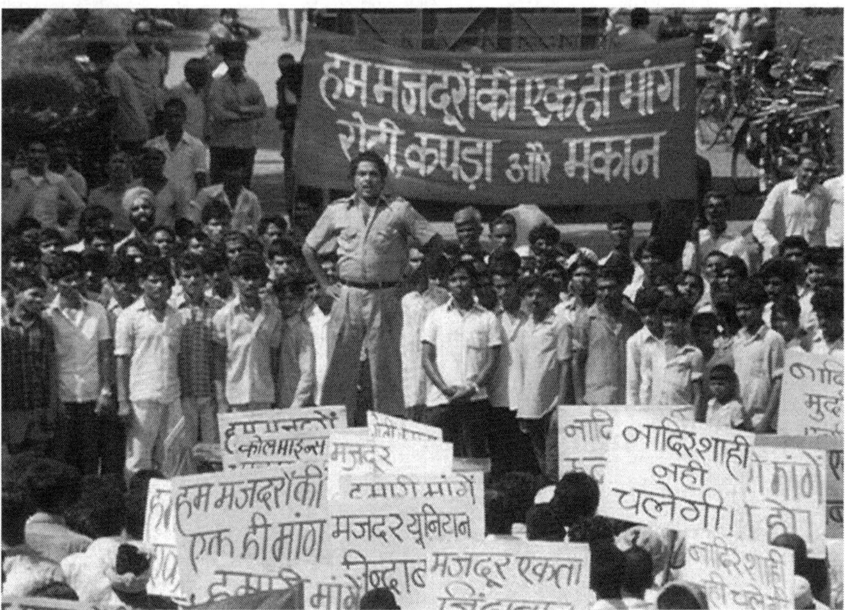

FIGURE 3.1 Anandbabu at demonstration before red flag ("Hum majdooron ki ek hi mang: roti, kapda, aur makaan"), in *Deewaar* (1975).

on to become #5 at the box office for the decade (ibosnetwork.com, for the 1970s). To quell the demonstration and the workers' demands, the organizer's family is kidnapped; he is coerced into accepting a bad contract; and his workers regard him a sellout. They beat him up, tattoo "my father is a thief" on his son's arm, and make life for the family miserable. Anandbabu, the disgraced organizer, abandons his family and disappears; his wife, Maa (played by the actress Nirupa Roy), takes her children, Vijay and Ravi (played as grown-ups by actors Amitabh Bachchan and Shashi Kapoor, respectively), from their comfortable bungalow to the streets of Bombay.

The now-single mother and her sons live under a bridge with other migrants to Bombay. Maa finds work carrying bricks for a high-rise apartment building under construction; Ravi longs to go to a school whose tuition the family cannot afford, so Vijay goes to work polishing shoes so his little brother Ravi can do just that. As young men, Vijay works in the Bombay docks as a coolie to support the family while his brother, now a college graduate, searches in vain for employment. Eventually, Vijay takes on the gangster who brutally exploits the dockworkers, joins a rival gang, amasses vast wealth, and purchases a lavish mansion for his mother and brother. Not long after, Vijay buys the high-rise that his mother's labor had built two decades earlier. Ravi, meanwhile, like most of India's youth of the period, has trouble finding work. He joins the police force, which offers him guaranteed pay and a squalid government-issued flat. Eventually, Ravi the policeman discovers Vijay's underworld connections and pursues Vijay's gang. Vijay meanwhile plans to end his association with crime and marry Anita in order to give his unborn son a different life than the one he had. The dénouement comes swiftly. Anita is murdered on her wedding day; at Maa's injunction, Ravi shoots Vijay in the back during a chase, and Vijay dies on his wedding night in a temple in his waiting mother's arms, breathing "I could never sleep away from you. Today, I'm lying in your arms. Make me sleep again." The police awards Ravi a medal for his bravery, which he publicly "awards" to his mother, and the film proceeds as a flashback of Maa's memories of the family's migration from Bengal to Bombay.

In the course of the film, the family's economic condition changes quite dramatically and with it their housing situation. Their comfortable Bengal bungalow recedes to a Bombay bridge under which the family resides with other homeless migrants; at some point they move to a room in a tenement. Vijay's earnings eventually bring them to a single-family home of some grandeur; and Ravi's police service brings him and his mother to a rundown flat where the water and electricity stop for days on end. Home for the Varmas brothers, though, is not where the hearth is: it is where Maa is. In the most famous scene from the film, all its major preoccupations come together: provision, property, criminality, law, justice, kinship, ideals, idealism, and home. Holding them together is the giant figure of Maa. The brothers meet under the bridge where they had lived during their childhood twenty years previously. Vijay warns Ravi of the underworld's price on Ravi's head and urges him to seek a transfer to a different town. Ravi refuses to give up the case against the underworld. "My ideals won't let me," he replies.

> VIJAY: Your ideals! Bah! What have your ideals given you? A scrappy uniform? A duty jeep? A rundown house? Look at me and look at you. We both came from this same footpath, and now look at what I have today. I have buildings, bank balances, cars. What do you have?
> RAVI: *Mere pas Maa hain.* [I have Maa.]

Countering Vijay's catalog of possessions with the same economy even while putatively critiquing it, Ravi's "I have Maa" is an awkward locution in any language. But the rhetoric of possession so permeates the film that it is the only way to claim kinship here. It is not that Maa lives with Ravi that matters; it is that he *has* her that makes him different from Vijay. At a time when very little could be owned, and much less provided, family relations, like ideals, succumb to the rhetoric of property and ownership. Thus, Ravi *has* Maa.[15]

But Maa is not just the biological mother. She is also Hindustan, undivided and free. Not only does the poet Muhammad Iqbal's patriotic anthem, "sare jehan se achcha," play each time the brothers are under the bridge, *Deewaar*'s mise-en-scène inverts the anthem's jingoistic ethos ("Our Hindustan is the best in the world . . . ancient Greece, Egypt, and Rome have all vanished without a trace, but we continue to shine in the firmament") in a deeply ironic comment on the bridge and on Hindustan. Rather than Hindustan being better than all lands, it is barely as good as them; rather than bringing the brothers closer, the bridge further estranges them. The bridge, thus, stands witness to the betrayals and failures of state and nation that this film marks, and it is in its presence that some of the most egregious betrayals of the film occur. Thus, it is under the bridge when Maa accepts Vijay's offer to be the man of the house and work so they can together send the baby of the house (Ravi) to school; and it is the consequence of the pact under that bridge that propels Vijay to do the things that men do for their women. But the pact they make is hideously corrupt, far more so than anything the gangster Vijay will do as a grown-up.

In accepting Maa's call to replace the father, to give her his childhood in order to be her man even though he is still a boy, Vijay is fulfilling not the

Oedipal wish, but the Jocasta wish: the desire of the mother for her son. In accepting Vijay's offer to work so that "their" baby, Ravi, can go to school, Maa has catapulted Vijay from being her son to being her provider. He is the husband she wants, not the husband she married. Her extramarital transgression is monstrous not because it is extramarital, but because it is intrafamilial. In taking her son as her mate, Maa's domination over him is complete. She is not just Jocasta; she is worse than Sophocles' doomed mother.

Jocasta's is the submission of desires for her son that comes from ignorance and avoidance; Maa's come from will and design. Having unwittingly "married" her son, Jocasta punishes herself with death when she discovers what she has done. Maa, in contrast, punishes her *son* with death in order to avoid discovery. Jocasta sought to evade her fate when she learns it at Oedipus' birth. Maa sought to embrace her fate, knowing she could evade its punishment. And the "punishment" has some cruel ironies. If a bride of Vijay's must die, Maa ensures it is Anita, the woman Vijay wants to marry, rather than herself, the woman who wants to "marry" Vijay under the bridge and cannot bear to share him with others. Maa commissions Vijay's murder after she learns of his plans to marry Anita, and she places herself at Anita's wedding altar in the temple to await her son, who spends his wedding night in his mother's arms rather than in Anita's.

Maa's is a terrible demand, far worse than Jocasta's in every way. Whereas Sophocles' mother simply took her child's adulthood away from him, Maa claims her son's childhood. For this obscene, unspeakable desire, *Vijay* (not Maa) must be punished. The mother will not accept what she has demanded under the bridge; she will not take responsibility for the violence that she causes. Maa's disavowal is so complete that it takes two decades and the news that Anandbabu has died riding the rails to permit the stirrings of her repressed to come to the surface. And when it does it is terrible. Her punishment comes brutally, and it is visited upon the son—the object of her desire—rather than on herself, its instigator. Maa conspires with the baby, Ravi, to shoot Vijay. "The woman has done her duty. Now a mother is going to await her son," she declares, heading off to the temple after handing Ravi his gun (fig. 3.2).

Like Ravi, Maa too objectifies kinship. Ravi regards a mother as something that can be owned. Maa regards kinship duties as something that can be disavowed, displacing the murder of Vijay to "the woman" and "a mother" rather than claiming it herself. Moreover, the twinning of her violence with the sanction of the state (the police force) and the piety of religion (the temple) is almost unbearable. But Maa knows that the perfect crime takes no prisoners. Vijay must die and she must do it in such a way

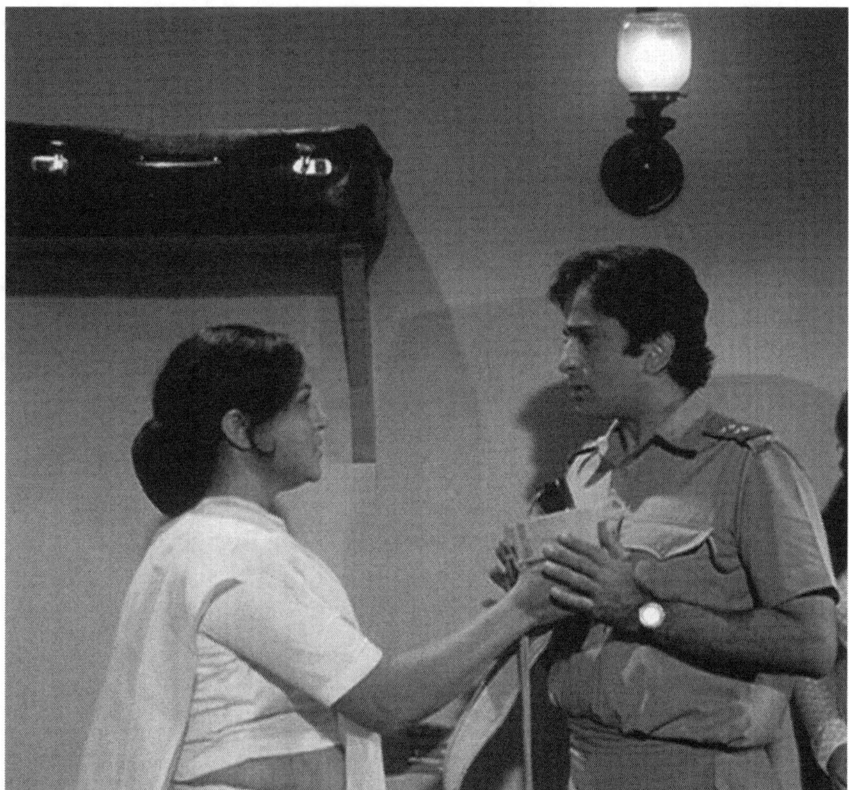

FIGURE 3.2 Maa handing Ravi his gun in *Deewaar*.

as to make it *her* sacrifice, not his. For this the state's participation is crucial. And the state, fully duped, hands Maa a medal for the murder of her son.

The family's vulnerability in their refuge under the Bombay bridge are heightened by the predation of their surroundings. Maa finds employment carrying bricks for a high-rise construction project, the only work available for the desperately indigent in megacities. Denied stable housing themselves, migrants are crippled by the labor of building it for others. Subjected to the unwanted attentions of an overseer, Maa is rescued by her new "husband," the adolescent Vijay, who stones the harasser. Years later, Vijay purchases the same high-rise for his mother at a price he is told is too high. The transaction between bridge and high-rise is not just one between economic orders and the individual's new purchasing power. It is the journey that signals both the fulfillment of a dream and a nightmare. For Vijay the migrant, purchasing a building signals his accomplishment.

He has succeeded in securing a roof and walls ("Deewaars") to shelter his family. More specifically, he has succeeded in achieving what his father had exhorted in the opening speech before the striking miners: he has achieved the dream of "roti, kapda, aur makaan."

However, the purchase of a place to call home comes at great cost. Vijay brings the building's title to Maa but she will not accept it, having just learned of his criminal activities. She moves out of his bungalow to Ravi's squalid flat, and Vijay is left tearing the title to shreds. The dream that Vijay has offered Maa—a home, respectability, security—covers a nightmarish secret that neither he nor she can speak. Maa's departure from Vijay's world marks this rift, though it is not yet one he can recognize. It is only when Vijay returns to the primal scene—the bridge—that the rupture becomes clearest. "I have buildings, bank balances, cars. What do *you* have?" he asks Ravi. Without missing a beat, Ravi claims Maa as commodity and gloats: "Mere pas Maa hain." Their conversation about who "has" Maa thus devolves into a contest not just about the rightful heirs of the nation, but the rightful vision of the state. One enables material plenitude ("buildings, bank balances, cars"), the other, purely symbolic substance ("Maa"). In Vijay's depiction, Maa is the nation, a nurturer. In Ravi's, she is a menacing figure akin to the state that stands behind her.

This dialogue, possibly the most famous in modern Hindi cinema history, forces a latent content on *Deewaar* and on its larger narrative of the migrant and home. Ravi's insistent claim that he *has* Maa makes explicit a circuit between mother, home, and nation. To have Maa is to have all three. Yet the possession of all three is largely symbolic: *Deewaar*'s manifest content is a symbolic solution to a problem that cannot be resolved. The dialogue between the brothers underscores the tenuousness of the mother–home–nation circuit. It is unavailable in real, material terms, which is precisely why it must be overstated in such grandiose rhetoric. Maa is neither able to feed nor shelter her children. "Roti, kapda, aur makaan" remain elusive in her domain.

DEEWAAR, THE LATENT NARRATIVE

Scripted during a particularly fraught moment in India's political and economic history, the migrant's journey in *Deewaar* plays a key role in dismantling the earlier nationalist fantasy of nation-as-home. Corrupting the circuit of mother–home–nation, *Deewaar*'s Maa not only displaces her children from their natal home, she also insists that they sacrifice their lives for her depravity. To confront this depravity head-on in the film, to give it voice and to speak its name, would topple the vulnerable edifice of the nation circa 1975. Moreover, it would be unacceptable in the terms of commercial cinema that *Deewaar* enjoyed. So *Deewaar* submerges its critique in a powerful latent narrative that connects the specifics of the Vijay story with the national one. If *Deewaar* is the story of a dream deferred, it is also a story of a dream that festers like a sore and then runs. The metaphor of "running" is not made in vain. Vijay's idealistic father, who rouses his fellow miners in a cry for "roti, kapda, aur makaan," pleas not to topple the system of capitalist wealth but to share it more equitably with labor. His abandonment of the family is in part enforced by the recognition of the terrible price Maa extracts from her citizen-children. Protecting Maa involves selling his brother miners to the mine-owner's interests; their wrath brings in Maa's henchmen (the police) to save him. It is an atrocious place to be caught, between the Scylla of ideals and the Charybdis of corruption.

Anandbabu's departure has conventionally been regarded as a flight from the family, but another way to understand it could be as a flight away from Maa and her impossible demands that no compromise but corruption can resolve. In fleeing Maa, Anandbabu flees not just the mother–home–nation circuit: he also publicizes its fraudulence. His alternative "home" is nowhere and everywhere. From the moment he leaves Maa, the film portrays Anandbabu roaming the ends of the nation in third-class rail compartments in which he eventually dies. His journey-without-destination not only disrupts the settlement narrative Maa promises her children; it also revises it. His is not an alternative to the state's vision so much as an indication of its impossibility and corruption. Anandbabu's aimless twenty-year train ride in the temples of industrial modernity testifies to the gulf between the soaring rhetoric and the hopeless reality of his situation. Vijay's tattoo ("mera bap chor hain") is not marking a theft by the father, but the theft *of* the father who is exiled from the family along with his efforts to secure it "roti, kapda, aur makaan."

And it is precisely Anandbabu's ideals that the film develops in the figure of Vijay. Unlike the father who flees his family and community when threatened, Vijay stays and fights. He emerges a criminal in Maa's and Ravi's eyes because he is willing to serve as their provider when those responsible fail. Early in the film, Maa berates Vijay for fighting back during the dockyard shakedown. "Why can't you be like your father?" she poses. "Would you really rather I were like him?" Vijay replies. "That I slink away?" She replies with a slap. But when he goes from activist to actor, she shoots him. In this case, he is reviled for being a smuggler, and the figure deserves some scrutiny.

Virtually every Hindi film in the 1970s created a villain called a smuggler in the Anglophone locution. The term's seventeenth-century origins of someone who conveys goods into a country to avoid paying legal duty is only one part of the Bollywood smuggler's portfolio. The smuggler that Vijay becomes is more closely allied with the later eighteenth-century meaning of one who "gets possession of something by stealth or clandestinely" (*OED*). Vijay's smuggling activities in *Deewaar* reveal him to be a figure of regulation and redress rather than corruption, as the episodes below adumbrate. Taking on the dockyard gangsters following the payday shakedown, Vijay encounters their operations in a giant warehouse. During a high-testosterone fight, sacks of grain and barrels of oil come crashing down. The gangsters, it turns out, are hoarders who acquire staple foodstuffs that they store in a godown and sell at high prices to the middle classes and the poor during periods of shortage. Rather than wiping out hoarders by providing subsidized staples inexpensively as promised, the state first creates the food shortages by mismanaging the supply chain, and then enables the black market to thrive by failing to stamp it out. India's considerable agricultural output is sold overseas to prop up its hard currency reserves; its population suffers rising prices and limited foodstuffs, and the hoarder is born.[16] Vijay's "victory" over the hoarder thus regulates and potentially restores a market that neither capitalism nor the socialist ideology espoused by the state can quite control.

In another instance, Vijay joins a rival gang and is commissioned with capturing a boatload of gold from Dubai. Despite being a heavy and cumbersome commodity that is hard to disguise and harder to transport, gold was the commodity of choice among Bollywood smugglers of the decade, including the infamous Robert in Manmohan Desai's *Amar Akbar Anthony* (1977), who loses crates of gold in a burning car (fig. 3.3).

Smuggling gold in *Deewaar*, like hoarding staple foods, also reveals a story of state ineptitude and failure. In India's economy of the period where land ownership was limited in part because land was limited (and in part because credit was hard to access), gold has historically been the investment of choice. There has always been high demand for it among individuals who find in it a security akin to that of real (or landed) property. Because of high demand, gold in India is always priced higher than it is on the world market. Thus, when gold arrives from Dubai as it does in *Deewaar*, it has been purchased at a lower price to be resold at the market price in India. The transaction is deemed illegal because the state collects no duty on it. However, the transaction also exposes the resistance of the state to free-market competition. In India's highly protectionist economy of the 1970s, "foreign" commodities were banned, industry remained lugubrious, innovation lagged, and those entrepreneurs (such as smugglers) who provided the masses access to security by procuring goods or services such as gold were criminalized. In this context, smuggling gold has a socialist patina of

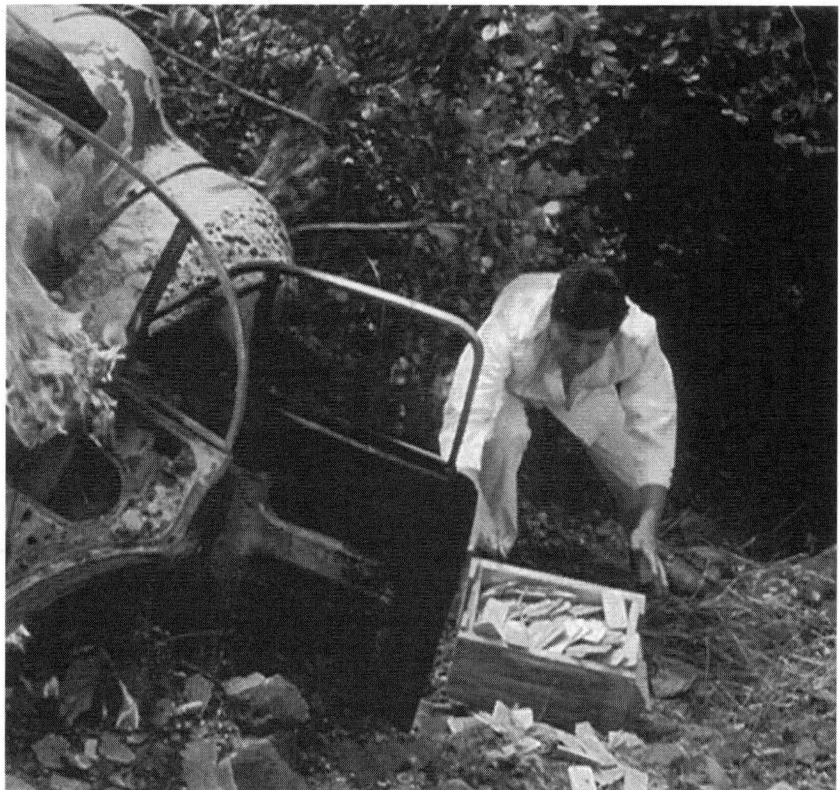

FIGURE 3.3 Crates of gold fall out of a burning car in *Amar Akbar Anthony*.

(COURTESY DEI ENTERTAINMENT)

sorts: the smuggler makes available a security that the state has withheld from its citizens.[17]

Vijay plays a role in the warehouse and during the gold raid in redistributing the resources the state keeps from its citizens. His activities underscore the fault lines of state competence and summon a combustible critique of the nation's myth as public provider. It is for smuggling in *this* critique in which the state is withheld its "due" that Vijay is eventually disciplined by a death planned by the state in the form of his mother, who hands the state (the police) a gun (fig. 3.2).

"INDIA IS INDIRA"

Assessing *Deewaar* two decades after its release, its scriptwriter, Javed Akhtar, offered his perspective on the zeitgeist that the film so starkly captured:

> When we were writing *Deewaar*, we were not aware of the sociological causes, implications, or symbolism. But the fact is that writers are also a part of society, and we were perhaps expressing the need prevalent at that time. The Emergency was imposed and the average Indian was losing faith in the various institutions—the police, courts, the government, the bureaucracy, and so on. When that happens, some kind of aggressive individuality develops. . . . In a society that lacked faith, it was natural that the gangster of *Deewaar* should take birth.[18]

Akhtar's remarks on the period bring a crucial point into focus. Not only did Indira Gandhi's Emergency evaporate the national ideals spawned during Independence, but she insisted on replacing earlier notions of Indian democracy with her own. Thus, "India is Indira; Indira is India" became her campaign slogan in 1971, and Mrs. Gandhi scripted herself as both mother and nation in speech and image to the extent that the hagiography persisted even after her death in 1984, as the election poster in figure 3.4 illustrates.[19]

Indira Gandhi's family psychodrama has unnerving resonances with *Deewaar*'s: like Maa, Indira Gandhi too prospered after she absented her husband, Feroze, from public life; like Maa, Indira Gandhi too anointed a younger son, Sanjay, her henchman; and like Maa, Indira Gandhi too commissioned the murder of the nation's young. In this case, the assassinations were accomplished quite literally through Sanjay's forced sterilization campaigns and more metaphorically by the Emergency and what Salman Rushdie named a "sperectomy: the draining-out of hope."[20] Indira Gandhi's reign inaugurated the evaporation of Nehruvian ideals and their replacement with corruption and cynicism. In this, Mrs. Gandhi, like Maa, rewrote the father's legacy and obliterated the father's inheritance from the child. Mrs. Gandhi's genius, like Maa's, lay in displacing responsibility for her crimes upon her perceived enemies and fabricating herself as the only figure equipped to save the nation from itself—and her.

The analysis of *Deewaar* establishes two kinds of outlaws and two kinds of gangsters. The manifest law that Javed Akhtar's comments gesture to is that of the state, a law that the executive has broken as the reference to the Emergency highlights. This law must be upheld even if those to do so are the very ones who have corrupted it in the first place. Vijay's transgression against the state must be punished even though his actions regulate society in a way that the state no longer can or will. Meanwhile, the second law is the law of the family. Here the conflict is sharper but also grayer, for the unit of discipline is the family itself, and it is its unspoken laws against desire and incest that Vijay is accused of disrupting. The real outlaw in this context, however, is Maa, the figure who takes a childhood from a son, a family from its father, a future from a brother, and returns a bullet in exchange.

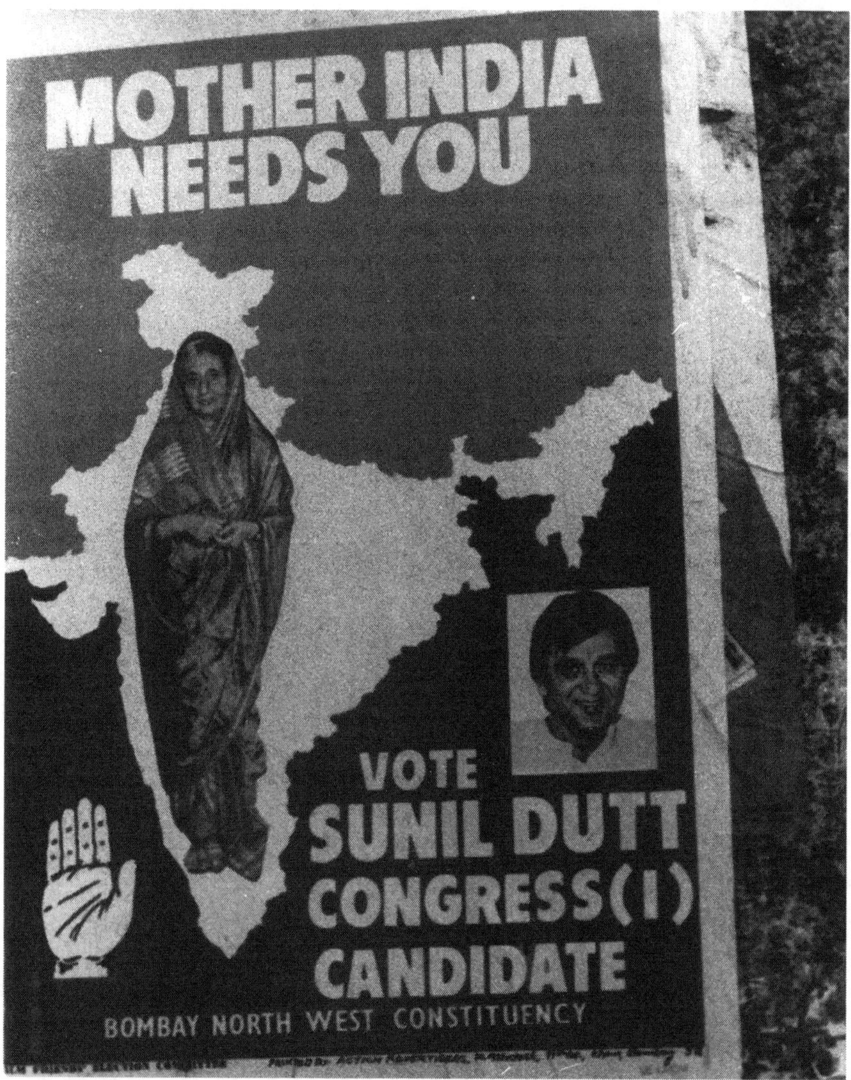

FIGURE 3.4 Indira Gandhi figured within the map of India in a 1985 election poster.

(COURTESY BEHROZE GANDHY)

Maa's infanticide was earlier compared with Mrs. Gandhi's and contrasted with the Oedipal story. In the Greek version, the mother Jocasta is an unwitting spectator to the initial attempt at infanticide (which was initiated by her husband, Laius) as well as of the later union with Oedipus. Her suicide follows the death of Laius and the revelation of the curse upon him for the long-ago rape of the young boy Chrissipus. *Deewaar*'s version of this story uses the same actors but fundamentally changes the point of view. Like the mythic father, Laius, Anandbabu too is absent for much of the action, though in marked contrast to the pederastic Laius, Anandbabu's nobility is unquestioned. Whereas the Greek myth focuses on patricide, the Indian version emphasizes infanticide. The difference is key.

According to the folklorist A. K. Ramanujan, there are scant instances of Oedipal narratives in India, and where they do exist, as in Kannada versions, they seldom have tragic consequences. The Jocasta figure marries her son or accepts her fate, and the father figure is *never* overthrown. From this, Ramanujan concludes that "the modern, Western quest is individualism, achieved through an overthrow of the father, whereas the Indian hero's quest is to fulfill his father. . . . A traditional culture needs to use and absorb the vitality of its young. . . . An innovative culture needs to overthrow its parents."[21] In the India captured in Ramanujan's research, stability prevails between the generations, and the father's power is always preserved in the proto-Oedipal oral folktales.

However, *Deewaar*'s Oedipal version reveals a very different India from Ramanujan's. It portrays a society that in Ramanujan's terms is paradoxically both highly modern (in which the father is overthrown) and deeply conservative (where the vital but renegade son must also be killed). At a time of political and social upheaval, youth in the film are a problem. Educated and unemployed like Ravi or charismatic and capable like Vijay, they represent challenges to a generational hierarchy and are criminalized or eliminated in the film's conservative plot. At the same time, those elements from the hierarchy (such as the father) that might compromise with youth or share its power with them are exiled, as Anandbabu is. In this, *Deewaar* presents a notably *authoritarian*—and eventually unstable—version of the Oedipal drama in which *neither* generation ultimately prevails. *Both* father and child are demolished, and power resides in absolutist fashion with a ruthless central authority that is unwilling to cede or share it. Thus, Maa — and Mrs. Gandhi. The oppositional political order has fully penetrated the family, and both are revealed as ruinous.

In its depiction of maternal power, *Deewaar*'s mother is closer to Kunti than she is to Jocasta—namely, the figure from the *Mahabharata* who tried to kill her firstborn, Karna, in order to preserve her social status and then, when he was an adult, asked Karna to sacrifice his life again in order to preserve the mother's future security. It is an impossible sacrifice to demand, and Karna refuses Kunti. The outcome is the apocalyptic battle in which the House of Pandu is destroyed. Much the same occurs in *Deewaar*'s cautionary fable where no happy ending is possible. Maa's infanticide destroys the family just as the state's infanticide deposes the political order and any belief in due process.

Unlike Ramanujan, who sees India's oral folklore as providing a flexible and comforting set of narratives that preserve the social order, *Deewaar*'s filmlore exposes a political and social order on the brink of collapse, willing to undertake the most egregious violence to kinship loyalties, as Vijay's murder depicts. *Deewaar* exposes the violence covered (up) by the mother-worship narratives so central to India's political culture and overplayed in cinema at especially anxious moments of national definition such as the 1970s.

DEEWAAR RETOLD, OR *TRISHUL* AND *SHAKTI*

I'll Die for Mama was one of *Deewaar*'s English titles that captured both the central plot conflict (for mother, with mother) and the thinly veiled allegory of the nation it signals. Vijay's "transgressions" in the film were described as inevitable by its scriptwriter: "In a society that lacked faith," Javed Akhtar averred, "it was natural that the gangster of *Deewaar* should take birth" (interview recorded in Gahlot 53). When asked if a criminal hero like Vijay was "justifiable," Akhtar riposted: "In this kind of society, what do you expect? . . . A hero at any given time is the personification of contemporary morality and contemporary ambitions" (interview recorded in Gahlot 53–54).

If Vijay was the outcome of his moment, he was also a marked departure from his cinematic predecessors. The criminal hero was hardly new in Hindi cinema: Raj Kapoor had developed him to popular acclaim in both *Awara* (1951) and *Shree 420* (1955). But whereas Kapoor's heroes eventually repent their crimes (murder and fraud) and are integrated back into society following appropriate penitence, usually in jail, *Deewaar*'s hero had no such luck. Vijay, who has done all that his mother asked for (provided for her, prayed for her), is nonetheless killed, and his death is meant to signal a sacrifice for Maa. Hence, *I'll Die for Mama*.

The state portrayed in *Deewaar* displaces upon the family the problems it creates but cannot solve. It criminalizes those whose efforts at regulation expose the state's ineffectiveness, and then calls upon the social order (in the form of the family) to restrain the monsters it has spawned. In this, *Deewaar* exposes the long-standing conflicts at the basis of Indian nationalism. The state espoused democracy, but the social order (with its caste and class hierarchies) abjured it. Rather than state and society being partners in a shared enterprise, they came increasingly into conflict. Whereas Nehru's vision tried to develop the state's institutions to nudge society's, his daughter's used the state to divide society. And no film better displays the bitter divisions as they came to a head in the 1970s than *Deewaar*, in which the menace of public life is reflected in the private.

Javed Akhtar may be correct to insist that Vijay emerged out of his moment, but Vijay's critical and commercial success notwithstanding, his was an uncomfortable emergence that had to be rescripted. If nothing else, the moment had changed with the fall of Mrs. Gandhi and the end of the Emergency in 1977, even if its legacies remained palpable. So, Salim-Javed killed Vijay in *Deewaar*, but it was not enough to quell the popularity of a hero who captured the day with his fists and his smoldering eyes. He may not have gotten the best line of the film ("Mere pas Maa hain"), but he became the best thing about the film. "A man who dies before his time lives to be a martyr," cautions the corrupt mine owner in *Deewaar* when his henchman offers to kill Anandbabu during the labor strike. Anandbabu is allowed to live but becomes utterly irrelevant. Vijay, on the other hand, achieves his diegetic and extra-diegetic stature by his death.

As if wishing to return the monster to his box, Akhtar and Salim Khan returned to *Deewaar* and rewrote it twice, revising the basic conflict and looking for more amenable solutions to it. If *Deewaar* is a raw exposition of conflict with the state, *Trishul*, which followed it in 1978, places its conflict solely in society and the family. If *Deewaar* is the story of the mother, *Trishul* is largely about the father. If Vijay is deemed a criminal in *Deewaar*, he is a successful capitalist in *Trishul*. If Vijay's romantic life follows his doomed family life in *Deewaar*, in *Trishul* he gets conjugal happiness along with restoration into a loving biological family. And where Vijay must be sacrificed in *Deewaar*, he thrives in *Trishul*. Above all, if the predominant conflict in *Deewaar* is the Kunti conflict in which Maa authorizes the murder of her firstborn, in *Trishul* it is a more conventional Oedipal conflict in which the son avenges his mother by killing the father.

While the basic structure of the two films remains the same, the point of view and the outcome vary dramatically. These variations say everything about the decade and the social work of popular film. Above all, the variations index the different "Indias" that popular cinema had to grapple with. In rewriting *Deewaar*'s master plot, its writers were drawing attention to very different citizen-protagonists in the nation. In this formulation, *Deewaar* tells the story of the child who bears witness and cannot forget; *Trishul* the story of an adult who is willing to forgive if not forget in order to move on. In *Deewaar*, Vijay's actions seek to regulate all society; in *Trishul*, they regulate only the family. *Deewaar* allegorizes the nation; *Trishul* largely ignores it. If politics and the state *are* the plot of *Deewaar*, in *Trishul* both politics and the state are detachable from the plot, and the film is an almost total retreat into family life and its melodrama.

Trishul softens many of *Deewaar*'s rawest referential allusions to the faltering state. It opens in Delhi with sepia-toned images of India Gate and

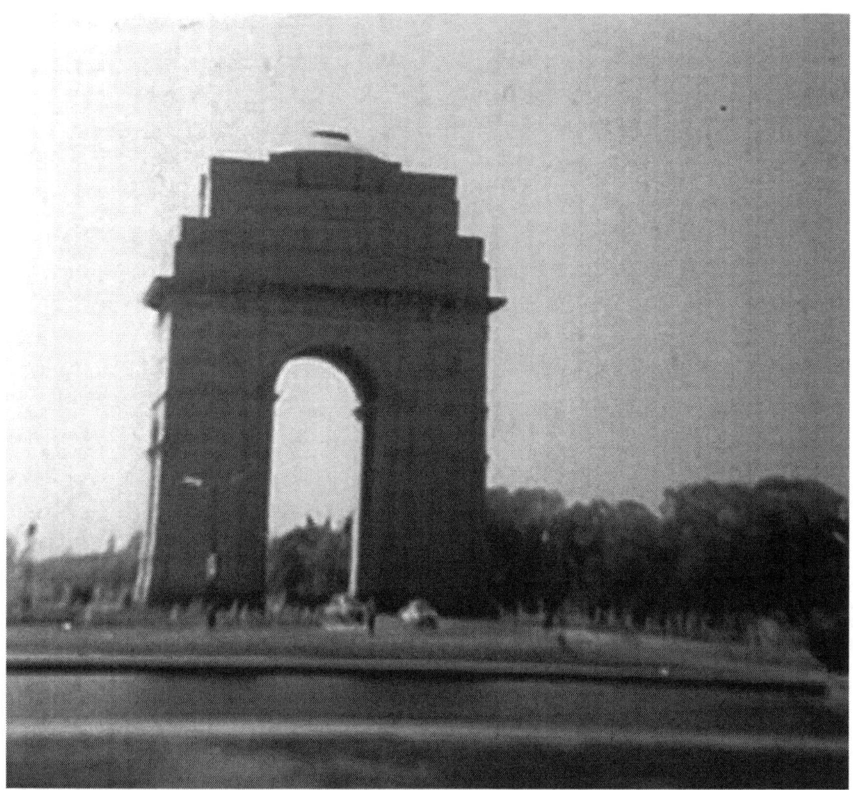

FIGURE 3.5 The opening credits of *Trishul* (1978) with India Gate.

Mughal monuments, recalling the two Indias antecedent to the modern nation (fig. 3.5). Here, a young civil engineer named R. K. Gupta (played by Sanjeev Kumar) romances an office worker, Shanti, and promises to marry her. His ambitious mother prefers that he marry the boss's only daughter, and the son obediently complies. Shanti leaves town and gives birth to a son named Vijay, who finds work as a laborer in a construction site. On her deathbed, she reminds him of his father's abandonment and makes him promise that he will always remember her, will never be weak, and will remember her life. (The song that plays during her funeral is more strident: "you must avenge my pain and death," it exhorts, as the flames from the pyre flicker on Vijay's eyes.) Thus burdened by a history not his own, Vijay moves to Delhi and discovers that his father is the city's most successful real estate developer. He buys a piece of land from him that has been occupied by squatters. R.K.'s numerous appeals to retrieve the land have been tied in court for seven years; he gladly sells to Vijay, who single-handedly clears the plot in a day and starts an empire. His goal: to best his father in the construction business. Vijay befriends his wealthy half-siblings, and his solicitude to them eventually fractures R.K.'s once-happy family. Facing fiscal and familial ruin, R.K. commissions Vijay's murder, not knowing Vijay is his son. When he discovers his paternity, R.K. repents and rushes to save Vijay. A showdown occurs in Pragati Maidan, the site of India's international trade shows where spectacles of national plenitude are routinely staged. R.K. takes the bullet intended for Vijay and dies. Vijay and his half-siblings reunite into a happy family, and the once-rival businesses are combined into a large prosperous one. ShantiRaj Enterprises is born, its name literally meaning the reign of peace.

Trishul's peace was a triumphant one; it remains today a major all-time grosser at the box office (at #12 to *Deewaar's* #11 in figures adjusted for inflation).[22] In it, all of *Deewaar's* signal preoccupations are replayed into happy endings. The preoccupation with "roti, kapda, aur makaan" is now just a preoccupation with makaan (housing). Both the protagonists are builders, and in *Trishul,* both Vijay and his father compete for a contract to provide low-cost housing for the middle classes, which they both succeed in providing. The state's ineptitude is irrelevant in *Trishul* because Vijay is allowed to prevail and provide security when the state (in the form of the courts) fails to protect R.K.'s title to the land. Vijay's law brings a widely accepted order. And if *Deewaar's* past is a haunted one that provides Vijay neither rest nor respite, *Trishul's* past dies out (with the mother) and allows the future to occur and with it a happy ending. In short, *Trishul* represents a compromise solution to the problem of *Deewaar.* The earlier film provided a powerful critique of the state and a stark depiction of its dystopian intrusions into private life. *Trishul,* on the other hand, erases the radical critique and gives the happy ending that was impossible in *Deewaar. Deewaar's* vengeful mother gets her way and is honored for punishing her son. In *Trishul,* the vengeful mother dies early so as to enable a happy ending that her bitterness would have prevented.

Trishul reassured audiences that the problems of *Deewaar* could be solved. The private could be separated from the political, and if one could be healed then maybe the other would follow. Above all, *Trishul* diffused the rage of the earlier film and integrated the protagonist not just into the social order, but also as the new head of the order represented by ShantiRaj Enterprises. Vijay is truly a victor in this film, unlike in *Deewaar,* where his name was profoundly ironic.[23]

But most happy endings invite one to ask, willfully, what unhappiness awaits around the corner. And in their final take on the "problem" of *Deewaar*, Salim-Javed scripted *Shakti* under Ramesh Sippy's direction. *Deewaar*'s legacy is scrutinized in a family that is everything that *Deewaar* was not: nuclear, contentedly middle class, professional, and stable. The public sphere does not just penetrate *Shakti*'s stable family and ruin it as well: the family *is* the state in the form of a father, a police chief who zealously pursues criminal elements to the letter of the law.[24] The main conflict occurs over whose law best provides justice. The father chooses to observe the state's laws even when his young son is kidnapped ("I refuse your call for a ransom," he tells the kidnapper). The boy, who overhears this remark, insists that the laws of kinship have been betrayed, and he strays from his father. Explaining his childhood to a lover, Vijay offers: "My father married twice. My mother and his job. I'm my mother's son; my stepmother's son is the law. The law is my stepbrother [kanoon mera sautela bhai hai]."

Rather than depicting the law as something that protects, *Shakti* reveals it as a weapon that creates a gulf between the weak and the strong, men and women, father and son. Rejecting this law, Vijay offers justice to those whom the law does not reach. A woman on the train being harassed by a gang of drunken men is protected by his presence (and his handy fists) when no cop is around. Unable to believe his son over the woman's harassers, who sue for injury, Vijay's father accuses him. Later, when a murder is pinned on Vijay based on circumstantial evidence, his father again believes the charge rather than the evidence. Though the film offers each conflict as a generational struggle, the conflicts also serve as tutorials about law and justice.

At a time when both law and order are shown to have frayed, the policeman's zeal comes with some irony in that rather than burnishing the law, it reveals that even following the law to the letter cannot bring order. The father cannot tell the difference between charge and evidence. For him, an individual (even his son) is guilty until proven innocent, and in this, the father's actions unwittingly end up underscoring the widespread view that *Deewaar* had captured in the previous decade. Rather than the well-intentioned father redeeming the law by "believing" it, he ends up revealing that even those best intentioned to uphold the law cannot conceal its irrelevance. In this, the law is in fact a stepchild *to* the family and the nation. Vijay's estrangement from his father in *Shakti* is a parable of the law's estrangement from the nation. Vijay chooses fathers in the film who protect him at the cost of biology; the state chooses laws that protect it at the cost of ideology. In both choices, the mother dies. She is literally shot in *Shakti*, just as the nation and its ideals metaphorically die in the conflict between her son (Vijay) and her stepson (kanoon, the law).

In a pivotal exchange in *Shakti*, when his father urges him to reform, Vijay replies: "How can I surrender myself before the law that made us strangers?" This law continues to estrange them till the end, when it is Vijay who guns down his mother's murderer (whom his father, helped by a busload of policemen, is unable to catch). Refusing to stop at his command, the police chief then shoots his son in the back, much as Ravi shot his brother in *Deewaar*. In a gasping, melodramatic death scene, the father embraces his son and by way of explanation offers:

FATHER: This was to happen one day. That's why it happened.
VIJAY: I tried really hard to remove the love in my heart for you but I always kept loving you. I tried not to but [*pause*]—Why did this happen?
FATHER: Because I too love you. I love you too.
VIJAY: So, why didn't you say so, Dad? Why didn't you say so, Dad?
[*No reply. Vijay dies in father's arms.*]

Ramesh Sippy, who used silence to virtuoso effect earlier in *Shakti* when a handcuffed Vijay in a long wordless sequence pays last respects to his mother's shrouded corpse, uses it again at Vijay's death. Vijay's question to his father gets no reply at the time. Decades later, Vijay's son asks his grandfather if he can join the police force, and this time the old man gives a voluble "reply." His memories *are* the film, diegetically, but the words and the actions are all Vijay's (and Salim-Javed's).

While the father cannot answer Vijay's question, he can answer his grandson's. And in this answer, we get the justification that is supposed to regulate society by conserving its energies. In *Shakti*, Vijay has done work that the father cannot. He has avenged both his mother's murder and restored his father's career. He can now be disposed of. The film ostensibly celebrates the father's law and his values in a way that the next generation wishes to emulate—as Vijay's son does when he determines to join the police force at the conclusion of his grandfather's story.

If *Trishul* undid most of *Deewaar*'s radical politics, *Shakti* renders those politics obsolete. *Shakti*'s manifest content is profoundly conservative: youth is co-opted into family, family prevails over romance, the authority of both family and state prevail over the individual, and the father is allowed to prosper and to determine the direction of the following generations. Meanwhile, where *Deewaar*'s latent content destabilized its manifest order, in *Shakti* the latent content is harder to discern within the terms of this single film. To do it, one needs *Deewaar* and the mythologies embedded in its filmlore.

CONCLUSION

Deewaar's displacement of national anxieties upon the family exposes key elements of social belief and public concern and transforms them. Far from providing alternatives to a painful present or reconciling with it, it followed the lead of Hindi cinema's most popular blockbusters of the decade and repeatedly scripted the family as the primary locus for national trauma. The cinema's blockbuster narratives simultaneously reveal extraordinary mechanisms for repression and renewal, and uncovering them underscores *Deewaar*'s critical role in a fuller reckoning of the decade.

However, Hindi cinema's Family Romances, as amplified in *Deewaar*, are neither typical liberation narratives nor exorcisms as psychoanalysis posited such narratives. The traumas they are intended to heal are paradoxically rendered more real on the screen largely because of their projections upon the familiar intimacy of the family unit. Rather than rendering the state abstract, and thus distant from the subject, these films render it closer to Vijay in the form of the brother who will gun him down and the mother who will authorize the killing, as in *Deewaar*. Rather than liberating the subject from his nightmares, they bring them to life for him. In this form, the films are a peculiar kind of political tutorial: neither exultant not exculpatory of the national myth, they serve to expose its fraudulence.

Deewaar is notable for embedding its extensive critique of India in the 1970s within the terms of popular commercial cinema. If the situation of the decade "created" the protagonist of *Deewaar* and ensured his currency at the time, the film's combustible counter-narrative nevertheless required some form of containment that its protagonist's death weakly provided. While Vijay's diegetic death illustrates the incompletely radical nature of popular cinema, it also stands as an indicator of popular cinema's opportunities. Because while Hindi film seldom provides sequels, it narrates the same story numerous times, with each retelling exposing or addressing anxieties that the previous one missed or was unable to pursue fully. *Deewaar*'s radical critique kills a semi-criminal Vijay while *Trishul*'s radical revision brings him back as an unambiguous hero, and *Shakti*'s radical burial renders him obsolete. Taken together, the three films serve not just as "contemporary folklore," as Javed Akhtar claimed in this chapter's epigraph. They also serve as cautionary fables about the power of stories.

Deewaar's volatile family drama, with its dramatic critique of state and nation, illuminated the corrosion in symbolic kinship units. Revising this story in *Trishul* generated the happy ending as well as a tutorial on the futility of such endings. In other words, utopia in *Trishul* proved as unsatisfactory as dystopia in *Deewaar*. Stories, in this context, have the power both to satisfy and to unsettle. In the tutorial that emerges from Salim-Javed's cinematic triptych, the pleasures of stories are contingent. They come with attendant cautions to qualify their satisfactions. But stories also expose and reconfigure the world in which they circulate. *Deewaar*'s critique, refashioned in *Trishul* then again in *Shakti,* serves a *restorative* function that first critiques the master narrative (of nation and family) and then provides a series of commentaries on it in the form of revisions. If *Trishul*'s ending of a peaceful ShantiRaj embeds a fantasy, it is a fantasy that powerfully underscores the unrelenting somberness in *Deewaar.* In this cautionary account, *Deewaar* exposes the corruption that pervades 1970s India as well as the futility of confronting it, *even while providing the short-lived satisfaction of Vijay's Pyrrhic confrontations. Trishul*'s ending is no more satisfying than *Deewaar*'s, even though both speak to the same desire for social justice.

Salim-Javed's cinematic triptych in *Deewaar–Trishul–Shakti* illuminates the many acts of storytelling central to all nation-building projects. The triptych provides a way to reconceive—perhaps even to restore—the national narrative even while critiquing its corruption. It purveys the notion that the art of the story carries the craft of life. For this, popular cinema is the nation's Family Romance, a space where the nightmares of the collective are addressed, where its public fantasies might be retrieved, and where alternatives can be scripted even if they must eventually be dismissed. Reading the manifest and latent narratives embedded in *Deewaar* and unraveled across the triptych exposes a set of pressing anxieties that found expression in the locus of the family and that required the countering impulse of the Family Romance for dissolution, if not resolution. In the Family Romance that emerges, Vijay becomes a symbol condensing all the forces threatening India—both the state and the nation—in the mid-1970s. *Deewaar*'s family sanctuary is revealed, like the nation's, as threatened by invasion from without and seduction from within (a preoccupation keenly observed by Michael Rogin in his work on U.S. Cold War cinema [Rogin 267]). These threats are narratively "undone" across the films that comprise the triptych as the originary film's murderous plot is rewritten in more conciliatory terms.

Recovering these acts of making and undoing exposes the anxieties of the decade and the powerful role popular Hindi cinema played in producing and then containing the combustible energies of the moment. In countering the brutality of the decade on screen if not on the street, cinema served to remind the state of the nation that preceded it. Both were acts of public fantasy, enabled and underwritten by the Family Romance. Cinema in this context stands for a recovered memory—flawed and faintly gesturing to a truth that cannot be spoken. The cinematic imagination of which the Salim-Javed triptych is a part enables a critique of the nation and the narrative fabrications that propel it. Suspended below the manifest narrative is a combustible latent critique, one that can only find voice in the displacement and hyperbole characteristic of the Family Romance. Popular cinema's genius lies in providing a space for these narratives that must not be recalled. At best, they have the sharpness and horror of all recovered memories, compared to which reality is neither as bad, nor as real.

BOLLYWOOD, BOLLYLITE

EIGHT OSCARS, SEVEN BAFTAS, FIVE Critics' Choice awards, and four Golden Globes: *Slumdog Millionaire*'s (2008) landslide victory in just about every international film award competition seems to echo a lesson from the year's triumphant Obama playbook: yes, Jamal can; yes, India can; yes, even Bollywood can. Danny Boyle's *Slumdog Millionaire* pays powerful *hommage* to popular Hindi cinema of the 1970s when that cinema was beginning to be named Bollywood. The first question Jamal is asked on the quiz show is the name of the actor who starred in the 1973 blockbuster, *Zanjeer* (Chains, Prakash Mehra). Jamal knows the answer, of course, just like most Indians would, regardless of their class or social status. Yet the real question is not who played the angry young man in *Zanjeer*, but why that figure continues to be relevant in the India of the 1990s and beyond, which is when Jamal, probably about six or seven years old, dives through a sewage pit to get Amitabh Bachchan's autograph when the screen god descends from the firmament in a helicopter. Jamal's devotion to a screen idol well past his prime is of a piece with the ecstatic, excessive response that certain blockbusters from Bombay enjoy, not just among slum dwellers like Jamal, but among viewers across many parts of the globe where Bachchan and Raj Kapoor and Nargis and Shah Rukh Khan among other Bollywood superstars elicit similarly frenzied adulation long after their blockbusters are decades old.[1]

Fans of Bombay films could multiply these anecdotes manifold for virtually every nation on the globe with one major exception: the United States. The popularity of Bombay's blockbusters provide invaluable insights into the travels of a truly mass culture in having taught Nigerian youth to weep for Nargis, Egyptian traditionalists to yearn for Dimple Kapadia, and Greek workers to hum Mukesh numbers in Hindi.[2] Yet their influence upon audiences in the United States has been hard to detect and even harder to ascertain. If Bombay films have a global centripetal flow, it appears to have stopped prior to reaching U.S. shores where these films exist far below the mainstream cultural radar. Until recently, occasional mainstream multiplexes in the United States might screen Hindi films for diasporic audiences on sporadic schedules advertised online or in the ethnic press, so the idea that *Amélie* might routinely share a screen with *A Wednesday* (Neeraj Pandey, 2008), or *Run Lola Run* might play alongside *Rang de Basanti* (Color it saffron, Rakeysh Omprakash Mehra, 2006) seems unfathomable to most filmgoers in this country.

Slumdog Millionaire's massive critical and commercial success seems to have transformed Bollywood's cultural invisibility in the United States to the extent that it invites a broader question: might the film's many Bollywood flourishes and its layered references to that cinema finally augur Bollywood's fuller penetration into the U.S. market that showered *Slumdog Millionaire* with such fulsome encomia? *Slumdog*'s remarkable journey from a small-budget film released in ten prints in U.S. art house theaters to one with almost 3,000 prints circulating widely in the U.S. suburban multiplex circuit makes some ask if it might have created a wider appetite for the film's "ancestors" from Bollywood.[3] Some film watchers insist that Bollywood's presence in the Western mainstream is widely evident in the new millennium, a phenomenon that a group of scholars recently dubbed "Bollyworld."[4] Even before *Slumdog Millionaire*, Baz Luhrmann's musical hit, *Moulin Rouge* (2001), had primed the Western market for things considered "Bollywood," followed by *Lagaan* (Tax, Aamir Khan, 2001), the anticolonial cricket saga that was nominated for a foreign film Oscar in 2002. The same year, spectacular Bombay productions such as *Kabhi Khushi Kabhi Gham* (Sometimes happy, sometimes sad, aka *K3G*, Karan Johar, 2001) crossed the Atlantic and did exceptionally well at the U.S. box office. Meanwhile, *Monsoon Wedding* (Mira Nair, 2001), produced in the U.S., pilfered aspects of the Bombay industry's formula, sterilized it, peopled it with Delhi's consumerist elites, and purveyed the confection with hitherto unimaginable success to multiplex audiences in the United States.[5] *Monsoon Wedding* remains the top-grossing Indian film in the U.S. at receipts of almost $14 million, with another Bollywood knockoff, Gurinder Chadha's *Bride and Prejudice* (2004), at second place with receipts at $6.6 million.[6]

This brief profile of Bollywood's travels to the United States underscores several details. The already unstable term from the 1970s has today mutated to incorporate any Indian-themed product, regardless of its site of production, distribution, or content. Thus, *K3G* (produced in India), *Monsoon Wedding* (produced in the U.S.), and *Bride and Prejudice* (produced in the UK) seem equally included in the vexed term, along with a film such as *Slumdog Millionaire*. As the film scholar Madhava Prasad poses: "could Bollywood be a name for this new cinema coming from Bombay, but also lately from London and Canada?"[7] Despite superficial similarities in theme and setting across the cinemas, there is much that separates the productions even when they are all dubbed "Bollywood." *Slumdog*'s insistence on conjuring 1970s blockbusters such as *Zanjeer* in order to comment sharply on an incredible India that frames slums alongside high-rises, criminals alongside pacifists, global industry alongside postindustrial squalor, often within a single shot, is nowhere visible in either Johar's Bombay-produced *K3G* or Nair's New York version. The confrontation with social problems that defined Bollywood's identity in the 1970s seems to have retreated in products such as *K3G* and *Monsoon Wedding* with their exuberant embrace of the culture of consumer capital. Yet these are some of the very films that have recently crossed over to a U.S. market that has long been indifferent to Bollywood. This chapter analyzes why. It studies two linked phenomenon associated with the term Bollywood. First, it analyzes the mutation of substance from its origins in the 1970s that accompanies the term Bollywood today. Second, at a time when India's media ecology has dramatically expanded, and popular film competes with modes of entertainment and media unknown and unimagined in the 1970s, Bollywood has had to make compromises.

This chapter analyzes what Bollywood does to survive both in India and in global markets that now include the United States. It addresses the question of Bombay cinema's penetration into the U.S. mainstream. It proceeds concentrically in three parts: first, it addresses why this cinema works when and where it does; second, it explores the influence that recent U.S. financial interests and industry practices are having over Bombay cinema's hitherto informal business model; and finally, it examines the select forms in which Bombay cinema has recently traveled into Hollywood's home turf and scrutinizes why.

The argument of the chapter turns closely on this last point. In many ways, the germane issue is not the influx of Bombay cinema *en masse* into America's screens but rather the *specific* forms from Bombay that have been able to capture the interest of audiences in the United States. This form is such a major departure from the internal conventions of Bollywood that it is more properly understood in a concept I define as *Bollylite*. Bollylite is a relatively recent fabrication that heavily pillages formal characteristics from Bollywood cinema while shearing much of that cinema's social substance and political edge. Thus lightened, Bollylite travels, though, in contrast to Bollywood, with a remarkably limited commercial and critical half-life. Observing Bollylite's fortunes and the material conditions that produce it allows one to observe the stubbornness of Bollywood's cultural product despite the onslaught of a renewed global machinery with new capital. At a time when increased despondency has accrued in many quarters at the apparent demise of popular culture, Bollywood's persistence as a form tells a very different story that shifts the locus of cultural study from the United States to a place where popular and mass culture have managed to coexist and even be the same thing.

THE WORLD ACCORDING TO BOLLYWOOD

Used both pejoratively and with pride, the term Bollywood has many faces and phases. It was initially used in 1976 to dismiss a cinema regarded as frivolous, spectacular, and escapist at a moment when the cinema's social purpose closely engaged with the public and political culture of its time. Today, the term Bollywood captures not just these engagements but also a culture industry that has become international in production and global in consumption. It conveys as much a kind of cinema as a kind of response to cinema, the extravagant spectacle of its productions being matched by the outsize popularity that its blockbusters enjoy. Thus, to use the term Bollywood is to convey the cinema of Bombay that is also a cinema of excess in all its forms.[8] In the usage I prefer, Bollywood is a heuristic device: neither epochal nor Bombay cinema *tout court*, it is a clarifying term to refer to a popular cinema made in Bombay that has claimed a social purpose and enjoyed a certain kind of popularity that it has maintained across time and audiences. Bollywood does not necessarily convey a national cinema, though Bollywood's nationalist imaginary is an important component of its success both in India and overseas.[9] In contrast to scholars such as Sangita Gopal, who remain sensitive to Bollywood's origins in the 1970s but insist that the period of its global ambitions in the 1990s is constitutively different (Gopal calls it the "New Bollywood"), the present study demurs. Bollywood is a *tendency* that had its clearest expression in the 1970s when the term emerged. Retrospectively, with caution, it might be applied to an earlier period, and it certainly persists into the decades following its origins when it continues its social purpose in different forms.

In her exposition of Bollywood's history, Sangita Gopal describes the period from Independence to the 1970s as the classic phase of Hindi cinema, characterized by what she calls a "socially responsive" national cinema (Gopal 2011:5). The events of the 1970s, Gopal contends, initiated a retreat from this project of national cohesion, and the cinema of "Bollywood" was born with a commitment toward mass entertainment. In this shift, according to Gopal, the social films that defined the classic period gave way to the masala films of Bollywood. Today, that entertainment- and commercially-savvy cinema of the 1970s has achieved new global ambitions in content and marketing, and Gopal characterizes it as the New Bollywood phase, which started around 1991 with the liberalization of the Indian economy. Gopal's taxonomy associates each phase with a form (classic phase with the social film; Bollywood with the masala film; New Bollywood with genre films), and with a set of dominant preoccupations (social cohesion, violent individualism, and urbanization, respectively).

The schema glosses over a number of practices that remain consistent across the three phases. The first is the "master genre" of the social film that Gopal avers declined with the ascendance of masala in the mid- and late-1970s (Gopal 2011:14). To the contrary, rather than being a "genre," the social film embodies a tendency of critique and response evident in virtually every phase of the cinema. As such, the social is more accurately a tendency that persists across *all* periods of Hindi cinema. It may be more or less prominent at a particular moment, but at no point have popular Hindi films ever abandoned the tendency. Similarly, the preoccupation with the nation suffuses the cinema at all moments. The *kind* of nation imagined in the 1950s differs from the one proffered in the 1970s or 1990s, but in each of its phases, Hindi popular cinema remains adamantly focused on the idea of a nation and actively engages in debating a variety of national fantasies. Exactly when the cinema is what Gopal calls "mere entertainment," Bollywood most urgently exposes deeply held national fantasies (Gopal 2011:12). For instance, preoccupations with the national converge in the landmark masala blockbuster *Amar Akbar Anthony* (Manmohan Desai, 1977), which rewrites the trauma of Partition and the assassination of M. K. Gandhi as a manic reunification caper. However, these preoccupations are also prominent in a more sedately social film such as *Mother India* (Mehboob Khan, 1957), which reviews the same traumas, albeit with apologia as melodrama. The preoccupations over the idea of nation persist in kind if not degree across other forms, including vibrant indie films such as *Kahaani* (Story, Sujoy Ghosh, 2012) and *Talaash* (Search, Reema Kagti, 2012), both of which include A-list stars with mainstream credits. Therefore, to define the cinema's historical phases by transhistorical tendencies such as the social is to reduce the industry to form at the expense of content.

Bollywood's popularity among close to a billion viewers in the Subcontinent (and close to a billion more elsewhere in the world) explains partly why it has not succeeded (and perhaps not even tried to succeed) in penetrating Hollywood's home turf. As a popular cinema deeply invested in the preoccupations of its domestic audience, it has traveled only as far as those preoccupations have. Mapping the success of Bollywood worldwide, one sees its appeal among a swathe of nations where modernity competes with tradition, where urban and rural commingle in uneasy proximity, where, as the scriptwriter Farrukh Dhondy perceptively noted, "underdevelopment meets development, where a peasantry and an urban population live side by side and are often the same people. It is that part of the world which lives through a clash of innocence and experience. . . . It is where the settled life of the village comes into contact with the temptation and even the routines of the city, the factory, the commodity, the market."[10] In these parts of the globe, audiences have flocked to Bollywood films as conveyers of a modernity that is neither American nor threatening to their fantasy of a "tradition" that they never quite had to begin with.

Where Hollywood mobilizes blockbusters to make money, Bollywood's blockbusters have made the nation. The typical Bollywood film, if there is such a thing, is a perfect compromise solution to the conflicts of its time. Wreathed in spectacle, suffused in song, the public traumas of the day—be they Partition, dowry murders, class violence, or political corruption—are given shape and voice in dark movie halls. Like dreams that process in the subconscious that which cannot or should not be brought to the surface, Bollywood's three-hour sessions in giant halls with names like Eros and Opera House address recurring fantasies that lie just below the surface. Bollywood exteriorizes and gives shape to the anxieties of its audience. It is a cinema that, to paraphrase the social theorist Ashis Nandy, is deeply invested in the psychic reality of its viewers, not its characters.[11] Therefore, while Western audiences balk at the many elaborate dance sequences and the musical interludes that they frequently complain are "unrealistic," for Bollywood's Indian audiences these "unrealistic" sequences become occasions to sort through the dilemmas and conflicts presented in the plot without sacrificing pleasure.[12]

Raj Kapoor's 1973 hit, *Bobby*, is as example of the cinema's ability to have it both ways. Kapoor's mastery over market and melodrama without compromising on either produced one of Hindi cinema's most renowned blockbusters, which remains, at #6, among an elite group of all-time top-grossing Hindi films in the worldwide market adjusted for inflation, below Aditya Chopra's *Dilwale Dulhaniya le Jayenge* (aka *DDLJ*, The man with the heart gets the bride, 1995, at #4) and Manmohan Desai's multi-starrer, *Amar Akbar Anthony* (1977, at #5).[13] Inspired by Kapoor's reading of *Archie* comics, *Bobby* appears to be an endorsement of the impetuosity of adolescent love. Poring over an *Archie* comic, Raj Kapoor recalls, "I came across a sentence . . . spoken by Archie himself, something like, 'Seventeen is no longer young—we have a life of our own too and we are aware of it!' This really got me. I felt, here is something very profound—and thinking about this resulted in my making *Bobby*" (figs. 4.1 and 4.2).[14]

Instead of "Fast Times at Riverdale High," Kapoor produced a cleverly refashioned account of his real-life courtship from the 1940s with the screen great Nargis (1929–1981), morphed onto concerns from the 1970s. Kapoor's son, Rishi, plays Raja, scion of wealthy industrialist Nath and his neglectful socialite wife. Nargis, known as "Baby" in her lifetime, is reborn in the figure of Bobby, granddaughter of Raja's Christian nanny, Mrs. Braganza.[15] Smitten by the 16-year-old Bobby (played by Dimple Kapadia), whom he sees for the first time on his eighteenth birthday, Raja courts her with her father, Jack's, consent. His own father is less welcoming, insisting that the family's social status forbids Raja's union with the nanny's granddaughter. The duo prevail across Kashmiri landscapes and Goan beaches, fleeing an increasingly incensed set of fathers intent of separating their offspring to

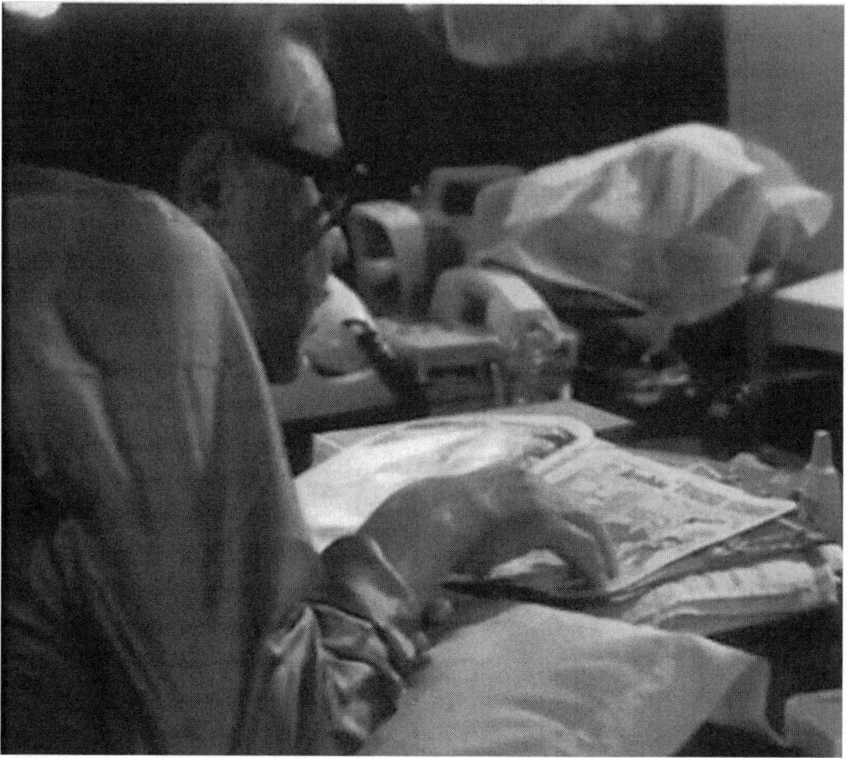

FIGURE 4.1 "To be honest, I am not a very well-read man." Raj Kapoor with an *Archie* comic book.

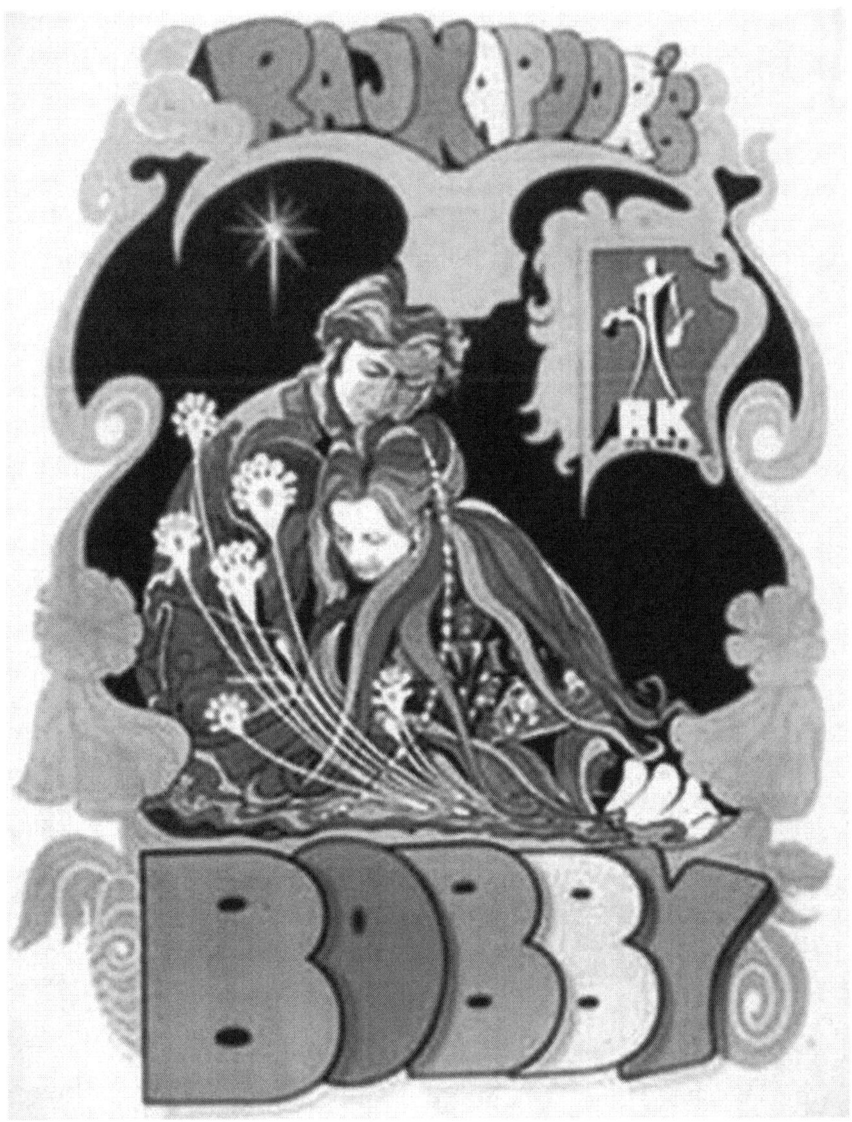

FIGURE 4.2 Publicity poster for *Bobby* (1973).

preserve their egos. Finally, with their fathers in hot pursuit, the couple decides that death together is better than life apart, and the two jump into some rapids. The fathers plunge in after them, each rescuing the other's child, and the four, reconciled after the cold dip, walk off arm in arm down a yellow dirt road in a shot seemingly borrowed from *The Wizard of Oz* (fig. 4.3).

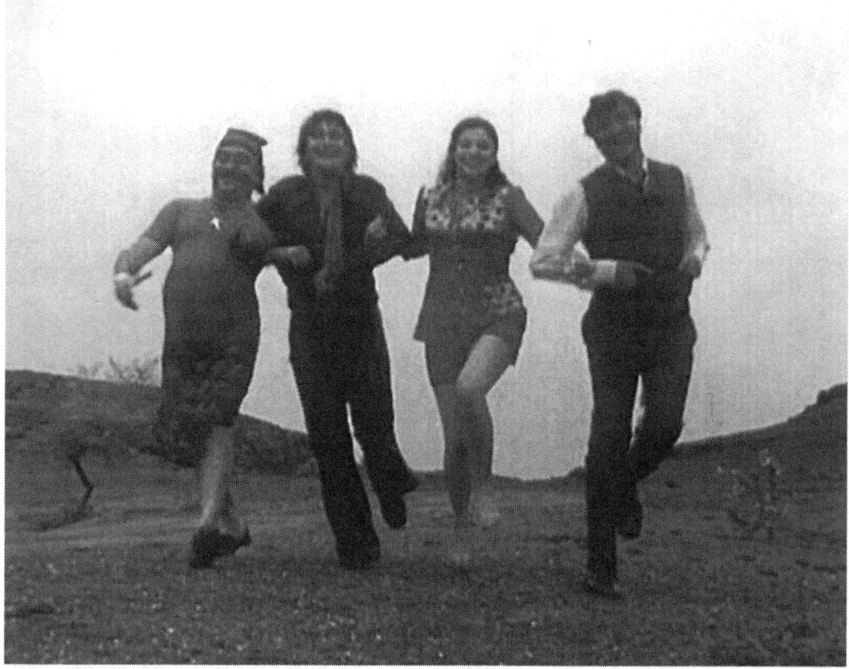

FIGURE 4.3 *Bobby*'s happy ending.

On one level, the film's conclusion and its lavish romantic staging celebrate the audacity of young love and its power over the forces of custom, family, and class. The lovers daringly act out throbbing pubescent desires during a school trip to Kashmir. "Imagine if we were locked in a room and the key got lost," proposes Raja in a famous song, "Hum tum ek kamare mein band hon." "I'd lose myself in the labyrinth of your eyes, and I'd come," Bobby replies boldly, flinging herself onto the bed with arms open to receive her lover (fig. 4.4). Dimple Kapadia's miniskirts, midriff-baring polka dot shirts, and her fabled red bikini were visual enticements of an audacious teenage sexuality hitherto unseen on Bombay's screens (figs. 4.4–4.6). The song about being locked in a room together, with its sly lyrics and double entendres, sent viewers into paroxysms of glee at Kapoor's naughtiness. Audiences love young love, apparently, and Kapoor was warmly recompensed at the box office for celebrating it.

However, a closer reading of the songs in the film, especially the contrasting back-to-back numbers sung during a neighbor's wedding, gives pause. Inspired by the wedding festivities, Raja promises Bobby his heart forever.

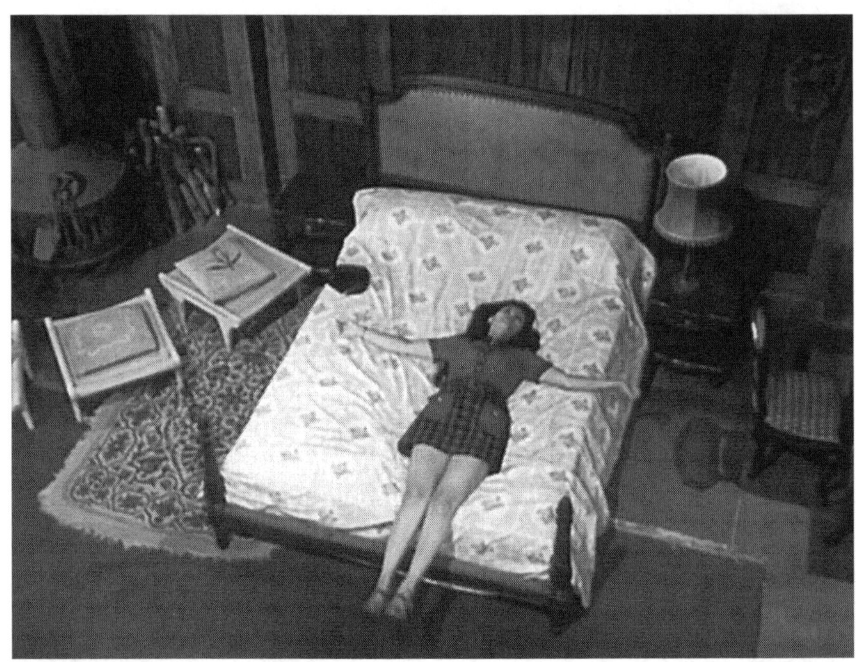

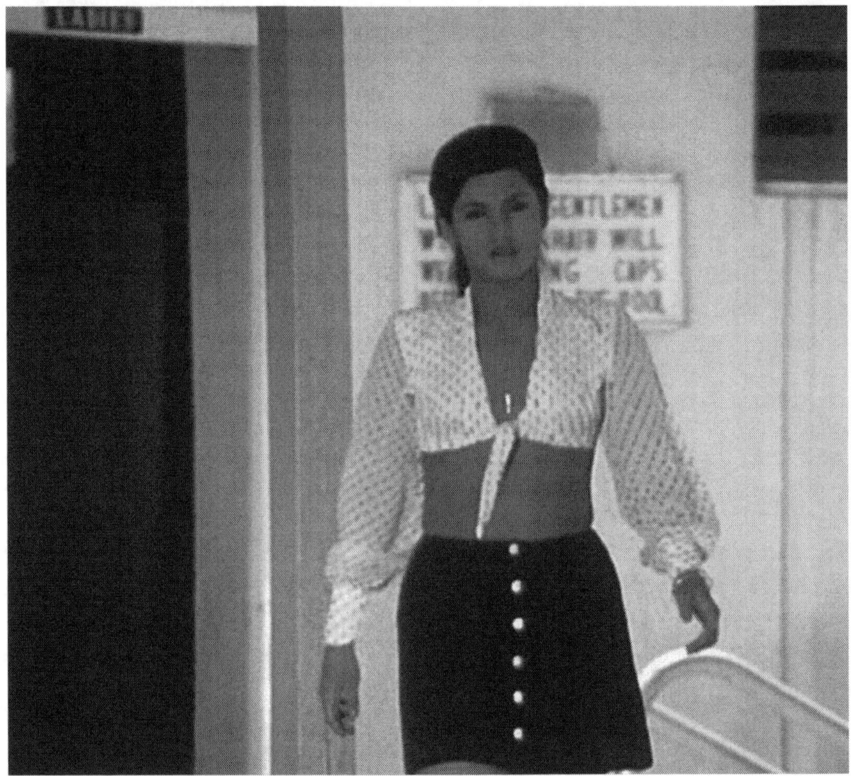

FIGURES 4.4–4.6 Dimple Kapadia as Bobby.

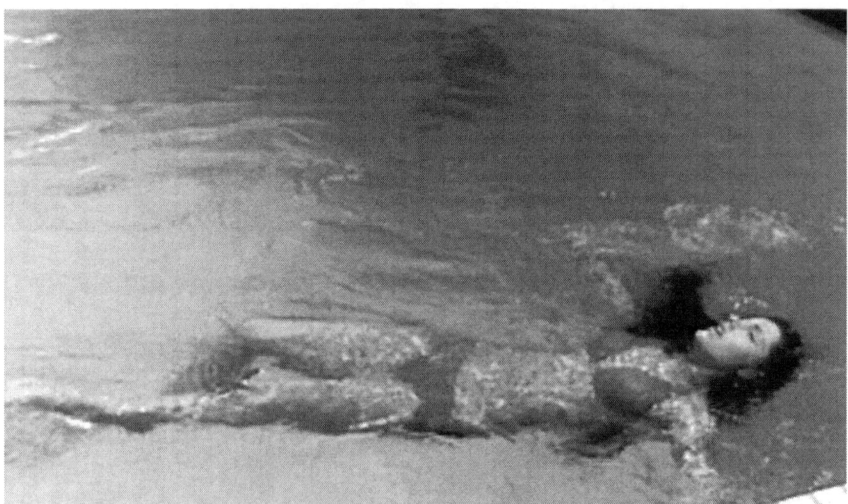

FIGURE 4.6

Na chahun sona chandi	I don't want gold or silver
na chahun heera moti	I don't want diamonds or pearls
Ye mere kis kam ke?	What use are they to me?
Na mangun bangla bari,	I won't ask for a bungalow or a house
Na mangun ghora gari—	I won't ask for a horse or a car—
Yeh to hain bas nam ke.	These are just things after all.
Deti hai dil de,	If you want, give me your heart and
badle me dil le. [. . .]	take mine in exchange. [. . .]
Pyar mein sauda nahin.	There's no trading in love.

Without missing a beat, a second song, "Jhoot boley kauwa kaatey," remarkably different in melody and mood, opens with Bobby threatening to leave for her mother's if Raja doesn't keep his vow. "Don't you lie to me," she trills, "or a crow will bite you, and besides if you lie, I'll leave you and return to my mother's house." The remainder of the song is an exchange between the lovers, its exuberant dance and playful repartee barely able to contain the violence of the exchange. The fact that this song is staged as a spectacle performed at a wedding with the once miniskirted Bobby now costumed as a fisherwoman (fig. 4.7) goes quite some way in heightening the playful nature of the threats. Yet because the game is part of a public performance, the threats are more intense, the violence spelled out more menacingly. The visual attractions of the cinematic reds and blacks and blues of Bobby's and Raja's costumes play no small role in cuing the sinister colors of injury alongside those of pleasure (figs. 4.7 and 4.8). The

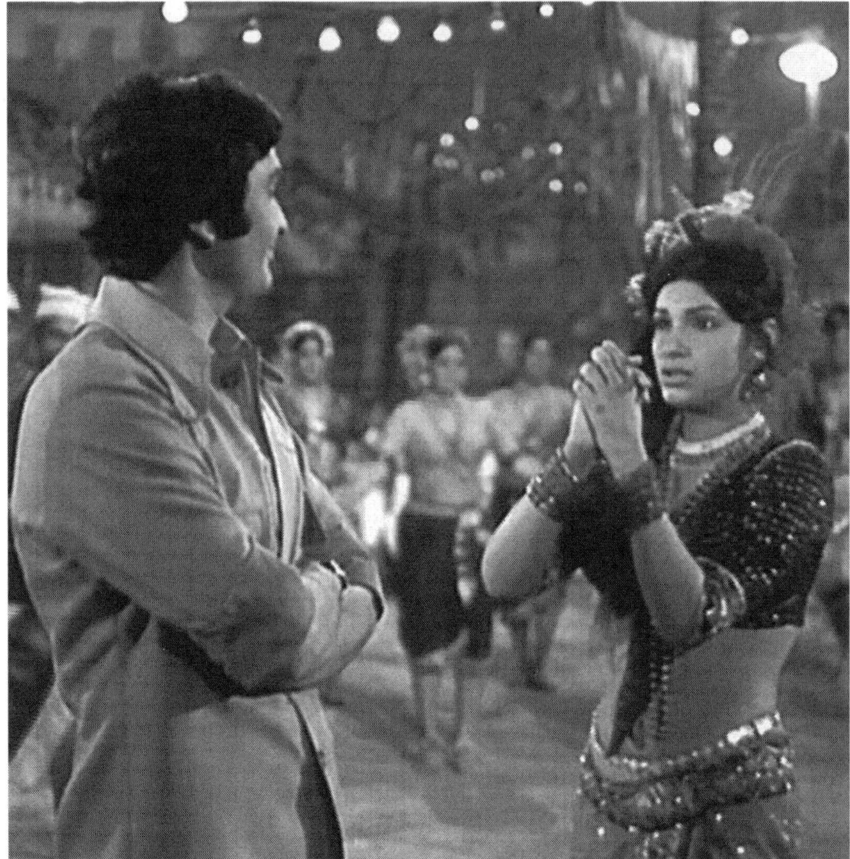

FIGURES 4.7 AND 4.8 "I won't leave you; I'll observe my marital vows." Rishi Kapoor and Dimple Kapadia in *Bobby*.

hitherto independent Bobby is transformed in the second song's ("Jhoot boley") lyrics into a wretched victim of domestic violence, with the baby-faced Raja her tormentor in a marriage from which she has no escape.

RAJA: If you go to your mother's, I'll come after you with a stick.

BOBBY: You do that and I'll jump into a well.

RAJA: I'll get you with a rope.

BOBBY: I'll climb up a tree.

RAJA: I'll cut down the tree.

BOBBY [*shocked*]: Are you my suitor or an axe man? Beware of such lovers. Watch out or I'll leave for my mother's. Don't you lie to me.

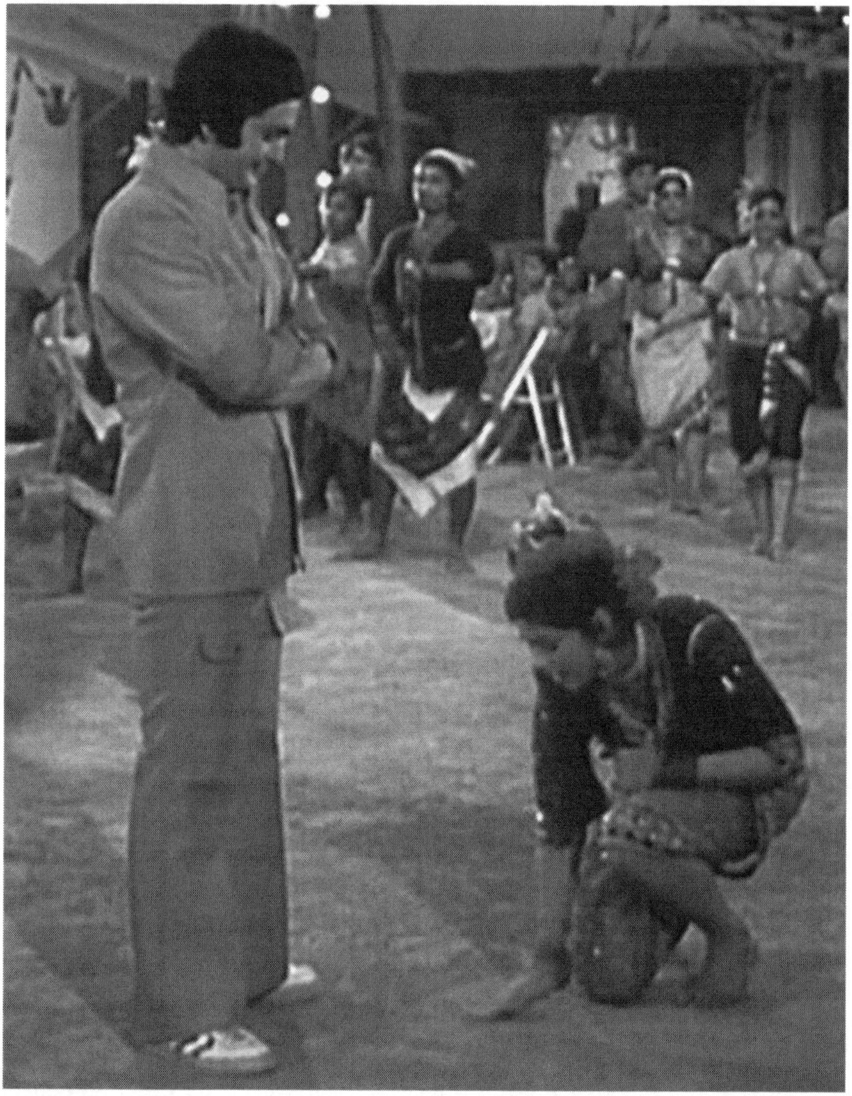

FIGURE 4.8

RAJA: Go ahead to your mother's. I'll get me another wife, you'll see!
BOBBY: *What?* You'll do that? [*song shifts tone dramatically; Bobby prostrates herself at Raja's feet; figs. 4.7 and 4.8*] OK, I won't go to my mother's. I'll serve you, I'll be your obedient wife, I promise. I'll observe all my marital vows. I won't leave you, I promise.
RAJA [*triumphant; dancing over the crumpled Bobby at his feet*]: Don't *you* lie, or a crow will bite you. And *I'll* get me another wife, you'll see.

Bobby's freedom to choose a mate and her doting father's support all end on her wedding when a lover can change into an axe man, and her only recourse from his abuse is the threat to return to a mother she does not actually have. While Bobby's only power is her words, Raja's is in brute actions. Unable to escape his stick, rope, or axe, she can only invoke her long-dead mother—or jump in a well to her death. Raja, on the other hand, always holds the upper hand, threatening her replacement with a second wife should she no longer please him.

The song's subtext is even more sinister than its physical violence. In the decade before death by fire became the preferred method in dowry murders, "falling" into a well was the preferred way of eliminating a bride who had run her use as a source of dowry.[16] Raja's catalog of commodities he putatively declines in the first song (gold, house, car) rehearses a typical list of dowry demands. Raja and Bobby's subsequent duet rehearses the preamble to a dowry death. Nothing, not even the threats, are innocent here. On any level, the sadism in the duet counters the utopian vow of true love in the first song, playing out the perils of adolescent love and serving as a cautionary tale of impulsive desire.

While the plot and staging of Kapoor's blockbuster manifestly celebrate the theme of adolescent passion, the songs interrupt that continuity and latently correct an overt endorsement. The Raja-Bobby duet, "Jhoot boley," cautions women in particular that leaving the family for a forbidden love is dangerous: love can turn and the woman, always vulnerable, has no recourse or support. Another narrative of social violence is marked behind *Bobby*'s frothy love story. The conclusion of the Raja-Bobby story re-creates the status quo of the capitalist male (Raja) claiming mastery over working-class labor (the fisherwoman Bobby) that remains typically female (figs. 4.7 and 4.8). That this ominous outcome is gestured in a song ("Jhoot boley") in which the fashionably modern Bobby is dressed as a fisherwoman underscores that, romantic love notwithstanding, Bobby's origins indicate her class's destiny in a union with Raja.

Rather than the two songs appearing to contradict each other, they provide a sobering account of an "ever after" that the commercial film cannot manifestly provide. *Bobby*'s cinematic closure turns to Hollywood fairytale (the dreamwalk from *Wizard of Oz*; see fig. 4.3) not because it believes in fairytales. It turns there to point out the fairytale's necessity against a violence that all fairytales both gesture toward and heroically contain. "They all lived happily ever after" is only comforting if one knows how *unhappy* ever after they might have been. Creating a space where the violent ever after can be enacted safely, in play, is caution enough. The point is to indicate a threat, not to eradicate it. What Bollywood's audiences observe in these lyrical interruptions is the even-handed depiction of desire, rather than a contradiction inherent in its representation. This form of narrative irony, where manifest and latent content coexist without apparent disruption to the pleasures of spectacle, is exactly what recedes in later Bollylite productions with their singular narrative planes.

Recognizing the disruption of such narrative moments, Bollywood's neglect in the United States lies less in American indifference to its stock formulae and musical numbers than in Bombay's insistence on targeting the interests and preoccupations of its domestic audience. For Bollywood is first and always staunchly grounded in its origins in the Subcontinent. Its overseas success is a *consequence* of its popularity in India, not a compensation for the lack of it. Yet it deserves mention that a cinema that can contain deadly serious caution in spectacular frivolity as Raj Kapoor did in *Bobby* is a cinema with a special gift for transmogrification. As Farrukh Dhondy observes about Bollywood's success outside India: "[Its films] carry abroad a nationalist message, but somehow that message is not narrowly Indian" (Dhondy 130).[17]

Outside India, in places such as post-Stalinist Soviet Union, Bollywood films provided occasions to debate sensitive topics such as ideology and pleasure publicly and safely. *Bobby* was voted one of the top five films in 1975 by readers of the biweekly film serial *Sovetskii Ekran* (The Soviet Screen, with a circulation of 2 million in 1975), who conducted a lengthy print debate about *Bobby* that many wrote "taught them how to love." As the scholar Sudha Rajagopalan documents, discussions about Hindi films over any other cultural form in the Soviet press demonstrate that "it was possible to have divergent opinions about what Indian films represented to the audience, voice them publicly, and continue to engage with each other in the public space of the movies in post-Stalinist society."[18]

Audiences in Nigeria, the anthropologist Brian Larkin has shown, flock to Bollywood films, preferring those from the Golden Fifties (such as *Mother India*, Mehboob Khan, 1957) to more recent offerings. As Larkin explains in his ethnography of media in predominantly Muslim northern Nigeria: "the visual subjects of Indian movies reflect back to Hausa viewers aspects of everyday life . . . [that] fit with Hausa society . . . [and] offer an alternative style of fashion and romance that Hausa youth could follow without the ideological baggage of 'becoming western.'"[19] A scene indicating similar preferences and even similar tensions is played out in *East Is East* (Damien O'Donnell,1999), when the miniskirt-clad British-born daughter of a Pakistani fish and chips seller joyfully dances to a song from the courtesan hit,

Pakeeza (The pure one, Kamal Amrohi, 1971), while her family has its one on-screen cuddly moment in a Bradford cinema's screening of *Chaudhvin ka Chand* (Moon of the 14th day, Mohammed Sadiq, 1960).

For Bollywood's fans in India and elsewhere, the cultural product represents a cognitive horizon crucial for organizing an understanding of modern life and enabling an acceptance of it. Its blockbusters provide a symbolic cultural space of social resolution for the many who were alienated (as in the Soviet example) or left behind (as in the Nigerian case) by the print industry and its putative work in fully literate societies. Not only are Bollywood's blockbusters products of the age in which they are made and circulate, they are also producers in their own right whose images, conflicts, and associations acquire a power and authority often independent from and in excess of the whole. The cinema works, as popular forms do, not just by reproducing itself or its main preoccupations. It works by enabling its consumers to nimbly refashion the text to their own ends. When modernity appeared more a threat than an opportunity in India, film played a role in appeasing its demons. Bollywood's enchantment lay exactly in its flexibility. Through image, lyric, and narrative, its multiple codes embody messages not always in concert yet always coherent. Thus, Bombay's confections trolled the globe, a traveling market of film capital that stopped short of U.S. borders.

THE WORLD ACCORDING TO HOLLYWOOD

In 1998 the Indian government granted "industry" status to commercial cinema, enabling productions to access bank financing and loans for film development. The influx of capital, combined with the release of crowd-pleasing films such as *Hum Aapke Hain Kaun?* (Who am I to you?, Sooraj Barjatya, 1994) and *DDLJ* (1995) renewed Hindi cinema and inaugurated a phase that some scholars name the New Bollywood. India's media environment continued to change rapidly: cable made way for satellite television and the internet, and wider distribution, new screening platforms, and a new professionalism seemed to gather around the Hindi film industry. If we began by asking whether Bollywood could make it in Hollywood's turf, it seems equally germane to ask if Hollywood's methods might transform Bollywood's ways. In other words, do funds create the cinema, or does cinema create the funds? A glance at Hollywood's "world" may be illuminating in understanding how differently the two major film industries work in their quest for global markets. In contrasting the Bombay film industry

TABLE 4.1 The Economics of Bollywood vs. Hollywood

	BOLLYWOOD	HOLLYWOOD
Worldwide revenues	\$1.86 billion[1]	\$10.8 billion[2]
Revenue source	Cinema ticket sales (70%)[1,3]	TV rights, DVDs, merchandizing (50%)[2,3]
Worldwide ticket sales	\$3.6 billion[1]	\$2.6 billion[2]
Major revenue growth	12–20% per year[1]	<5% per year[2]
Star salaries as proportion of film budget (in %)	>40%[3]	<20%[3]
Major funding sources	Intrinsic to industry	Extrinsic to industry
Film considered "blockbuster" if it grosses more than	\$2 million[3]	\$200 million[2]
Average cost to make and market a film	\$1-3 million[1,3]	\$96.2 million[2]
Total number of screens available domestically	14,000[1]	40,000[2]
Percent of screens that are multiplexes	7.9%[1]	81%[2]

1. KPMG-FICCI, *Digital Dawn: The Metamorphosis Begins*, Indian Media and Entertainment Industry Report (2012), 59–76 (revenues reported in INR are converted at the 2012 rate of INR 50 to US\$1); see www.in.kpmg.com/securedata/ficci/Reports/FICCI-KPMG_Report_2012.pdf (accessed June 2013).

2. Motion Picture Association of America, "Theatrical Market Statistics: 2012"; see mpaa.org (accessed June 2013). The 2012 global box office for all films is reported at \$34.7 billion, with \$10.8 billion from U.S. and Canadian sources (ibid., 1).

3. Yassir A. Pitalwalla, "Hollywood vs. Bollywood," *Fortune* 152.10 (Europe), November 28, 2005.

with Hollywood, the profoundly different fiscal logics and loci that organize each are immediately apparent.

Table 4.1 provides a snapshot of the Bollywood and Hollywood industries from reports compiled by official sources.[20] Three main points are immediately evident. First is the scale of the Bollywood industry in contrast to Hollywood's and Bombay's notable undercapitalization in the comparison. Revenues from Bollywood's productions (\$1.86 billion) comprise only roughly 5 percent of cinema's global revenues at the box office (\$34.7 billion). Second, Bollywood's revenues are less than 20 percent (i.e., 17 percent) of Hollywood's (\$10.8 billion). Nevertheless, despite lagging in global revenue and gross earnings, Bollywood's worldwide ticket sales (\$3.6 billion) are almost 40 percent *higher* than Hollywood's (\$2.6 billion). Third, despite the chaos in funding, a business model that makes most financial managers cringe, and the fact that according to an Ernst and Young report, 30 percent of Bollywood's films that start shooting are never completed and

90 percent of Bollywood's films fail to recover their costs,[21] the Bombay film industry has seen an annual growth rate of between 12 and 20 percent. In contrast, Hollywood's industry, famously overseen by corporate managers, has been steadily dwindling in growth to under 5 percent a year while it loses domestic and worldwide audiences and sees losses at the U.S. box office. In short, the Bollywood profile appears to challenge any positive correlation between business oversight and economic return.

Prior to being recognized an industry in 1998, Bollywood was quite literally a cottage industry, absent reliable financing for its projects. The cottage industry, which was heavily taxed by a suspicious state, was mainly self-funded by sources intrinsic to it, such as film distributors. There were sporadic influxes of capital from private sources such as rice farmers after a particularly good harvest,[22] or diamond merchants such as Bharat Shah, who produced *Devdas* (Sanjay Leela Bhansali, 2002), once the most expensive Bollywood film ever made (at the cost of $10.2 million).[23] Notable among these sources were distributors with their intimate knowledge of regions and audience, who provided financing for productions that would appeal to their target region. It is arguably the case that it is distributors and their insistence on serving their audiences (rather than serving their directors or producers) that made Bollywood what it has become.[24]

This erratic funding created a cinema of great internal variety, with forms including mythologicals, action and stunt films, Muslim socials, dramas and melodramas, detective and crime thrillers, historical sagas, social films, romances, war films, and slapstick. The diversity of offerings includes within it common formal elements of music and dance around a shared cinematic vocabulary—a particular handling of shots, an increasing affection for exotic locations, a persistent crossing of generic boundaries, an acting style that veers toward skiagraphia (which emphasizes broad gestures rather than lexical precision), and a frequent disregard for the unities of time, place, and action. The typical Bollywood film still screens in a large theater not unlike a nineteenth-century opera house (also the name of one of Bombay's grandest movie theaters) with thousand-plus seats divided into carefully niched classes according to a staggered economy that places the unwashed masses in the front stalls, on benches, or on the floor, with ladies and middle-class families spread across the balcony and the highest price dress circle. The railway is the only other public space in India where such social diversity voluntarily occupies such a limited space. Like the train, the movie audience is separated according to class in regulated but porous compartments, each class aware of the other's presence but spared physical and often even visual contact. Because of the sheer size of such theaters, a film had to play to every sector of the audience enough of the time to draw every sector in for the three bread-and-butter showings at noon, 3, and 6 p.m.[25] Under these material conditions, a Bollywood film must purvey a bedrock of familiarity to signal its widest possible appeal. A filmmaker could not make a niche film and expect financial success; nor could the theater owner count on a niche audience to fill a thousand-seat hall day after day, year upon year.

In an industry dominated by exigencies of production and distribution such as this, it is no wonder that a cinema that could fill thousand-seat theaters with homemakers, adolescents, retirees, factory workers, domestic servants, families, taxi drivers, bureaucrats, and college students came to be associated as the national cinema. One conundrum that many ask is why Bombay travels as well as it does. Part of the answer must surely lie in the industry's unwillingness or inability to circumvent the material challenge of filling the thousand-seat theater. It made movies to fill them and ended up with a cinema for the billions. The filmmaker Shyam Benegal calls Hindi cinema "pan Indian, and a generalist cinema," elaborating: "Hindi films tend to travel much more than regional films. . . . Its common denominator has to be extremely wide and it has to appeal to a very large number of people. So the subject matters and treatment of the subject matters in a Hindi film tend to be far more generalized."[26]

Both the financing of Hindi films and their distribution and screening have begun to change markedly. The thousand-seat movie palaces have rapidly begun to be replaced by multiplex screens in large metropolises and midsize cities. The justification has been that the smaller screens encourage a diversity of content. No longer will a film need to appeal to a broad audience day after day. Rather, the smaller screens, it has been argued, allow distributors to pick up films earlier deemed too risky or too specialized for the mass audience. "The era of big cinema is out," claimed Raj Chopra of the Competent Group in 2002.[27] Multiplexes enjoy tax-free status on profits in many states where their construction in malls twins retail with entertainment, both intent on capturing a demographic that the anthropologist Ron Inden has dubbed the "bubblegum crowd."[28] In contrast to single-screen theaters that were constructed in densely populated urban areas easily accessible by public transportation, sociologists Adrian Athique and Douglas Hill document that "multiplexes have been constructed in suburbs . . . [that] must be reached by private rather than public transport." The result is what Athique and Hill call a "sufficiently sanitized and controlled public space where the behaviour of patrons corresponds with middle-class norms and where the overwhelming numerical superiority of the mob is mitigated."[29] The "big cinema" appeal to "big audiences" of the past half century is now reconfigured in what the media scholar Amit

Rai has dubbed the "malltiplex," where middle- and upper-class viewers can make a "lifestyle statement" (Athique and Hill 67) as they view similar statements projected by the content on screen.[30] The process of gentrification that Tejaswini Ganti observes in Hindi cinema is not just a matter of gentrifying content for smaller screens. The construction and location of multiplexes also gentrifies the screening experience and isolates it from the masses putatively dreaded by the middle and aspirational classes.

Alongside changes in screening, the elevation of film from cottage industry to a state-recognized industry in 1998 ameliorated the hitherto in-house financing situation in Bollywood. Now "bonafide" financing sources such as multinationals and venture capitalists see film as a ripe space for investment. Even India's Catholic Church has gone Bollywood, producing a film about sex, religion, and AIDS called *Aisa Kyon Hota Hai?* (Why does it happen like this?, Ajay Kanchan, 2006).[31] A special report in *India Today* describes how such corporate efficiency works in the industry: "Audited by Ernst and Young, a specially designed software programme breaks down the entire screenplay of the film, taking stock of every detail: from the budgeting to the colour of Bipasha Basu's clothing for a particular shot."[32]

The old Bollywood was characterized as a place penetrated by *Archie* comic books and divine inspiration (*Sholay* was germinated from a four-line idea that Salim Khan and Javed Akhtar sold to the Sippys in 1973).[33] It is a cinema that made history—and the nation. Backers of the new Bollywood include global media giants such as Sony and Twentieth Century Fox and global steel magnates such as Lakshmi Mittal, who financed the media arm, B4U, Mittal's first non-steel venture. Banks, which had shied away from the industry since its inception, are now eager to support it with loans, though the onerous paperwork requirements keep borrowers away. According to one insider, "financial institutions are not very happy with the number of loan applications they receive for movie projects. The Industrial Development Bank of India, for example, gets only 30–40 applications a year. Most producers are not willing to get involved with the documentation and paperwork that precedes the sanction of a loan."[34]

The "reformed" film industry, run by MBAs and accountants, is now rife with practices apparently learned by business school case-study methods, echoing Hollywood's focus groups. As Gitanjali Kirloskar of the venture capital arm of the multinational, Lintertainment, claims: "We want to help in professionalizing the industry from developing scripts to testing storylines."[35] Meanwhile, iDream, an offshoot of the securities firm SSKI, is reportedly "keeping an eagle eye on the finances of debutant director Robby Grewal's *Samay*. Bhatnagar [the back office suit] won't even look at films with no bound script or storyboard. His aim: 'We want to produce sensible cinema as well as make money.' "[36]

Bhatnagar's is a lofty aim, though it remains to be seen whether the "sensible cinema that makes money" actually comes off of a bound script, or whether it was better inspired from the legendary late-night sessions at Raj Kapoor's cottage in Chembur that produced hits like *Awara* and *Bobby*. Notwithstanding claims of professionalizing this informal culture, recent reports seem to indicate as high a failure rate as Bollywood itself. Only about a dozen or so of the films made with the new corporate financing mantra have actually made it to screens. The year 2002, when the influx of new capital was at a high point, has been regarded as one of the worst in Bollywood's recent memory.[37] Indeed, 94 percent of the films released that year (or 124 of 132) were flops incurring losses of $58 million.[38] Meanwhile, the dark cloud in the multiplex boom already seems evident. While the break-even point in Western multiplexes occurs with 10 percent occupancy, in India, with higher infrastructure costs and building taxes it is 40 per-cent.[39] And that, it seems, brings the multiplex back to where the movie palace once was: obliged to screen films for the multitudes.

The details on the new corporatized industry underscore what might yet happen in Bollywood, that it too might follow the uninspiring destiny that Hollywood has claimed and become that abhorrent form of mass culture instrumental in the alienation of its audiences. But Bollywood has yet to succumb. The influx of new funds has not seen many results. Sony got burned after its venture in 2000 with *Mission Kashmir* (Vinod Chopra), which grossed only $590,000 in the U.S. box office. The Industrial Devel-opment Bank of India has more funds to loan than applicants, and its one "hit," *Mangal Pandey: The Rising* (Ketan Mehta, 2005), appears nowhere in the top 200 list of box office grossers.[40] Most film IPOs on the Bombay Stock Exchange are trading for paisas despite their initial buzz, even while the broader stock market sees double-digit increases. A report in the *Wall Street Journal* cautions that "investors might want to stick to buying cinema tickets rather than shares in the country's moviemakers." With its "opaque management practices and unclear, if not downright murky, deals for fi-nancing and distribution," the industry is considered too "difficult" and "fragmented" to be understood by outside investors, be they Indian or not.[41]

Overall, the Bollywood industry remains a diffuse site of production with intimate if unsystematized ties to its audiences. Aditya Chopra made film history with *DDLJ*, the longest-running Hindi film at over 800 weeks, by making a film for his friends, scoring again with *Bunty aur Babli* (Bunty and Babli, 2005), a runaway hit among small-town youth audiences whose frustrations it affectionately portrayed. Meanwhile, *Kabhi Khushi Kabhi Gham* (*K3G*), made by Chopra's childhood friend and colleague, Karan Jo-har, is one of the most successful Hindi films to circulate in the United States and the UK. (Johar's earlier film, the trendsetter *Kuch Kuch Hota Hai*

[Something happens, 1998], earned £1.75 million in the UK and $2.1 million in the United States; *K3G* almost doubled that amount in 2001.) However, these films never enjoyed screenings for U.S. critics or distribution amongst U.S. audiences, so they never made it to the mainstream multiplex at the mall. As one scholar documents, *K3G* created a "minor scandal" when "the film should have appeared within the top-10 box office in the United States on *Variety*'s lists for late 2001, but [it] was omitted because the [*Variety*] editors apparently couldn't believe that an 'unknown' film was doing 'house full' business in American theatres (albeit those catering to Indo-American audiences)."[42] The neglect of Hindi films by mainstream U.S. outlets has changed considerably in the last decade, and it is now commonplace at the time of writing to encounter reviews of Hindi films in the *New York Times* on Fridays alongside the latest Brad Pitt or James Bond release.

Reviewing these statistics, it is evident that Bollywood's presence is already apparent in the United States even if its popularity seems largely a diasporic phenomenon.[43] Its box office returns might appear small when compared to Hollywood's on table 4.1, but they are in fact substantial in Bombay's own terms when its lower production costs and purchasing price parity (PPP) are taken into account. These observations urge a renewed reckoning of Bollywood and Bollywood-themed imports into the United States. Might reviewing *which* films succeed over others render clarity over what imports travel better than others into U.S. markets?

BOLLYLITE IN AMERICA

The data on table 4.2 illuminate several points. First, of the five top-grossing Indian films in the U.S. market, those from the "real" Bollywood, made in Bombay in Hindi with locally grown directors, financing, production, and distribution, trail in the U.S. box office far behind the carefully deracinated versions that grossly copied its affects (thus, *K3G*'s $3.1 million in the United States in contrast to *Monsoon Wedding*'s $13.9 million).[44] Second, returns in the U.S. box office notwithstanding, the three top-grossing Bombay-produced films in the U.S. market are in fact considerable laggards among the 200 all-time top-grossing Bombay films (adjusted for inflation). In this pantheon, the trio on table 4.2 appear nowhere near the top. *K3G* is at #72, *3 Idiots* at #33, with *Don 2* entirely absent from the list at the time of writing. Meanwhile, seventeen of the top twenty all-time highest-grossing Hindi films through 2012 (adjusted for inflation) were made in the long 1970s, with the list including *Sholay* at #1, *Amar Akbar*

TABLE 4.2 The Five Top-Grossing Hindi Films in the United States

FILM	U.S. BOX OFFICE GROSS
Monsoon Wedding (2001)	$13.9 million
Bride and Prejudice (2004)	$6.6 million
3 Idiots (2009)	$6.5 million
Don 2 (2009)	$3.7 million
K3G (2001)	$3.1 million

All figures adjusted for inflation.

Sources: "International Business Overview Standard" at http://ibosnetwork.com/usatopgrosses.asp; http://ibosnetwork.com/uktopopenings.asp (accessed June 2013) and boxofficemojo.com (accessed June 2013).

Anthony (#5), *Bobby* (#6), *Deewaar* (#11), and *Trishul* (#12).[45] These two details hint at a complex backstory about the nature of Bollywood's hits that is worth scrutinizing.

There is no doubt that the financial data that profile these films are highly suspect. The industry notoriously underreports its profits at every level to avoid tax liability, and the figures are routinely "adjusted" to account for this. Yet the statistical corruption is so widespread and widely acknowledged that the figures, however distorted, are the best index (in fact the only one) to profile the industry. They provide quantitative corroboration to the symbolic capital that specific films have accrued as evident from qualitative sources, which affirms the data's general, if not particular, accuracy.

The continued box office dominance of films from the 1970s underscores the influence that the decade and its products continue to have almost half a century later. Furthermore, in a marketplace dominated by the domestic box office, films that are top grossers in the United States flounder.

It should be no surprise that films that are popular in one context may not be in another. Therefore, that a version of Bollywood I name Bollywood Lite—or Bollylite—sold better in the U.S. multiplex than it did in India is not particularly unexpected. Bollylite's specially charged confection with sexual predation, expensive automobiles, and romance appears destined to cross borders with little obstacle, as *Monsoon Wedding* so successfully demonstrated. In this context, the director Mira Nair called *Monsoon Wedding* "a Bollywood movie, made on my own terms."[46] The critical story, however, lies in the U.S. fortunes of the films listed in table 4.2 (such as *K3G*), which were produced and made in and for an Indian audience before traveling West. Examining the success of these Bombay productions in U.S. theaters may explain something about the forms of Bollywood that can make the journey to the United States and find commercial success there.

Unfreighted of many of Bollywood's familiar locational and cultural markers, Bollylite is both leaner than its shaggy antecedents, and possibly lesser. The suffix "lite" gestures at least initially toward the pruning of a cultural brand in preparation for the U.S. market. Whether "lite" also comments on the substance in these films will become clearer shortly.

K3G

The U.S. success of a film such as *K3G* has often been explained by its extraordinary production savvy, which can hold its own against just about any Hollywood export. Packaged for theatrical release and video sales with slick advertising and catchy bylines that circulated on the internet, the film is subtitled in more languages spoken outside the Subcontinent than within, including French, German, Spanish, Arabic, Dutch, Malay, Japanese, and Hebrew. Its content reveals a skillful command over style, fashion, editing, color, and makeup to render it visually current with global trends if not fully coherent. *K3G*'s non-resident Indians (NRIs) with their Armani suits, designer saris, and flashy gemstones provide a relentless spectacle of an *au courant* consumer utopia unfettered by taste or modesty to become one of the highest-grossing Bombay exports in the U.S. box office.[47] "Bollywood" in form, this film departs markedly from earlier blockbusters in its systematic embrace of the material world. Produced at a moment when the new financial instruments and technological innovations described earlier enabled the enhancement of the Bombay industry, Bollylite films illuminate a cinema in which new technology and financial priorities have penetrated and become the inner logic of everyday life. No film better elaborates the idea of Bollylite than Karan Johar's *K3G*.

Dubbed "The Indian Family" in France and Germany, *K3G* paired reigning screen star Shah Rukh Khan with Amitabh Bachchan in a reprise of their blockbuster pairing from *Mohabattein* (Lovers, Aditya Chopra, 2000). Inhabiting a Delhi house curiously identical to Baron Ferdinand de Rothschild's Waddesdon Manor in Oxfordshire, this Indian family consists of a stern industrialist father, played by Amitabh Bachchan, a successful corporate son, played by Shah Rukh Khan, and a bevy of doting and devoted wives alternating saccharine smiles and domestic piety as if their lives depended on it. The remark is not in vain: their lives *did* depend on diligent devotion to something Corey Creekmur has wryly called industrial strength patriarchy. The son crosses the father by marrying a woman of his choice; the father disowns the son, who leaves India for London where he makes easy millions at an unspecified job where he can leisurely get to work by lunchtime; the two eventually remeet in a British shopping mall and tear-fully reconcile after a decade-long estrangement.

It is no coincidence that labor is invisible in *K3G*: it tends to be that way in most Bollylite films that showcase wealth in an effort to capture the attention of the aspiring classes.[48] What *is* visible in this film is surplus capital, repeated over and over again in the lavish display of name-brand luxury. That the estranged father and son can reconcile, not in the family home in Delhi but in that special emporium of consumption, the mall, is an irony unremarked upon in this connection, for Bollylite has little time for such narrative subtleties.

In *K3G*, the logic of the marketplace replaces all human relations, even filial piety. Whereas the mother cuddles her son in the prayer room at home, the father reserves parental cuddling for his place of worship, namely, a well-appointed suite in his corporate headquarters where he emotionally hands *his* family (i.e., his business) to his heir (see fig. 4.14). The son reaches his father's stature not by his moral integrity (in keeping his word to the woman he loves) but by the acquisition of millions, which makes them equals by the end of the film. The father punishes the son's breach to family honor not so much by cutting family ties, but by cutting him from his share of the family corporation. The exile the son chooses is not to remove himself from his father, but to find economic opportunities to best his parent's. While in London yearning for the paternal embrace, the son reverentially places a giant photo of his parents above his household gods, specifically, a giant state-of-the-art flat panel television (fig. 4.9).

"It's all about loving your parents," claimed the publicity banner (fig. 4.10) for a film in which that love finds its best mediation in models learned from the media and television that the flat panel displays. Media is the message here, and it could not be more severed from substance.

Larded with patriotism stirred by the indiscriminate playing of all three of India's patriotic anthems, the son's diasporic family gets teary-eyed longing for "home" all the while impervious to the transformations that "home" is undergoing as a consequence of the market values they usher into it. The concepts of family, duty, and nation exist largely in relation to the market in the film. Economic liberalization and its aftermath provided new capital and social impulses that *K3G* exploits in its treatment of the familiar trope of family melodrama. As the scholar Meheli Sen observes, in the 1990s "Bollywood fashioned a new family to articulate the nation's vicissitudes."[49] In this "new" family, both tradition and patriarchy are skillfully retrofitted within the logic of the market and made to reinforce the market's priorities. The refurbished "family" is an extension of the corporation, supported by

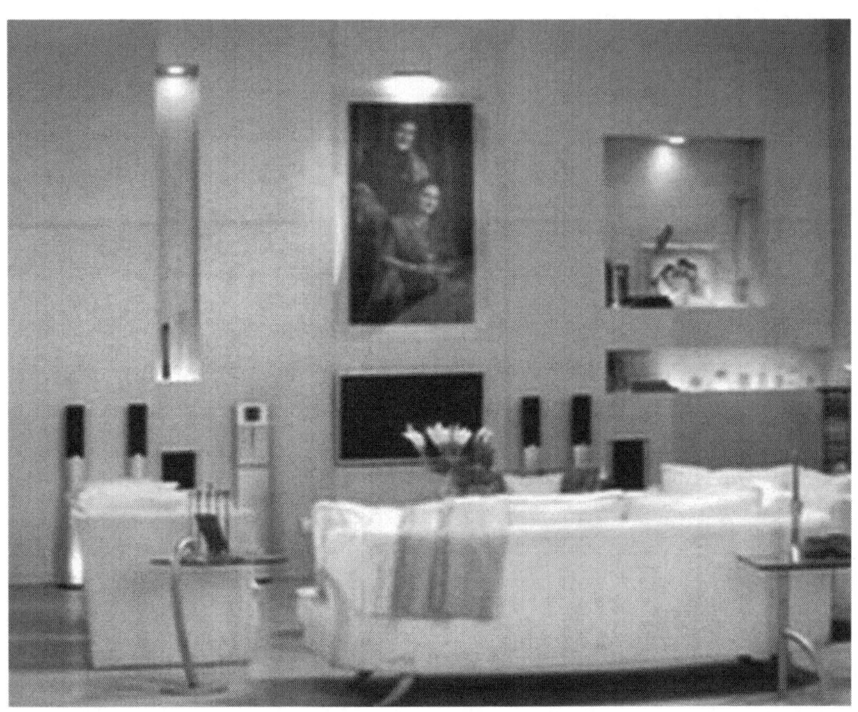

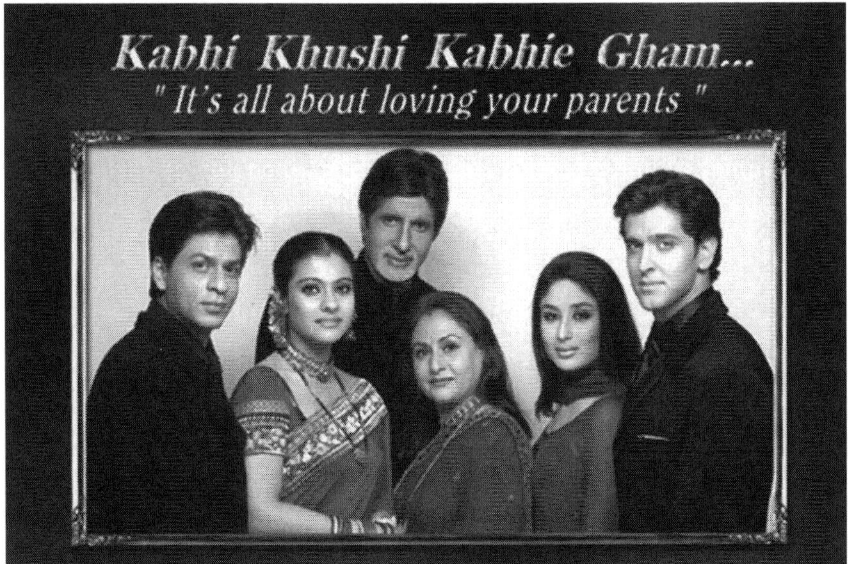

FIGURES 4.9 AND 4.10 The immigrant home in London, where "it's all about loving your parents"—and your stuff (*K3G*, 2001).

mergers (marriages) that extend the corporate entity. Boardroom protocols dictate kinship alliances. Infractions within the family—such as the son's refusal to marry a woman of his father's choice—lead to ejection from the boardroom *and* the family, as the son's exile in *K3G* underscores.

Anchored to a fantasy of "tradition" comprised of consumer goods and massive mansions, *K3G* provides a special form of comfort to salve the nostalgia of India's prosperous diasporic elite. Money, love, and family become interchangeable: having the first generates the others, or some simulacrum thereof. The prayer room has given way for the mall, the family for the television. Cinema's self- critique of media made famous in Douglas Sirk's *All That Heaven Allows* (1955)—with Jane Wyman's despair blankly reflected off the new television set meant to assuage a loneliness that only the forbidden Rock Hudson can fulfill—has gone the way of irony in Johar's Bollylite exemplaire.

These remarks underscore the superficiality of a hit that even its director has since called "candy floss."[50] The earlier gulf between a film's manifest and latent content evident so consistently in blockbusters such as *Bobby* has largely disappeared. *K3G*'s conservative social values and misogyny are rendered attractive by the visual glitz of its production. Form *is* content in Bollylite, and the two are seamlessly packaged to slide by an onerous demand for value. Paradoxically, the forms in which Bollylite travels to the West shear its politics and social critique but preserve its formal features. Thus, if *K3G* is a reliable indicator, there is more dance, not less in it; more melodrama, not less; more family, not more individuality. Rather than diluting form, Bollylite *concentrates* it. What it dilutes are political and social substance. What you see is what you get in this new kind of blockbuster that played so well to the diasporic crowd at the U.S. multiplex. The multiplex's smaller screens were warmly justified in India on the grounds that they enabled smaller films to prosper: those made on smaller budgets, with smaller stars, for a smaller audience—such as indie films (sometimes called *hatke*) that have prospered in this new screening opportunity. But Bollylite's offerings have equally prospered in the multiplex, with their large production budgets and scale balanced by a considerable diminishment in subtlety and substance. The exigencies that dominate the thousand-seat theaters still operating in most parts of India mean that film producers still have to entice a variety of viewers in order to expect predictable returns. Smaller screens both in India and elsewhere remove some of that urgency. They offer the promise of more diverse fare, but at the cost of a fully diverse audience. The outcome is a diminished cinema and product, as *K3G* demonstrates.

It would be too simple to claim that multiplexes create vapid fare. But the changing economics of the Bombay film industry, with new forms of financing, new business models, new investors, new distribution networks, and new corporate ownership of exhibition spaces is certainly having an effect on the industry's products. In 2002 an optimistic entrepreneur exulted at the "latent demand for destination entertainment" in the country.[51] The rise of the multiplex alongside India's new shopping malls gave new purpose to brand identities. The cinema spun a visual fantasy that the mall then delivered in the commodities it purveyed. The two became what the writer Ratna Bhushan calls "synergistic retail partners," both hedging risks on their investment. Should the film not deliver a purchasing fantasy, the mall and the film both flop in this sort of relationship. To avoid that outcome, one multiplex executive insisted, "we will backward integrate into film distribution and subsequently into film production. That will evolve as a general industry trend."[52] How plausible that relationship might be for the long term remains to be seen.[53]

Products like *K3G* point to one possible outcome of the new relationship. There is no evidence available of backward integration in producing this film, but there is every evidence that its content collaborates well with the consumer values of the new post-liberalization economy both in India and in the United States. *K3G*'s success as a top-grossing Hindi film in the U.S. says as much about the particular film's ability to travel as the conditions under which that journey is possible. While the considerable industry muscle of Johar's company, Dharma Productions, got the director permission to shoot lavish dance sequences in Leicester Square and even at the venerable British Museum, none of that gave *K3G* the symbolic (or even box office) capital that *Sholay* and *Awara* continue to enjoy in the decades since their release.

I do not for a moment mean to suggest that blockbusters of the earlier period did not contain their own commodity fantasies. Both *Awara* and *Sholay* are centrally about the quest for stability that comes with financial security. When Veeru asks Jai in *Sholay* about settling down in Ramgarh, it is fully evident that the migrant laborer can only dream of acquiring a home because the cash to purchase it has finally come into sight. In *Awara*, the quest for financial stability is layered with the search for paternity and the social integration it affords. Yet the fiduciary objects are not ends in themselves as the luxury goodies in *K3G* are. Virtually all the protagonist's exploits in *Awara* involve getting things for the women in his life that his biological father has withheld from them. In these earlier films, commodities, economic stability, and the market are means to an end far bigger than the sum of the parts. At the same time, the parts are subject to critique for obstructing individual agency and social decency. Thus, when Raj in *Awara* attempts to reform from a life of crime, his exploitation in the hands of a local factory owner is critiqued as well as the poverty that criminalizes him in the first place. Neither the commodity nor the market of which it is part is fully embraced in these films, even while both are being eventually mastered by protagonists as different as Raj and Veeru. In Bollylite, to the contrary, the market *is* the end, and mastering it *is* the happy ending that arrives in a mirage of goodies meant to fill a void that must not be named.

As India's economic liberalization program concludes its third decade and the distance between it and the West shrinks, the earlier clashes with modernity have now become full-fledged warfare. If Raj Kapoor's *Awara* showed the clash between three generations and three economic orders (the feudal class of landed property, the professionalized post-Independence elite that sprang from the squirearchy, and the "new" class represented by the tramp; see figs. 4.11–4.13), the clash these days is between two generations (father and son in *K3G*), inhabiting the same economic order (fig. 4.14).

The earlier critiques of a market-dominated logic, the insistence on separating economic wealth from social worth that was so keenly detailed in

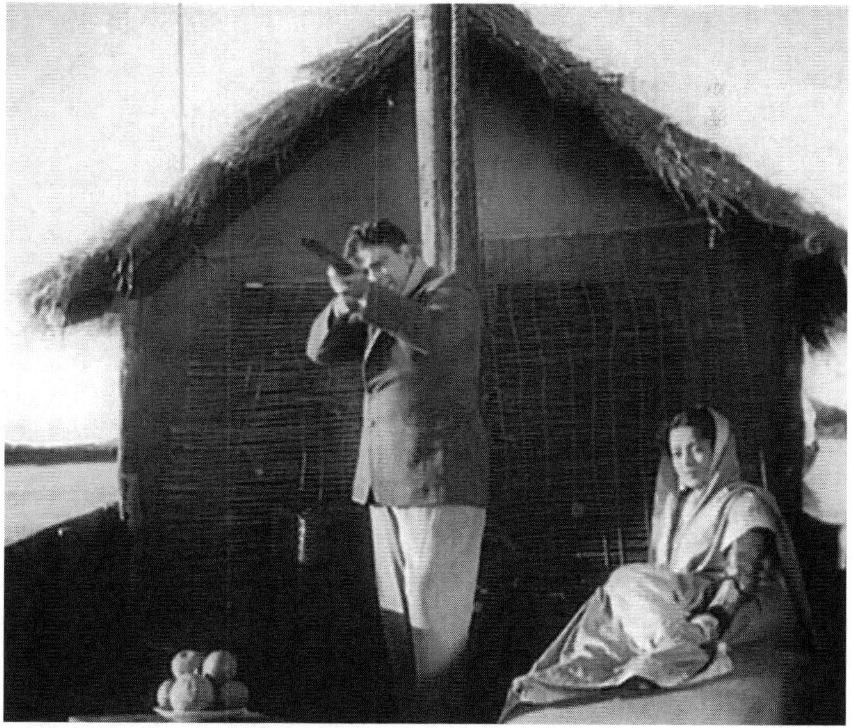

FIGURE 4.11 Prithviraj Kapoor as landowner in *Awara* (1951).

(COURTESY YASH RAJ FILMS)

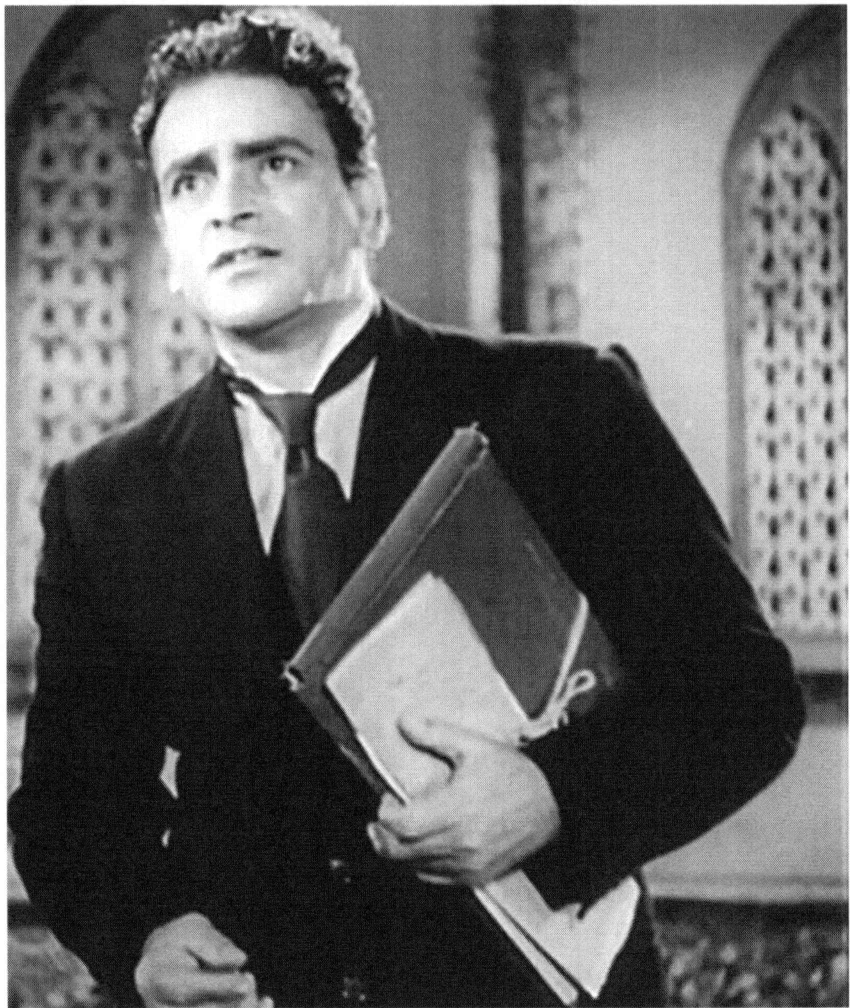

FIGURE 4.12 Prithviraj Kapoor as judge in *Awara* (1951).

Kapoor's films of the 1950s and that persisted in Hrishikesh Mukherjee's 1970s comedies of the middle classes and Manmohan Desai's blockbusters for the masses have largely disappeared.[54] The subalterns and their struggles have no place even in Bollylite's hairline margins. Bollylite's issue is no longer making it ("it" being financial security, social position, community integration): those things are given, if we believe Bollylite's tales of the fabulously wealthy. The real issue now is *being it:* "it" being the good Indian who has evaded any conflict from succumbing to the pleasures of material

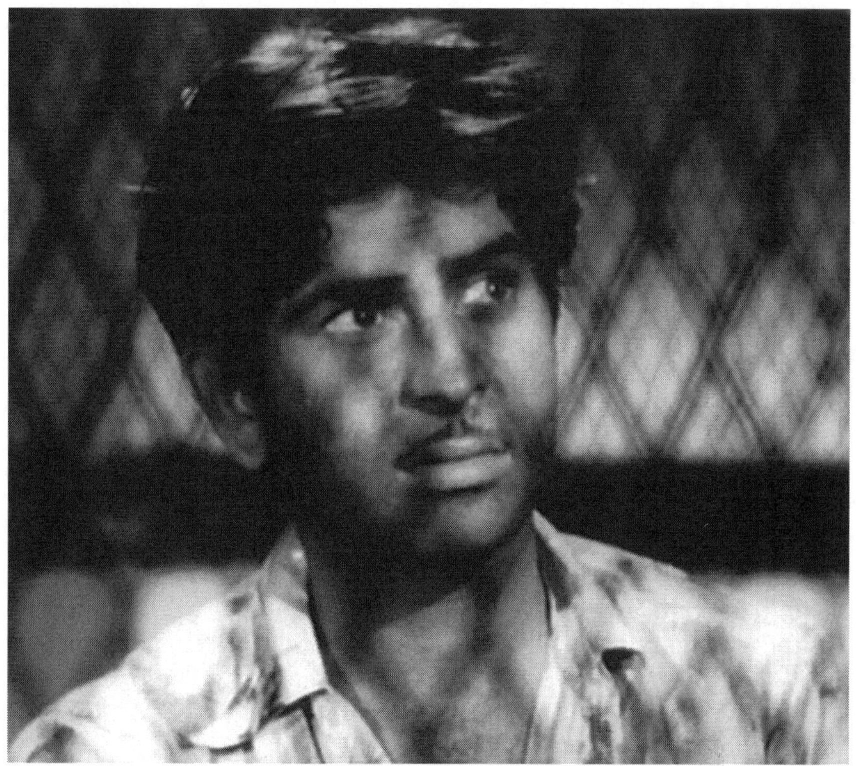

FIGURE 4.13 Raj Kapoor as tramp in *Awara* (1951).

(COURTESY YASH RAJ FILMS)

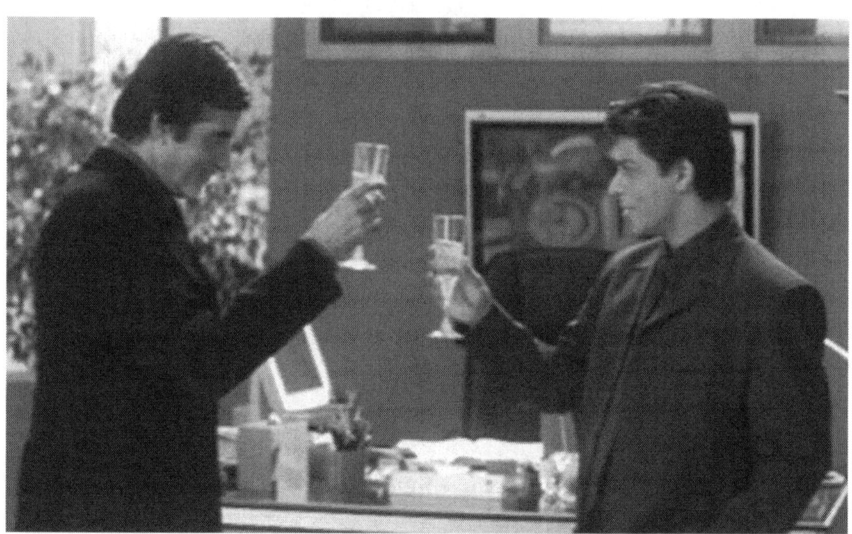

FIGURE 4.14 Amitabh Bachchan and Shah Rukh Khan in *K3G* (2001).

(COURTESY YASH RAJ FILMS)

TABLE 4.3 Bollywood vs. Bollylite

DOMINANT FEATURES	BOLLYWOOD	BOLLYLITE
Family	dislocated, incomplete, truncated	entrenched, extended, established
Social space	city, slum	home
Economic order	in transition	stable
Social mobility is	governing ethos and *raison d'être*	irrelevant to plot
Conflict and/or violence occurs	between classes	within family
National identity conveyed by	struggles within and for the public	struggles and anguish within the individual
Cinematic meaning resides	between latent and manifest content	in manifest content; latent content largely eliminated

desire in the climate of economic liberalization and Westernization. In this regard, *Monsoon Wedding* may not be as different from *K3G* as its box office returns in the United States might anticipate, even as both are profoundly dissimilar from the cinema christened Bollywood and detailed in the first section of this chapter.

Table 4.3 gathers some of the most striking differences between a cinema of substance and one of image conveyed in the terms Bollywood and Bollylite, respectively. For Bollywood to travel to the U.S. multiplex, it needs to be shorn of its substance, its contradictions, and its coherence. Indian modernity in the new iteration is one that carries a sacrosanct tradition untouched, unmodernized, and unexamined with it.

The table is indicative rather than prescriptive. It condenses the analytic arguments of this chapter in an effort to sharpen an understanding of a cinema at a moment of transition as that cinema crosses its Rubicon—or the Mississippi. One could immediately think of exceptions: Bollywood films such as *DDLJ* with many of Bollylite's formal characteristics, or Bollylite films such as *Hum Aapke Hain Kaun?* with numerous typically Bollywood features. Both sorts clearly proliferate and coexist. Table 4.3 highlights a set of dominant features of the cinemas that I differentiate into the forms Bollywood and Bollylite. These are by no means the only features that characterize the differences between the two. They simply happen to be most marked in this analysis. The seepage of features across the two cinemas is to be expected. Bollylite owes its identity and origin to Bollywood and adeptly borrows from it when it can, even as it brutally unfreights itself of matter deemed too heavy for its global travels. Thus, the clarity of formal features as outlined in table 4.3 is not perfectly reflected in this fecund industry, nor should the difficulty with taxonomic precision necessarily obviate the larger argument in table 4.3.

In the end, the real question may not be so much whether Bollywood travels to the United States as Bollywood's travels in multiplex circuits both in the U.S. and in India. The Indian multiplex phenomenon indexes a larger transformation of a booming globalized economy and its domestic social changes. For some observers, this "new" Indian world resembles the United States in more ways than one, with a markedly alienated and depoliticized relationship between culture and consumption. Social capital is in decline in this world; commodity capital appears in some quarters to have taken its place. In such an environment, where the NRI and the wannabe NRI are such visible players, films such as *K3G* have considerable appeal. *K3G*'s travels gesture toward the proliferation of a set of values that coexists with those that Bollywood purveyed in the post-Independence period and that Farrukh Dhondy observed a quarter century ago.

Bollywood, however, has yet to disappear as the success of hits such as *DDLJ* and *Bunty aur Babli* attest. For now, it coexists with Bollylite. Both products in this iteration serve as compensatory narratives in all senses of the term. The greater India's embrace of modernity, the firmer its step into the dance of global capital, the stronger the likelihood of Bollylite's proliferation. But that proliferation remains destined for the multiplex, and its fortunes tied to a form that even today plays to a minority of the twelve million a day who go the movies in India. KPMG's 2012 industry report (*Digital Dawn: The Metamorphosis Begins*) observed the multiplexes' "dismal footfall over weekdays" and cautioned: "High property prices and recent recessionary conditions have slowed the expansion of malls and corresponding footfall growth which has directly affected the growth of multiplexes" (KPMG 2012:65).

At a moment where a little over 1,000 (or approximately 8 percent) of India's 14,000 cinema screens are multiplex, large-capacity single screens still dominate with their content devoted to capturing the largest audience possible (see KPMG 2011:61; 2012:64). With twelve screens per million people in India (or approximately one screen for every 83,000 people), going to the movies is a crowded undertaking.[55] The malltiplex has done much to ease the gentry into more comfortable seats, and Bollylite's offerings have helped further anesthetize their sensibilities from civic engagement. The political and social responsiveness that dominates Bollywood have become economic farces in Bollylite's offerings. If Bollywood, exemplified by the cinema of Raj Kapoor and blockbusters such as *Deewaar*, captured national fantasies to bring everyone along rather than alienating one section from another, Bollylite's offerings erase whole sections of the public altogether. Its India is scrubbed clean of labor and poverty. *K3G*'s Chandni Chowk comes in soothing pastels without open drains or germ-infused chutneys. Its Delhi mansions look awfully like English country houses, the weather is always amenable, and perilous Delhi buses are replaced by sleek private helicopters that deliver Shah Rukh Khan home in time for a party to celebrate his father's most recent corporate takeover.

But the India of slums coexists alongside its high-rises. This is the India that *Slumdog Millionaire* insists on recalling when it opens with another screen god, Amitabh Bachchan, descending from another helicopter by a garbage heap. The film retrieves Bollywood's core plot and reminds its viewers of the nation that inspired the state and the cinema that sustained it. Bollywood is always the story of slumdogs who become millionaires, of men of multiple faiths who make it in a flawed secular democracy, of movements from innocence to experience, of the hero who gets the girl and his pawned honesty medal, and of protagonists who conquer the metropolis and their lesser selves. As India changes, the cinema does as well—to an extent. It remains national, if increasingly less nationalist.

Above all, the cinema named Bollywood remains insistently a form of critique and renewal. Through the long 1970s that critique was directed at a political horizon that seemed to have failed its citizens. With economic liberalization, as several hundred million people entered the middle classes and beyond, the object of critique moved from the political back to the social and the economic. Raj Kapoor's *Shree 420* comes to an end when a group of con artists desperately chase a bag of money that eventually bursts and dooms them. The scene is oddly prescient of what occurs today in an India eager to integrate more completely into global capitalism. The bag of money has now come "home," and everyone has a shot at getting it. Many do. However, the money brings little solace—either to the Raichand family estranged in London in *K3G*, or to Salim Malik, Jamal's brother in *Slumdog Millionaire*, who is shot in a bathtub full of rupee notes. Bollywood, and the forms that honor it, allow one to see that.

The United States proclaims its multiplexes break even with 10 percent occupancy. With such figures, one has little to fear that the multiplex will transform a cinematic form that has kept billions rapt across the last century. Bollywood may not travel to the U.S. multiplex; but Bollylite will, and it will likely prosper there. And one day it may even awaken its audience for the real thing.

EPILOGUE

ANTHEM FOR A NEW INDIA

BOLLYWOOD HAS IT ROUGH IN the new millennium. The cinema competes in a dense entertainment ecosystem that includes television, print, the internet, radio, cricket, social media, and gaming, all nimbly delivering content skillfully niched to consumers. In 2013 the Indian film industry of which Bollywood is a part came third in revenues behind television and print.[1] Meanwhile, as the previous chapter detailed, the influx of capital into the newly recognized industry in the millennium failed to deliver the anticipated hits. In a 2012 industry report commissioned by the Federation of Indian Chambers of Commerce and Industry (FICCI), the consulting firm KPMG cautiously names the year a moment of "Digital Dawn" (the title of the report). Bollywood's A-list producers, Yash Chopra and Karan Johar (who coauthored the report's foreword), remark on the "mixed fortunes" and "hyper competition" that India's media and entertainment industry faces. Any certitudes on what audiences "wanted" seem up for grabs in this new dawn, they conclude.[2] Anil Arjun, the CEO of Reliance MediaWorks, one of the largest corporate entities to enter Indian film, observes that "films which are termed 'Mass' . . . and expected to do well in Tier 2 and 3 locations have also done extremely well in urban centers with Tier 1 audiences. . . . Alternatively, the urban centric stories . . . which were traditionally targeted towards metro audiences have done extremely well in smaller centers." Arjun's remark illuminates a cinema whose audiences create its fortunes largely on their own, apparently ignoring the corporate interests that manage distribution and screening by establishing "tiered" markets. Notwithstanding predictions, films defy their destined tiers and routinely reach audiences outside them. Observing this trend, Siddharth Roy Kapur, CEO of UTV Motion Pictures (an Indian subsidiary of the Walt Disney Company), offers: "such cinema works at [the] box office provided it guarantees entertainment to the audience."[3]

Neither Arjun nor Kapur addresses *how* cinema works at the box office or what entertainment it guarantees to its audiences. In a document invested in quantifying the industry and reporting on outcomes not processes, KPMG's report relegates content to the general category "entertainment," leaving the substance of the cinema absent from discussion. In KPMG's 2013 report, film's revenues behind other media such as television and print are explained by market fragmentation. Here as well, content is largely ignored, even when the industry's main stakeholders ponder ways to reach a broader audience: "The vision set out for the sector, of engaging communities, entails reaching out and understanding multiple segments, creating greater connect, and leveraging this connect to influence for the greater social good."[4] At a moment when distribution, exhibition, and markets are being exhaustively analyzed, when single-screen theaters are being refurbished for digital screening, when the multiplex is expanding vertically to provide luxury entertainment at the hitherto unimagined cost of INR 1,000 a ticket (approximately $20) and downwards to Nukkad theaters (*literally*, corner theaters) with tickets priced at INR 15, or 30 cents,[5] the industry underscores its seriousness about "reaching multiple segments" absent a recognition of content's central role in "creat[ing] greater connect" and "influence[ing] the greater social good."

Bollylite's strategies from the early years of the twenty-first century to focus on well-heeled viewers by purveying content and exhibition targeted to gentrifying tastes seem to be nearing a conclusive demise. Niche production and marketing still prevail, but without providing the returns that make them worthwhile. The multiplex boom documented in the previous chapter continues, but not quite in the form anticipated a decade ago when it was regarded as auguring the single screen's death. At the time of writing, single screens continue to bring in box office revenues, and industry figures document that "in reality, the per show revenue of the single screen is higher than that of multiplex[es]," which are now obliged to program broadly popular fare such as World Cup cricket matches to offset declining feature film revenues from the distracted middle- and upper-middle-class viewer.[6] As chains like Nukkad take off, a version of the single screen is being reborn for lower- and lower-middle-class viewers in previously underserved regions.[7] The masses, such data underscore, are getting content and exhibition venues much as they did in the previous century. Moreover, as content destined for one tier crosses over to others, the margins are closer to the mainstream than their designation implies.

Concluding a book about Bollywood as public fantasy when both Bollywood and public fantasy remain present has challenges, but also opportunities. *Bollywood's India* focuses on the content in the cinema and outlines a set of preoccupations that characterize the cinema called Bollywood. As some of the procedures within the cinema have changed, as its financing, production, distribution, and exhibition are transformed, as the relation between the cinema and its audiences undergoes shifts in a media environment dominated by the internet and the opportunity for on-demand viewing, the cinema's social responsiveness has persisted even when the subjects of response are different today than they were in previous decades.

This Epilogue sketches Bollywood's persistence in what some claim to be a "New" India. It outlines the cinema's skillful retrofitting of novelty in remarks framed around two recent blockbusters, *Lage Raho Munnabhai* (2006) and *3 Idiots* (2009). Rather than being full-scale critical analyses of these films, the remarks are illustrative of trends in recent cinema and are applicable to other blockbusters as well. The Epilogue concludes by offering areas of further research in a rapidly transforming environment.

Bollywood is thriving in spirit and substance in the current moment. The cinema's continued ambition to reach the widest audience in the present media environment echoes aspirations from the decades immediately following Independence when it confronted a different set of challenges. During that moment, as this book details, the industry had little state support, infrastructure and exhibition were cottage industries, studios were in decline, notwithstanding which the cinema secured audiences across regions and classes and kept them there for almost half a century. A large reason it did so resides in the *content* of particular blockbusters that captured the public fantasies of the day in an enduring cocktail of stories, stars, music, and tropes.

This study identifies social responsiveness as the defining feature of the cinema named Bollywood and shows how Bollywood's appeal lies in its ability to capture audiences by addressing dispersed apprehensions and aspirations. The content of the cinema—its narratives, their treatment, the constellation of tropes, and their mise-en-scènes—became features that conveyed cultural capital upon Bollywood's blockbusters that made, remade, and unmade "India." Ideas about "India" were a central preoccupation of the cinema, and the cinema nimbly evolved to address them.

With the onset of economic liberalization in the 1990s, India's economic and social landscape changed. More people joined the middle classes in the decade following economic liberalization in 1991 than they did in the four decades following Independence in 1947.[8] The gentrification of the social order ushered a gentrification in the cinema as well. The influx of capital from new corporate partners in the millennium ushered global ambitions that have led some to claim the cinema of the post-1990s as the cinema of global capital addressed to those who aspire to it.[9] What gets lost in the bland summary is the unevenness of neoliberalism's economic and social processes that occurred fitfully and sporadically across the past quarter century, leaving large swathes untouched or unfairly touched by liberalization's bounty in India. The social tensions of the 1970s have persisted in kind if not degree alongside other tensions introduced by the neoliberal economy. The cinema continues to address these anxieties frontally in blockbusters that, like those of the preceding decades, travel widely, reaching the fragmented market lamented in the KPMG media industry reports.

Cinema remains a key player in India's public culture despite lagging behind television and print in revenues. Much of cinema's content gets another run on television and the internet. Its blockbusters continue to address the anxieties of the moment. If the state is no longer the sole object of critique, its institutions are. Rather than the police and judiciary being singled out as they were in films such as *Ab Dilli Dur Nahin* (1957), *Shree 420* (1955), *Sholay* (1975), *Deewaar* (1975), and *Shakti* (1982), other institutions such as the education system, healthcare, the media, and the labor market come under scrutiny alongside corruption, land grabs, terrorism, organized crime, social stigmas, and what some identify as the "new" Indian family. In its responsiveness to the idea of "India," Bollywood today remains consistent with its past from the 1970s, even as its treatment and emphases have inevitably evolved, occasionally borrowing from the procedures identified with Bollylite as detailed in the previous chapter.

Blockbusters such as *Lage Raho Munnabhai* (Keep at it, Munnbhai, 2006) and *3 Idiots* (2009), both directed by Rajkumar Hirani and produced by Vinod Chopra, skillfully manage corporate interests (inserted in lengthy opening slides that preface both films) and the media (the theme of *Lage Raho*) in works that radically critique the nature of new wealth in twenty-first-century India. Unlike the tortured Vijay from *Deewaar* who roves Bombay as a solitary fixer for the criminal underworld, *Lage Raho* features the affable gangster, Munna, in the company of his loyal sidekick, Circuit, who calls him Bhai (brother) and is always nearby, even when Munna has his morning tryst over the airwaves with the radio jockey, Jhanvi. Where *Deewaar*'s dark violence is visually paired with its somber colors and claustrophobic cinematography, *Lage Raho*'s violence is coated in cheerful South Beach hues accompanied by a kinetic camera. When Munna discovers Jhanvi's devotion to Gandhian principles, he rushes to acquire them as well, eventually hallucinating that M. K. Gandhi himself is standing and speaking by his side.

Lage Raho's latent critique of ruthless land grabs obliges Munna to make choices between accumulating kinship (the woman of his dreams) or capital (from his criminal activities). His transformation from being street muscle to hosting a live radio call-in talk show in which he espouses a version of Gandhi's nonviolent philosophy that he delivers in Mumbai gangster argot spawned critical detractors who found the film's resolution superficial and distracting from the crises it identifies.[10] Notwithstanding *Lage Raho*'s manifest protests over the consumerism and the superficiality of Mumbai's yuppies, youth prevail in the film over the aged; violence, or its threats, prevails over Gandhian nonviolence; and humor, music, and Munna's hallucinations of the nation's great soul cheerfully accept quite a bit of chicanery. Munna's fusion of selected Gandhian philosophy with gangster efficiencies fixes quite a few problems. It enables rapprochements between Munna and Jhanvi, and between parents and children; it publicly exposes a corrupt astrologer; and it reforms the rapacious land developer threatening Munna and Jhanvi, transformations all achieved by Munna's earnest radio broadcasts, or his (and Circuit's) weapons.

The critical insistence that *Lage Raho* is not serious or serious enough misses the point of both film and Bollywood. The density of M. K. Gandhi's philosophy, its idiosyncratic nature, and its rambling articulations do not lend themselves easily to film of any kind, much less to popular cinema.[11] For a man whose image appears on Indian rupee notes of every denomination, whose name appears on a street in virtually every Indian city, whose image graces interiors in most public institutions, Gandhi is curiously absent from popular culture. For the scholar Ashis Nandy, "Gandhian values are more like a potentiality incompatible with both classical and some aspects of the popular and can appeal to these sectors only under specific conditions."[12] *Lage Raho*'s revival of the Mahatma gives him a second inning, and the figure *has* to appear as hallucination, a shadow of Gandhi's "real" self that was incomprehensible even to those who knew him.[13]

The Gandhi that script writers Rajkumar Hirani and Abhijat Joshi fabricate in the Bollywood blockbuster is a device, much as Nehru was in Raj Kapoor's films, a figure both borrowed and abstracted from history. Bollywood's Gandhi provides not a tutorial on the author of *Hind Swaraj* (1909) but a tutorial on modern citizenship. Surrounded by forces immune to decency, the desperate citizen of post-liberalization India learns to conduct his own version of passive resistance by offering his underwear to a corrupt pension officer demanding a bribe. The public self-humiliation works, and the pensioner rapidly receives his pension.

Such is Bollywood's version of Gandhi's message, not espousing nonviolence, per se, but providing appropriate weapons for the weak. For scholars such as Nandy, Gandhi's appearance in *Lage Raho* offers a reminder to a new generation that "someone in this very country dared to experiment with another kind of politics, defying the academic and bureaucratic canons and, while this other politics might be taboo in the high culture of the Indian state, it still makes sense to millions in the world."[14] Nandy's account of *Lage Raho* places Gandhi as the engine of critique, rather than the cinema of Bollywood, as this study does. Likewise, others remarking on *Lage Raho* observe the blockbuster's inevitable refashioning of the historical figure, missing perhaps that the film is not about Gandhi. *Lage Raho* is about Munna—and India.

The figures of Gandhi and Munna become ways to address an India entirely alien to the Mahatma—and itself. Confronting a moment when the state, corporate interests, global ambition, and outsize greed collaborate on massive land grabs that remove inconvenient residents from prized real estate by any means possible, Gandhi's methods against the colonial state from the previous century are remade, this time to address the enemy within. The arrival of this Gandhi—of any Gandhi—in popular film absorbs attention away from the conflicts the figure putatively addresses. Thus, *Lage Raho*'s detractors reference the film's contradictions and inaccuracies over the biographical record, rather than its depiction of practices convulsing many parts of India caught in the often destructive vortex of neoliberal development.

Like Bollywood's blockbusters from past decades that form the core of this study, contemporary blockbusters such as *Lage Raho* continue to play a role in addressing public fantasies, without necessarily redressing them. *Lage Raho* has no "solution" to offer in the battles against real estate developers. Its comic depiction of passive resistance barely hides the brutality inflicted on an aged schoolteacher who has to beg for his pension. However, alongside *Lage Raho*'s skillful cinematography, which renders Mumbai a convivial media utopia, the film's pitch-perfect casting and toe-tapping music also deftly convey a ruthless India where a home for senior citizens can be razed for its valuable land on a bureaucratic technicality, where a son exiles his inconveniently ageing parent, and where the only choice available is a wallet or a bullet as Lucky, the real estate developer, offers his victims.

Land grabs, which are *Lage Raho*'s core conflict, have long been present in Bollywood as *Shree 420* (1955), *Deewaar* (1975), and *Trishul* (1978), among others in the present study, reveal. However, in the earlier blockbusters, land was grabbed *for* and *by* the working and middle classes—as Raj tried to do in *Shree 420* or as Vijay and his developer father attempted in *Trishul*. In today's India, on the other hand, land is grabbed *from* the middle and working classes, as *Lage Raho* underscores with Lucky's efforts to claim the senior residence for a high-rise. No one and nothing are safe in the greedy neoliberal race.[15] Bollywood's articulation of this violence and the cinema's representation of its widespread practice, much like the cinema's articulation of gendered violence in films such as *Bobby* (chapter 4), underscore the form's engagement with and as public culture. *Lage Raho*'s manifest visual and aural pleasures sugarcoat its more sinister latent content, much as Bollywood's blockbusters from the past half century did for the anxieties of the day.

Across the decades of this study, Bollywood's blockbusters have conducted a dialogue over the idea of "India," recognizing that cleavage rather than coherence is its dominant topos. In recent blockbusters, the social embrace of what the anthropologist Ron Inden called "commercial utopia" (characteristic of films from the early moment of economic liberalization in the mid-1990s) is balanced in the cinema with caution over liberalization's social costs.[16] Thus, the extraordinary wealth of a Lamborghini-sporting Raj in *DDLJ* (1995) is considerably tempered a decade and a half later. The 2009 blockbuster *3 Idiots* opens with a successful engineer gloating over a photo of his Lamborghini and swimming pool in Silicon Valley, sneering that a long-desired meeting with a reclusive Indian inventor, Phunsukh Wangdu, will propel him to unimaginable wealth. "Look at me, and look at you idiots!" he boasts to his former engineering college classmates. The film closes with Phunsukh Wangdu being none other than the Silicon Valley engineer's one-time college nemesis, an inventor who checked out during the rush for global gold for a more rewarding alternative far outside the corridors of soul-destroying corporate labor. The Lamborghini and private plane that featured so flamboyantly in *DDLJ* give way to solar-powered vehicles and bicycle-powered washers in Wangdu's social utopia, which concludes *3 Idiots*. Bollywood refocuses the novelist Chetan Bhagat's reform-of-Indian-education novel, *Five Point Someone* (2004), into a wider critique of neoliberal social values that prioritize economic wealth over individual worth, objects over subjects.

3 Idiots's exuberant conclusion has dissenters from India's neoliberal dream convene in a border zone resembling an ashram. There, a woman who fled a loveless trophy marriage, an engineer who tossed a career to pursue a calling, and the reclusive inventor-turned-teacher stage a romance to counter the aspirational world of Lamborghinis that now grovels before them. The film concludes in Ladakh, a state on India's political borders far outside its metropolises and their hubs of economic production. The "idiots" in the film have to rove all over India in a Volvo (a brand associated with a country fabled for its "Third Way") in search of it. When they finally arrive and find Wangdu, they discover a place both within and without, an alternative to and a reminder of the "India" that should be but is not. The entrepreneurial zeal that takes India's engineers to Silicon Valley is refashioned in Wangdu's borderland "ashram" where young inventors propose human and bio-power solutions to address *India's* needs, not Silicon Valley's. Lambdas replace Lamborghinis in Wangdu's "Ladakh," where everybody is equal, educated, and has electricity. If all this sounds somewhat "Gandhian," it is, recalling Gandhi's Sabarmati Ashram with its social experiments in equality and entrepreneurship. Of course, somewhat typically, Bollywood's Wangdu is rich, far richer than Sabarmati's, capable of buying out the Silicon Valley braggart.

Meanwhile, in a series of political films that contend with the threats of global terror and the state's feeble responses to it, Bollywood stages the ideals of India more directly. In the thriller, *A Wednesday* (Neeraj Pandey, 2008), the call against a hamstrung state apparatus is delivered by a lone vigilante who holds Bombay captive while he executes four men responsible for masterminding a decade of terror on the citizens of India. The vigilante's critique of the state and its defunct due processes is so persuasive that it has to be expunged from official records and can only be recalled in the twilight memories of a retired police commissioner who finds himself unable to confront or arrest the vigilante. In *Kahaani* (Story, Sujoy Ghosh, 2012), an India that has turned against itself in the form of a rogue double agent who drops chemical weapons in a subway car can only speak from the grave, leaving its future stillborn. The film's female detective insists on speaking to a dead man whose child she pretends to carry, articulating the direness of a political identity whose past and future are largely inconceivable.

These concluding remarks about the socially responsive and engaged popular cinema named Bollywood reveal both similarities and differences across the decades of this study and usher directions for future research. In India's present media ecology, the travel of films across carefully tiered and niched markets is also accompanied by the arrival of new forms that include indies, fanvids (fan videos), and local productions, all enabled by inexpensive technology and new media platforms for production, distribution, and exhibition. Beyond the notion of Bollywood, the very concept of "blockbuster" now needs to account not just for films that break national records as those in this study have. As Hindi cinema moves into the new millennium, the concept of "blockbusters" that guided the present study may need to be reconsidered to include films that sustain *local* records and *regional* capital in claiming the popular (thus, blockbusters with the emphasis on "block" as a smaller unit than current). If Bollywood today is being remade elsewhere as some are beginning to suggest, future scholarship will need to contend with Bollywood's legacies and afterlives outside the mainstream and beyond the prism of the 1970s, as *Bollywood's India* pursues.[17]

Above all, the industry's own bafflement over its product and processes as captured in KPMG's reports underscores this study's core claims. Narrative and content dominate in the cinema; production and distribution practices play a smaller part in determining the overall product. In India's evolving public culture, the stories in the cinema and their forms of appeal play the major role in finding and preserving audiences, a detail evidently overlooked by the corporate moguls and A-list producers who collaborated on the KPMG reports. What some name India's global self is engaged and refuted in this cinema across the decades. The diaspora that once was the global self in Bollylite hits (see chapter 4) is now reconstituted, even rebuffed, in the more recent iteration, as blockbusters such as *3 Idiots* adumbrate. Globalization in the present cinema is often regarded as a means to an end, rather than a destination in itself.

Rather than narrowing the notion of "India," Bollywood's blockbusters continue to expand it, remaining the site where versions of the nation are played out and retrieved. As long as the cinema engages with public fantasies of the day, there will continue to be a Bollywood, even if one day it migrates from Bombay.

NOTES

PREFACE: THE SOCIAL WORK OF CINEMA

1. Bunny Reuben, "An Open Letter to Raj Kapoor," *Star and Style*, April 30, 1971, 10. Chapter 2 further addresses Raj Kapoor and his funk in Chembur following the failure of *Mera Nam Joker*.

1. BOLLYWOOD'S INDIA

1. In 1938, to celebrate the twenty-fifth anniversary of Indian film, M. K. Gandhi was asked for a message to congratulate the film industry, to which his secretary responded as above, noting: "As a rule, Gandhi gives messages only on rare occasions—and these only for causes whose virtue is ever undoubtful." From *Dipali*, June 16, 1939, as quoted in Erik Barnouw and S. Krishnaswamy, *Indian Film*, 117n63.

   Interviewed a decade earlier (in 1927) by the Indian Cinematograph Committee, Gandhi primly voiced his objections to the cinema: "Even if I was so minded, I should be unfit to answer your questionnaire, as I have never been to a cinema. But even to an outsider, the evil that it has done and is doing is patent. The good, if it has done any at all, remains to be proved." Indian Cinematograph Committee, 1927–28, v. 3 (Calcutta: Govt. of India Central Publishing Branch), p. 56, as quoted in Rachel Dwyer, "The Case of the Missing Mahatma: Gandhi and the Hindi Cinema," *Public Culture* 23.2 (2011): 349. Dwyer notes that Gandhi only saw part of one feature film during his lifetime, Vijay Bhatt's devotional *Ram Rajya* (1943). Prime Minister Nehru meanwhile took an active interest in Indian film, dashing off letters on official stationary to filmmakers whom he personally admired, cultivating others such as Raj Kapoor, and serving, on occasion, as unofficial consultant to films such as Mehboob Khan's *Mother India* (1957), to which he advised adding more songs and shooting a new beginning to celebrate industrial India besides the rural. Chapter 2 develops these themes.

2. Raj Kapoor as recorded in Siddharth Kak's documentary, *Raj Kapoor Lives* (Bombay: Cinema Vision, 1987).

3. Jawaharlal Nehru, "Tryst with Destiny" (1947), in Salman Rushdie and Elizabeth West, eds., *The Vintage Book of Indian Writing, 1947–1997*, 1, 2.

4. Benedict Anderson develops the role of "imagining" national consciousness, which he locates in two transformative innovations of print capital: the novel and the newspaper. In the case of India, neither form of print was likely to reach more than the 16-odd percent literate at Independence in 1947. Other forms of public transmission in India have more vitally played the role of "imagining" that print did in European nationalism. As Anderson acknowledges in a revised edition of his foundational work: the advent of broadcasting and what he elaborates as "advances in communication technology, especially radio and television, give print allies unavailable a century ago" (135). Film was one such ally in imagining modern India which, in Anderson's evocative language, "helped give shape to a thousand inchoate dreams" (140). See Benedict Anderson, *Imagined Communities: Reflections on the Origin and Spread of Nationalism*.

5. See M. Madhava Prasad, *Ideology of the Hindi Film: A Historical Construction*, 9; Sumita Chakravarty's pioneering, *National Identity in Indian Popular Cinema, 1947–1987*; and Jyotika Virdi, *The Cinematic ImagiNation: Indian Popular Films as Social History*.

6. In Max Weber's memorable phrase, the state has "a monopoly on legitimate violence" that it affirms through institutions such as the army, the civil service bureaucracy, the judiciary, and elected representatives. See Weber, *Politics as a Vocation*, trans. H. H. Gerth and C. Wright Mills.

7. The concept of third space was developed by Ray Oldenburg in *The Great Good Place: Cafés, Coffee Shops, Community Centers, Beauty Parlors, General Stores, Bars, Hangouts, and How They Get You Through the Day*. The historian Bryant Simon has a powerful chapter on Starbucks' claims over Oldenburg's concepts; see Simon, "It Looks like a Third Place," in *Everything but the Coffee: Learning About America from Starbucks*, 82–121.

8. Freud's analytical project has tended to be remembered by this phrase alone, and not by the equally important sentence that follows which underscores how crucially narration enables the "transformation" of misery to unhappiness: "With a mental life that has been restored to health, [the patient] will be better armed against that unhappiness." Sigmund Freud, "The Psychotherapy of Hysteria," in Josef Breuer and Freud, *Studies on Hysteria*, trans. James Strachey with Anna Freud, 305.

9. Fredric Jameson, *The Political Unconscious: Narrative as Socially Symbolic Act*, 61–62.

10. Chapters 2 and 3 elaborate on these themes more fully. Consider two titles (of many possible) that use concepts developed in psychoanalysis to understand very different historical phenomena: Lynn Hunt, *The Family Romance of the French Revolution*, and Françoise Vergès, *Monsters and Revolutionaries: Colonial Family Romance and Métissage*.

11. Ernst Renan, "What Is a Nation?" (1882), trans. Martin Thom, in Homi Bhabha, ed., *Nation and Narration*, 19.

12. The political theorist, Sunil Khilnani, has called Bombay with its cinema industry India's "cultural capital . . . permanently lodged in the popular imagination as a totem of modern India itself." See Khilnani, *The Idea of India*, 137.

13. It is remarkable how little scholarship there is on the Emergency in contrast, for example, to the aftermath of Mrs. Gandhi's assassination in 1984 or the destruction of the Babri Mosque in December 1992. Until recently, those interested in studying the

Emergency had to turn to fiction (which added to the mythology of the period). Salman Rushdie's *Midnight's Children* (1981) has a dark chapter on it called "Midnight"; and Rohinton Mistry's novel, *A Fine Balance* (1995), is more centrally focused on the period. Nayantara Sahgal's *Rich Like Us* (1985) is set during the Emergency, but it focuses on a set of social and domestic crises for which the period seems a backdrop.

Even recent scholarly works seem to echo this strange diplomacy toward the Emergency: the index to Ramachandra Guha's *India After Gandhi: The History of the World's Largest Democracy* provides no listing for the Emergency, whose events are instead indexed under Indira Gandhi, "authoritarian methods." Popular film, meanwhile, has addressed the period as an inscribed absence: never quite frontally, but always with presence and persistence in works as widely different as *Sholay* (1975; chap. 2), *Deewaar* (The wall, Yash Chopra, 1975; chap. 3), and *Roti Kapda aur Makaan* (Food clothing and housing, Manoj Kumar, 1974). In contrast to Bollywood, the New Cinema of the 1970s that addressed political topics of the day more frontally "appears, in hindsight, relatively marginal" contends Ashish Rajadhyaksha in "The Indian Emergency: Aesthetics of State Control," *Indian Cinema in the Time of Celluloid: From Bollywood to the Emergency*, 241. Meanwhile, the pogroms that followed Indira Gandhi's assassination in 1984 rapidly received serious scholarly attention by figures such as Veena Das and Amitav Ghosh; and the riots of 1992–93 have an entire library call number devoted to them. Neither popular cinema nor fiction have been reticent on these latter moments either; both powerfully contributed to the public conversation as films such as *Bombay* (Mani Ratnam, 1995) and *Zakhm* (Wounds, Mahesh Bhatt, 1998) among many others show. The Emergency period is an anomaly for its dearth of scholarly analysis, one that this study along with other works cited throughout attempts to redress (see Rajadhyaksha, Tarlo, and Vitali for notable contributions). For an elaboration of some of these themes, see Priya Joshi and Rajinder Dudrah, eds., *The 1970s and Its Legacies in India's Cinema*, and also Joshi and Dudrah, "The 1970s and Its Legacies in India's Cinema," in a Special Issue of *South Asian Popular Culture* 10.1 (2012): 1–5.

14. Emma Tarlo, *Unsettling Memories: Narratives of the Emergency in Delhi*, 2; see also Arvind Rajagopal, "The Emergency as Prehistory of the New Indian Middle Class," *Modern Asian Studies* 45.5 (2011): 1003–1049.

15. Indira Gandhi's Twenty-Point Programme, instituted during the Emergency, was ostensibly initiated to eradicate poverty, but it equally skillfully set up mechanisms to further class divisions. Items #1–12 of the Programme were pro–rural poor (involving land redistribution, housing, the elimination of bonded labor and rural indebtedness; more delivery of power, water, etc.). Items 12–16 leaned toward an anti-wealthy platform (#12: "special squads for . . . conspicuous constructions and prevention of tax evasions"; #13: "confiscation of smugglers' properties"; #14: "action against misuse of import licenses"). The last four were reserved for middle-class interests (#17: "income tax relief for the middle classes"; #18: "essential commodities at controlled prices to students"; #19: "books and stationary at controlled prices"; and #20: "new apprenticeship scheme to enlarge employment."

On paper, the revolutionary socialism of the Programme looks assured: to help India's poor and working families by pursuing conspicuous excesses of the rich. In practice, the Programme underscored Mrs. Gandhi's fabled divisive tactics: to regulate the rich by fear (of confiscation of property or prosecution for corruption) and to placate the poor by programs designed to capture their votes. (Ironically, even after Mrs. Gandhi's electoral defeat in 1977, the TPP, as it is called, remains in effect, and a 2006 version eliminates the anti-rich and pro-middle-class points for a program almost entirely targeting rural poverty.)

16. Valentina Vitali's *Hindi Action Cinema: Industries, Narratives, Bodies* usefully connects the economic environment of the 1970s with films that were produced during the decade. See esp. 184–229.

17. The notion of cinema "gentrifying" has been developed with nuance in Tejaswini Ganti, *Producing Bollywood: Inside the Contemporary Hindi Film Industry.*

18. Ashis Nandy, "Indian Popular Cinema as a Slum's Eye View of Politics," in Ashis Nandy, ed., *The Secret Politics of Our Desires: Innocence, Culpability, and Indian Popular Cinema,* 5.

19. The term "malltiplex" is Amit Rai's; see his chapter "On the Malltiplex Mutagen in India" in *Untimely Bollywood: Globalization and India's New Media Assemblage,* 133–78 .

20. See H. R. F. Keating's *Filmi, Filmi, Inspector Ghote* (1976), credited in the *OED* for first using the term "Bollywood" in print. It bears mentioning that film was obliged to function through informal networks of accounting, distribution, and finance since it was denied industry status that would have allowed access to low-cost bank loans and other forms of secured financing. All this changed in 1998 when the state conferred industry status on film, and much changed again in the new millennium (see chapter 4).

21. See Madhava Prasad, "This Thing Called Bollywood," *Seminar* (May 2003). Sangita Gopal cites an Indian journalist, Bevinda Collaco, for using the term in 1978, a few years after Keating's coinage. See Gopal, *Conjugations: Marriage and Form in New Bollywood Cinema,* 11.

22. Amitabh Bachchan's discomfort of the term has been widely recorded. "Today when I go abroad, and I am introduced . . . they refer to me as a Bollywood star. Why? For a country that produces the highest number of films, why must we carry a Hollywood crutch? Why *that* word? Why not something else? Don't we deserve better? In the final analysis, it all stems out of a deep-rooted complex." Recorded in Bhawana Somaaya, *Amitabh Bachchan: The Legend,* 197 (emphasis in original).

23. Ashish Rajadhyaksha, "The 'Bollywoodization' of the Indian Cinema: Cultural Nationalism in a Global Arena," *Inter-Asia Cultural Studies* 4.1 (2003): 25–39. Rajadhyaksha's work serves as a reminder of other preoccupations and productions from the 1970s that the term "Bollywood" neither captures nor coincides with.

24. The ideological commitments associated with the cinema called Bollywood have been propelled to a new level by an influx of capital. And with this influx, as the anthropologist Tejaswini Ganti shows in her decade-long ethnography of the industry, the cinema underwent a process of what she calls "gentrification" which displaced "the poor and working classes from the spaces of production and consumption" (Ganti, *Producing Bollywood,* 4; also her chapter, "From Slumdogs to Millionaires: The Gentrification of Hindi Cinema," ibid., 77–118). Sangita Gopal's schema of Hindi cinema identifies the cinema following liberalization as "New Bollywood," claiming it a "radically new *art*

form that must be analyzed on its own terms." See Gopal, *Conjugations*, 14, emphasis added. For Gopal, aesthetics ("art") rather than ideology differentiates the cinema following liberalization from what preceded it. In short, she sees ruptures in the cinema where others see continuities.

25. In a vivid ethnography of Indian elections, the anthropologist Mukulika Banerjee documents: "The electorate [in the national elections of 2009] has nearly 715 million voters, 1 million voting machines, nearly 7 million polling stations, and 543 constituencies in a country of enormous linguistic, cultural, and physical variety. Two million people serve as officials to conduct the elections and the results are declared within less than 12 hours of the final vote being cast, and with negligible instances of recount." See Mukulika Banerjee, "Elections as Communitas," in *Social Research* 78.1 (Spring 2011): 88–89 (in a Special Issue titled *India's World*, ed. Arjun Appadurai).

26. Sudipta Kaviraj, "The Imaginary Institution of India," in Partha Chatterjee and Gyanendra Pandey, eds., *Subaltern Studies VII: Writing on South Asian History and Society*, 2.

27. Mani Ratnam, *Dil Se* (From the heart, 1998). Author's translations.

28. As reports concur, "India Now" was a major branding exercise involving a $5 million budget with key support from business and political leaders. See "Delhi in Davos: How India Built its Brand at the World Economic Forum," Knowledge at Wharton, February 22, 2006 (http://knowledge.wharton.upenn.edu/article.cfm?articleid=1394).

29. In a widely cited paper from 2003, Dominic Wilson and Roopa Purushothaman argue: "If things go right, in less than 40 years, the BRICs economies together could be larger than the G6 in US dollar terms. By 2025 they could account for over half the size of the G6. Currently they are worth less than 15%. Of the current G6, only the US and Japan may be among the six largest economies in US dollar terms in 2050. . . . India's economy, for instance, could be larger than Japan's by 2032." Following the 2008 economic crisis, growth stalled in most G6 countries. India, on the other hand, has seen a "downturn" in growth from almost 9% to 5% in 2013, a figure that would be enviable in the United States as well as other G6 nations. Thus, while the Goldman Sachs paper predates the economic crisis, its conclusions about India's growth prospects have yet to be obviated by the aftermath of the 2008 global collapse. See Dominic Wilson and Roopa Purushothaman, "Dreaming with BRICs: The Path to 2050," Global Economics Paper #99 (Goldman Sachs, October 2003) (see www.goldmansachs.com/ceoconfidential/ CEO-2003–12.pdf).

30. Rachel Dwyer makes a similar point about Shobha Dé's novels where " 'foreign' is a place without foreigners for it is always peopled exclusively by South Asians" (as cited in Christopher Pinney, "Public, Popular, and Other Cultures," in Rachel Dwyer and Christopher Pinney, eds., *Pleasure and the Nation: The History, Politics and Consumption of Public Culture in India*, 13).

31. Rushdie, *Midnight's Children*, 130.

32. For a fuller elaboration of these themes, see Joshi and Dudrah, "The 1970s and Its Legacies in India's Cinemas," 1–5.

33. For key examples of research primarily focused on industry practices rather than on narratives of the cinema, see Ashish Rajadhyaksha, *Indian Cinema in the Time of Celluloid*; Valentina Vitali, *Hindi Action Cinema*; Tejaswini Ganti, *Producing Bollywood*; Adrian

Athique and Douglas Hill, *The Multiplex in India: A Cultural Economy of Urban Leisure*; Amit S. Rai, *Untimely Bollywood*; and Swarnavel Eswaran Pillai, "The 1970s Tamil Cinema and the Post-Classical Turn," *South Asian Popular Culture* 10:1 (2012): 77–90, with Pillai's especially useful discussion of how the arrival of the lightweight Arriflex 35-2c camera enabled location shooting and loosened—literally—the studio's "hold" over Tamil cinema and its stars (see Pillai, pp. 82–85).

2. CINEMA AS PUBLIC FANTASY

1. Raj Kapoor, "Self Portrait," *Filmfare* 15.24 (November 23, 1956): 7.

2. Some researchers such as Firoze Rangoonwalla observe that "Nehru brainwashed Mehboob Khan to make *Mother India* [1957, a remake of Mehboob's 1940 *Aurat*]. He was looking for a more positive vision of Indian nationalism, not a grim reproduction of Indian rural life." What Nehru got was an extended opening sequence with its docu-realist paean to 1950s agricultural hardware (tractors and earth movers) sutured on to a rural life whose grimness even lavish color could not redeem. (Rangoonwalla interview with the author, Mumbai, June 2003.)

3. Raj Kapoor, "My Films and I," *Filmfare* 9.22 (October 21, 1960): 51.

4. Khilnani, *The Idea of India*, 137.

5. Ashis Nandy, "The Popular Hindi Film: Ideology and First Principles," *India International Centre Quarterly*, 92.

6. "One must analyse the *particular illusion* that the serial novel provides the people with and how this illusion changes through historical-political periods." See Antonio Gramsci, *Selections from Cultural Writings*, ed. David Forgacs and Geoffrey Nowell-Smith, trans. William Boelhower, 376

7. Derek Malcolm, "Monarch," *The Guardian*, June 4, 1988, 34.

8. The third major hit of the 1950s was Mehboob Khan's *Mother India* (1957), which is discussed later in this chapter and figures again in chapter 3.

9. See "Raj Kapoor and the Golden Age of Indian Cinema," Toronto International Film Festival (June 2011), at http://tiff.net/filmsandschedules/tiffbelllightbox/2011/201104270054032 (accessed June 2011). Kapoor's fame following *Awara* (1951) brought him to the United States and an audience with Harry Truman and another U.S. president in the making, Ronald Reagan, then president of the Screen Actors Guild.

10. Madhu Jain, *The Kapoors: The First Family of Indian Cinema*, xvi. Jain reports that Indira Gandhi once sought the hand of Raj's daughter, Ritu, for her son, Rajiv, a match that never took place (xv). "While the political family impinges on our public lives, the show business originals inveigle themselves into our intimate lives and fantasies, feeding our notions of romance, and even our notions of history," she concludes (xvi).

11. Raj Kapoor's penchant for spectacle had its origins in *Awara*'s fabled 9-minute dream sequence that transformed the film from a family melodrama to passionate social commentary. For a discussion, see Gayatri Chatterjee, *Awara*, 81–88; and Wimal Dissanayake and Malti Sahai, *Raj Kapoor's Films: Harmony of Discourses*, 44–45. Later Kapoor films such as *Sangam* (1964) included an hour-long honeymoon sequence in Europe,

though in contrast to *Awara*'s spectacle, the extended travel sequence did little to advance *Sangam*'s plot.

12. K. A. Abbas, "Raj Kapoor and the Writer," *Cinema India International* (April–June 1985): 16.

13. See K. A. Abbas, "Thanks, Raj—and Damn You!" *Filmfare* 19.25 (December 4, 1970): 38 and 39, respectively. Abbas collaborated with Kapoor on numerous films for which he received the writing credit. In a reminiscence from 1970 published in a special issue on Raj Kapoor in *Filmfare*, Abbas recalled: "It is Raj Kapoor's uncanny mastery of the box office, the intuitive grasp of what will appeal to the public, his subtle way of weaving in music, as an integral part of the narrative, his almost unequalled ability to purvey popular entertainment without pandering to the popular bad taste. It makes him, and his films, a uniquely powerful and potent medium for the transmission of ideas. Being a peddler and purveyor of ideas, that is very important for me. While no great ideologue, Raj Kapoor is not allergic to ideas. Indeed, with his basic sympathy for the cause of the common man, he is more than amenable to socially progressive ideas and humanist ideals, so long as their presentation does not interfere with the popular potential of his films" (Abbas, ibid., 39).

14. Allahabad's role as a crucible for India's democracy took an unexpected twist under Nehru's daughter, Indira Gandhi. Her 1971 election victory in Allahabad was challenged in the high court, and Mrs. Gandhi was found guilty of fraud. Shortly thereafter, she declared the state of Emergency, suspending democratic processes and the Constitution for twenty-two months.

15. Not only was *Awara*'s court scene impressive; the set itself became one of the most sought-after locations among other Bombay filmmakers, according to Vishwa Mehra, Raj Kapoor's uncle and close assistant at RK Studios (interview with the author, June 19, 2003).

16. At no moment is the public trial by judiciary more crucial than in the period immediately following a national struggle. Thus, the assassination of M. K. Gandhi in January 1948 saw an elaborate public trial with an extensive set of documents made publicly available to underscore the message that *all* criminals had access to due process in the new nation. The assassin's defense, made in his own voice and words, remains in print today: see Nathuram Godse, *May It Please Your Honour: Statement of Nathuram Godse*; see also Ashis Nandy, "Final Encounter: The Politics of the Assassination of Gandhi," in *At the Edge of Psychology: Essays in Politics and Psychology*, 70–98.

17. Despite claims that *Mother India* has played in one theater or another every day since its release, its infanticide was hardly a satisfactory solution to the problems of the village. The film's narrative core was refashioned numerous times, and chapter 3 addresses three symbolic remakes in Hindi cinema. On *Mother India*'s popularity, see Gayatri Chatterjee, *Mother India*, 9; see also research by Rosie Thomas and Paroma Roy on the figure of Nargis in her role in *Mother India*.

18. See Lalitha Gopalan on the modes of "interruption" constitutive of popular Hindi cinema (*Cinema of Interruptions: Action Genres in Contemporary Indian Cinema*); see also the collection edited by Sangita Gopal and Sujata Moorti meditating on song's particular form of "interruption": *Global Bollywood: Travels of Hindi Song and Dance*.

19. Rishi Kapoor, quoted in Rana Siddiqui Zaman, "Blast from the Past: *Ab Dilli Door Nahin*," *The Hindu*, October 10, 2004.

20. The scholar Nandini Chandra regards Nehru the "poster patriarch" in *Dilli*. See Chandra, "Merit and Opportunity in the Child-Centric Nationalist Films of the 1950s," in Manju Jain, ed., *Narratives of Indian Cinema*, 130.

21. See Sangita Gopal's *Conjugations* for an exposition on the social work that the couple performs in Hindi film narratives.

22. Bunny Reuben, "An Open Letter to Raj Kapoor," *Star and Style*, April 30, 1971, 10.

23. The following is a report on Kapoor following Nehru's death: "When Nehru died, Raj was abroad, but soon after he returned, he went to Shantivan to lay flowers. He met Nehru's gardener who gave him a marigold. The era of the red rose had ended." See "Behind the Showman," *Filmfare* (December 4, 1970): 17. As if to emphasize Kapoor's relationship to the new India now characterized by Nehru's daughter, two of his leading ladies were appointed MPs to Parliament, Vyjyanthimala and Nargis. Kapoor's loyalties, however, remained with Nehru, not with Congress, and his cinema receded from a direct engagement with New Delhi following Nehru's death.

24. The remark on Kapoor's waning popular presence in the 1970s is not fully accurate: in the 1970s, Kapoor's *Bobby* rivaled *Sholay* and *Jai Santoshi Maa* in the box office and in popular memory. It is #11 in the list of all-time worldwide box office grossers of Indian cinema, just behind *Amar Akbar Anthony* (#10) and *DDLJ* (#9). See "Biggest Worldwide Grossers of All Time (adjusted for inflation)," www.ibosnetwork.com/asp/actualalltime_worldwide.asp (accessed June 2013).

25. Anupama Chopra, *Sholay: The Making of a Classic*, 19.

26. Raju Bharatan, "1975: The Year of Violence and Sex in Films," *The Illustrated Weekly of India*, December 28, 1975, 24–29.

27. Raju Bharatan, "*Sholay*: Anatomy of Violence," *The Illustrated Weekly of India*, August 31, 1975, 35.

28. *Sholay*'s record remained unbroken till *Dilwale Dulhaniya le Jayenge* (*DDLJ*, The man with the heart gets the bride, Aditya Chopra, 1995) played continuously for over 700 weeks at the Maratha Mandir in south central Bombay. Industry insiders and some scholars note that this "continuous" run is subsidized by the Yash Raj production house: the film played only once-a-week in the unpopular morning slot in 2007 when this scholar attempted to see it, and then too, screenings were mostly cancelled if a more lucrative film could be booked at the theater.

29. *Sholay* today remains the #1 all-time grosser at the box office in figures adjusted for inflation, towering over *Hum Aapke Hain Kaun?* (Who am I to you?, Sooraj Barjatya, 1994), *DDLJ* (1995), *Amar Akbar Anthony* (1977), and *Bobby* (1973), which rank #5, 9, 10, and 11, respectively. See "All Time Worldwide Box Office Grossers of Indian Cinema," www.ibosnetwork.com (accessed July 2012). Other accounts of *Sholay*'s status can be found in Wimal Dissanayake and Malti Sahai, *Sholay: A Cultural Reading*, and Anupama Chopra, *Sholay*.

30. The writer, Ziauddin Sardar, recollects his dismay at watching *Sholay* for the first time in the UK: "The children with whom I watched the film knew Gabbar's lines by heart: every time he appeared on the screen, they would repeat his dialogue and imitate his

actions." Recognizing the wide enthusiasm for the film, Sardar's own view was quite different: "I was appalled by what I saw. Here was the complex world of Indian culture filtered through a western lens and rendered totally incomprehensible." See "Dilip Kumar Made Me Do It," in Ashis Nandy, ed., *Secret Politics of our Desires*, 49 and 47.

31. See Chopra, *Sholay*, 161.

32. Bindu Batra, "Kiss Kiss, Bang Bang," *India Today*, May 15, 1976, 31.

33. Javed Akhtar, *Sholay*'s coscriptwriter, cites *The Magnificent Seven, The Five Man Army*, and *A Fistful of Dollars* as influences, describing in particular Sergio Leone's influence on Gabbar and the massacre scene. "We were very influenced by Sergio Leone. I would say there is some Mexican blood in Gabbar. He's a bandit, not a *dakku*" (recorded in Nasreen Munni Kabir, *Talking Films: Conversations on Hindi Cinema with Javed Akhtar*, 58).

34. Javed Akhtar, as recorded by Nasreen Munni Kabir, *Talking Films*, 75.

35. As quoted in "Fundamental Blunder," in Ayaz Memon and Ranjona Bannerji, eds., *India 50: The Making of a Nation*, 130.

36. See Wimal Dissanayake and Malti Sahai's research on this phenomenon in *Sholay: The Making of a Classic* (especially the ethnographic interviews in the concluding appendix).

37. For instance, Jai and Veeru, not the police, protect the villagers and the Thakur from Gabbar's raids; Thakur-sahib is the only effectual police officer in the film; a Hitleresque parody of another jailer actually lets Jai and Veeru escape through his incompetence; and so on.

38. Other differences mark the sedate *Aurat* and its more political 1957 remake as *Mother India*. In *Aurat*, the husband, Shamu, leaves the family because of poverty; in *Mother India* the husband's departure is engineered by the moneylender; in *Aurat*, the moneylender undergoes a change of heart; in *Mother India* he remains rapacious till the end; in *Aurat* Radha pays off her debt to Sukhi; in *Mother India* the debt remains unpaid and thus justifies Birju's vigilantism against the moneylender. Finally, *Aurat* is *about* the woman, and it ends with Radha dying of a broken heart with Birju (as she does in the mythic story of Radha and Krishna/Birju). In *Mother India*, the film leans more closely on Birju, whom the mother shoots to death, while she lives to a ripe old age. Not surprisingly, the filmmaker, Mehboob Khan, seemed to want it both ways: to introduce a revolutionary figure like Birju as a critique of an unacceptable social order, and then to insist that the diegetic focus be on the saintly mother, Radha. In a 1955 script, Khan explains the film's title: "We have intentionally called our film *Mother India* as a challenge to [Katherine Mayo's] book in an attempt to evict from the minds of the people the scurrilous work that is Miss Mayo's book" (as quoted in Gayatri Chatterjee, *Mother India*, 20). Grateful thanks to the staff of the National Film Archive in Pune for enabling a private screening of *Aurat*. A useful summary of the film can be found in Shampa Banerjee and Anil Srivastava, *One Hundred Indian Feature Films: An Annotated Filmography*, 39–41.

39. The film's original ending (the director's cut) in which the Thakur kills Gabbar and falls weeping into Veeru's arms was ordered cut by the Censor Board who, according to Anupama Chopra, "objected to the suggestion that a police officer—even one who was no longer in the service—would take the law into his own hands and commit a murder" (Chopra 2001:148). Despite the Sippys' appeal, the Censor Board's ban held, and a new

ending had to be shot in which the police appear just as the Thakur is about to crush Gabbar to death with his nailed shoes. This version remained in circulation for the first quarter century and includes cuts to many of the most violent scenes, including one in which the young Ahmed is tortured over fire and another in which Veeru drags a lassoed bandit over a mountain. A Sippy family dispute left *Sholay* the property of G. P. Sippy, its producer, and not Ramesh Sippy, the director, who lost control over its rights and distribution (author's interview with Ramesh Sippy, Sathe House, Khar, June 21, 2003).

In 2002, an unmarked DVD of the director's cut was released by Eros Entertainment, apparently made available from Sippy Films' vault absent any commentary on the different version of the film put in circulation. In an interview, Eros' distribution arm had had no knowledge that the print was a substantial departure from the version that had been in circulation since 1975 (author's interview with Arjun Lulla, Eros Entertainment, March 17, 2003). The two DVDs are virtually indistinguishable in their covers save that the "original" is noted at 189 minutes, and the director's cut at 204.

40. To underscore Jai and Veeru's mercenary natures, when the Thakur's safe promises a larger payout than their contract with him does, it becomes their object early in the film.

41. During the Emergency, a piece of graffiti allegedly appeared on numerous city walls in Bhopal: "Swarag se aie Nehru ki pukar / Indira beti, mat kar itna atyachar" [Up from heaven, Nehru called down: "Indira, stop these atrocities, won't you."]. The graffiti was probably apocryphal, though the verse (linking Nehru's vision with his daughter's practice) was repeated endlessly and has persisted in public memory of the period.

42. For a report of over 200 interviews conducted among *Sholay*'s viewers, see Dissanayake and Sahai, *Sholay: A Cultural Reading*, 69–131.

43. See Peter Manuel, *Cassette Culture: Popular Music and Technology in North India*.

44. Ramesh Sippy in an interview with the author, June 21, 2003, in Sathe House, Khar.

45. Gulshan Grover, as quoted in Nasreen Munni Kabir, *Bollywood: The Indian Cinema Story*, 90.

46. Prasad, *Ideology of the Hindi Film*, 155 and passim.

47. Fareed Kazmi, *The Politics of India's Conventional Cinema*, 224.

48. Reflecting on Hindi cinema a year after *Sholay*'s release, its director Ramesh Sippy observed with rare candor: "It is ironic that while so much care is showered on making every aspect of the film functional to the achievement of the desired impact on the mass audience, nobody seems to bother whether the end product, the film itself, is functional to society. . . . This is precisely the tragedy of commercial films and the justification for replacing them with a new cinema." Taken in the context of the films Ramesh Sippy made and continues to produce, his remarks are not to be mistaken as a manifesto for an alternative cinema (that was already prospering in India during the period). Rather, they underscore a new calculus of consumption at play in which popular cinema's social work was resonant with its society's desires, however unarticulated and inchoate. Ramesh Sippy as quoted in Bharat B. Dogra, "*Sholay*: The Tragedy of Commercial Films," *Filmfare* (November 12–25, 1976): 23 (emphasis added).

49. Javed Akhtar in Kabir, *Talking Songs: Javed Akhtar in Conversation with Nasreen Munni Kabir*, 51.

3. CINEMA AS FAMILY ROMANCE

1. Emergency Broadcast as recorded in "Fundamental Blunder," in Memon and Bannerji, eds., *India 50*, 130.

2. See Rushdie's account of Mrs. Gandhi's defamation suit against him in Salman Rushdie, "His Own Mt. Sinai," *Outlook India*, May 8, 2006 (outlookindia.com; accessed June 2013).

3. See Dilip Bobb, "*Kissa Kursi Ka*: The Case of the Missing Film," *India Today*, June 1–15, 1978, 24–33; Padmini Sukumar, "*Kissa Kursi Ka*, End of a Controversy," *The Illustrated Weekly of India*, June 16–22, 1985, 40–41. According to Ashish Rajadhyaksha and Paul Willemen, the anti-Gandhi themes notwithstanding, the film's director, Amrit Nahata, "later joined the Congress Party and disowned [*Kissa Kursi Ka*]." Rajadhyaksha and Willemen, eds., *Encyclopedia of Indian Cinema*, 432.

4. My thinking and phrasing here borrow heavily from Jane Tompkins' work on the popularity of *Uncle Tom's Cabin* in nineteenth-century America, a work that Tompkins argues "retells the culture's central myth (crucifixion) in terms of the nation's political conflict (slavery) and its most cherished social belief—the sanctity of motherhood." See Tompkins, *Sensational Designs: The Cultural Work of American Fiction, 1790–1860*, 134.

5. Michael Rogin, "*Kiss Me Deadly*: Communism, Motherhood, and Cold War Movies," *Ronald Reagan the Movie and Other Episodes in Political Demonology*, 238.

6. Laura Mulvey's foundational work on early Hollywood melodrama inspired the phrase and insight on cinema's role as primal scene of India's modern mythologies. See Mulvey, "'It Will Be a Magnificent Obsession': The Melodrama's Role in the Development of Contemporary Film Theory," in Jacky Bratton, Jim Cook, and Christine Gledhill, eds., *Melodrama: Stage Picture Screen*, 121.

7. "International Business Overview Standard," see ibos.network.com/topgrosserbyyear .asp?/year+1975 (accessed March 15, 2006).

8. Jyotika Virdi, "*Deewaar*: Fact, Fiction, and the Making of a Superstar," in Raminder Kaur and Ajay J. Sinha, eds., *Bollyworld: Popular Indian Cinema through a Transnational Lens*, 238. See also Ranjani Mazumdar, "From Subjectification to Schizophrenia: The 'Angry Man' and the 'Psychotic Hero' of Bombay Cinema," in Ravi Vasudevan, ed., *Making Meaning in Indian Cinema*, 238–66; and Vijay Mishra, *Bollywood Cinema: Temples of Desire*.

9. Jyotika Virdi further observes that not just *Deewaar*, Hindi cinema *tout court* "projects the imagined nation on the terrain of the family . . . through contestations that throw into relief its social structures and realignments." See Virdi, *The Cinematic ImagiNation*, 7.

10. To a degree hitherto unprecedented in Hindi commercial cinema, Salim-Javed's scripts profoundly shaped the films that emerged from them. The writers were known to present bound scripts to directors who made virtually no changes to them. The director and producer had the choice over stars, music, movement, but little else. "Prakash Mehra . . . likes to tell a story, not to disturb the frame. . . . Yashji always zooms, for every shot. . . . Movement means a lot to him," noted Bachchan of the directors of, respectively, *Zanjeer* and *Deewaar* (as recorded in Rachel Dwyer, *Yash Chopra: Fifty Years in Indian Cinema*, 98.) Recalling *Deewaar*, director Yash Chopra observed: "That was one script

and screenplay where you didn't have to delete anything after making, it was such—such a perfect script. We didn't do anything [to it]" (as recorded in Dwyer, ibid., p. 100).

Both Bachchan and Shashi Kapoor concur, the latter in a 2003 interview with the author. Bachchan, in particular, held the writer's words sacred: "He never messes with a writer's lines," recalled Yash Chopra of his star. "[Bachchan's] maxim being if the writer has spent so much thought on the choice of words, it must have a reason, and altering them would alter the mood and the message of the film" (as recorded in Bhawana Somaaya, *Amitabh Bachchan: The Legend*, 123).

11. According to "International Business Overview Standard," *Trishul* ranks #25 among Hindi film's worldwide all-time grossers adjusted for inflation, while *Deewaar* comes in at #23 (see ibos.network.com/asp/actualalltimes.asp; accessed June 2013). If returns just for the decade are reviewed, the rankings are higher, and the same source has *Trishul* at #8 and *Deewaar* at #7 (see ibos.network.com/topgrosserbyyear.asp?/year+197; accessed June 2013). In contrast, BoxOfficeIndia.com, another industry source, provides returns by decade, according to which *Deewaar*'s earnings place it at #11 and *Trishul*'s at #15 (see www.boxofficeindia.com/showProd.php?itemCat+124&catName+MTk3MCOxOTc5, [accessed November 17, 2010]).

12. Other differences across the films: in *Deewaar*, the father's ideals absent him from his family; in *Trishul*, his ambitions absent him from his son but keep him at the center of the family; and in *Shakti*, the father's ideals preserve him in the family and exile the son from it. Mothers are central in all three, but in *Deewaar* the mother is vengeful and prevails till the end; in *Trishul* she is vengeful but dies so her son can achieve a happy end; and in *Shakti* she is portrayed as a gentle figure seeking compromises that eventually kill her, a fate in which her son joins her. Infanticide, or its threat, plays a role in all three: in *Deewaar*, it disrupts the family altogether; in *Trishul*, where the threat is headed off, the family reconstitutes itself in a happy unit; and in *Shakti*, infanticide is a sacrifice that is tragic but necessary to assure the stability of a now-truncated family and the nation.

13. Sigmund Freud, "Family Romances" (1909), in vol. 9 of *The Standard Edition of the Complete Psychological Works of Sigmund Freud*, trans. and ed. James Strachey, 238–39.

14. Madhava Prasad, among others such as Jyotika Virdi (2003) and Sumita Chakravarty (1993), provides a genealogy in which Hindi cinema through the 1960s is characterized by a focus on the family structure that Prasad names "the feudal family romance" (Prasad 1998:64). For Prasad, the term simply refers to a story in which the ideology of the family is central. In contrast, my usage of the term develops Freud's, and I use the upper case throughout to signal the technical (vs. colloquial) referent (see Prasad 1998:30–31).

The concept of Family Romance has been used in other ways as well. Some scholars such as the historian Lynn Hunt see the family as the unconscious unit underlying national politics and thus use the concept of Family Romance to understand different models of the family that underwrote revolutionary politics in eighteenth-century France. Others such as the political theorist Françoise Vergès consider the family as a myth imposed by colonial rulers for manufacturing consent, as Vergès shows in the case of France in Réunion. Both scholars focus on the family (which provides the unit of analysis for broader social and political events) rather than the romance, and both see the Family Romance as a mechanism deployed by authorities for manufacturing consent among subjects. In contrast to Hunt and Vergès, I regard the Family Romance as a mechanism fabricated by subjects for *evading* consent to authority. See Hunt, *The Family Romance of the French Revolution*, and Vergès, *Monsters and Revolutionaries*.

15. The historian Vinay Lal regards Ravi's locution of ownership as the "voice of patriarchy" in which Ravi has become the "reincarnated husband." In contrast, my analysis reveals a patriarchy that is overtaken by the castrating figure of Maa, who has ambushed its traditional authority. Ravi represents the intrusion of the state onto the family: he is neither the husband Maa married (Anandbabu), nor the husband she chose (Vijay). Unlike both males marked (literally and figuratively) by the ideals by which they live, Ravi is a figure marked exclusively by ideology. All his actions require the instruction and sanction of others and the grandiloquence of rhetoric that issues from "Mere pas Maa hain." See Lal, "The Impossibility of the Outsider in the Modern Hindi Film," in Ashis Nandy, ed., *The Secret Politics of Our Desires: Innocence, Culpability, and Indian Popular Cinema*, 241.

16. The specifics of India's economic turbulence in the 1960s and 1970s were to have consequences not just on the lives of its citizens but also on the Hindi film industry more broadly, a point noted by Madhava Prasad (1998), Rajadhyaksha (2009), and usefully detailed by Valentina Vitali. Prasad and Vitali propose that the "rise" of Bachchan occurs as a consequence of transformations wrought by Mrs. Gandhi's rollback of economic liberalization and the ensuing urgency to locate capital for film production. As Vitali documents: "Larger amounts of money were thus wrapped around those narrative ingredients that proved to sell at the lower end of the market, including and above all action. . . . Over less than four years, the combination of these selling points . . . led to the landmark action films of Amitabh Bachchan." See Vitali, *Hindi Action Cinema*, 203.

17. There is a twist to the story of gold and India. In July 1991, India pulled itself back from the brink of default by transferring—literally—47 tons of gold to the Bank of England as surety in order to secure credit on the world market. The desperate situation—and the gold that staved off disaster—inaugurated a policy of economic liberalization that soon brought about astonishing economic growth that has (almost) wiped out the destitution of the 1970s. For a dramatic account of what the gold transfer enabled, see Ajit Balakrishnan, "India's IT Industry: The End of the Beginning," in *Social Research* 78.1 (Spring 2011): 1–20 (in a Special Issue titled *India's World*, ed. Arjun Appadurai).

18. As recorded in Deepa Gahlot, "Look Back in Anger," *Cinema in India* 3.12 (1992): 53.

19. The "India is Indira" slogan was developed by Dev Kant Baruah, an Assamese politician and Indira Gandhi loyalist who was president of the Indian National Congress during the Emergency. Many thanks to Mrinialini Pande and Kumud Pant for providing this detail. The scholar Rosie Thomas reproduces the 1985 election poster in "Sanctity and Scandal," her classic 1989 essay on *Mother India*. Special thanks to her and to the photographer Behroze Gandhy for its use.

20. Harleen Singh's comments to an early version of this chapter spawned the associations that led to these insights on Indira Gandhi and Maa. In *Midnight's Children* (1981), Salman Rushdie memorialized the Emergency as the particular nightmare of midnight, creating a devouring mother, the Widow, who sets up special torture factories to crush

her children and prevent them from reproducing. "Test- and hysterectomized, the children of midnight were denied the possibility of reproducing themselves . . . but that was only a side-effect, because they were truly extraordinary doctors, and they drained us of more that that: hope, too, was excised, and I don't know how it was done." Rushdie, *Midnight's Children*, 523.

21. See A. K. Ramanujan, "The Indian Oedipus," in *The Collected Essays of A. K. Ramanujan*, ed. Vinay Dharwadker, 394. Javed Akhtar arguably claims that "in our country we don't have a strong tradition of bonding between father and son anyway" (as recorded in Kabir, *Talking Films*, 24).

22. Figures provided from ibosnetwork.com, "Biggest Grossers of All Time (adjusted for inflation)," ibosnetwork.com/asp/actualalltime.asp (accessed June 2013).

23. Javed Akhtar mentions a key detail about *Trishul*: "The first time we [ever] revised a script was for *Trishul*." See interview recorded in Nasreen Munni Kabir, *Talking Films*, 56. It was a script, moreover, that Akhtar and Salim Khan wrote with Yash Chopra at their side, though Akhtar would not elaborate on what aspects of *Trishul*'s script or its tone Chopra shaped. Following its box office success in Hindi, *Trishul* was remade in Tamil as *Mr. Bharath* (dir. S. P. Muthuraman), starring Rajnikanth, its new title underscoring the film's claim to a symbolic *national* culture (Bharat).

24. The scriptwriter Salim Khan was the son of an Indore police officer, which might partly explain the depiction of semi-benevolent police patriarchs in Salim-Javed films such as *Shakti* (and, above all, *Sholay*).

4. BOLLYWOOD, BOLLYLITE

1. In 1988 when he died, the front pages of major Soviet newspapers carried lengthy obituaries of Raj Kapoor. A few years previously, one observer of the Soviet Union had remarked: "Anyone who has visited the Soviet Union, either its European or Asian wings, will confirm that it has three Indian heroes: Jawaharlal Nehru, Indira Gandhi, and Raj Kapoor, although not necessarily in that order. Probably the reverse." From A. Malik, "Who's the Hero of the Soviet Union?," *The Statesman* (August 25, 1985), as quoted in Wimal Dissanayake and Malti Sahai, *Raj Kapoor's Films: Harmony of Discourses*, 19.

   In China at about the same time, the novelist Vikram Seth unexpectedly received a forbidden travel pass to Tibet because he was Indian, and the local police chief in a remote province thought Hindi films in general and Kapoor's *Awara* (1951) in particular provided recognizance enough for Seth's intentions. Seth records the anecdote in *From Heaven Lake*, a book of his travels to Tibet that came about from his familiarity with *Awara*.

2. The popularity of Hindi films around the globe has been analyzed in a number of studies, including a special issue of *South Asian Popular Culture* 4.2 (2006), titled "Indian Cinema Abroad: Historiography of Transnational Exchanges," guest edited by Dimitris Eleftheriotis and Dina Iordanova. See also Sangita Gopal and Sujata Moorti, eds., *Global Bollywood: Travels of Hindi Song and Dance*; Sudha Rajagopalan, *Indian Films in Soviet Cinema: The Culture of Movie-Going After Stalin*; and Anjali Gera Roy and Chua Beng Huat, eds., *Travels of Bollywood Cinema: From Bombay to LA*.

3. For statistics on *Slumdog*'s circulation, see www.thenumbers.com/movies/2008/SLUMD.php.

4. The transformative presence of Bollywood in a global frame has been explored in Raminder Kaur and Ajay J. Sinha, eds., *Bollyworld: Popular Indian Cinema through a Transnational Lens*; also Anandam Kavoori and Aswin Punathambekar, eds., *Global Bollywood*; and Rajinder Dudrah, *Bollywood Travels: Culture, Diaspora and Border Crossings in Popular Hindi Cinema.*

5. The story of Bollywood's travels to the West has a UK dimension to it as well: in 2002, Andrew Lloyd Webber's Bollywood-inspired musical, *Bombay Dreams*, opened in London's West End. Madame Tussaud's unveiled a wax figure of Amitabh Bachchan, voted the greatest star on stage or screen in a 2000 BBC Millennial poll in which Bachchan beat out Laurence Olivier (#2) and Charles Chaplin (#3) for the honor. (Tamil cinema's Govinda made #10, following Marilyn Monroe at #9. See http://news.bbc.co.uk/hi/english/static/events/millennium/jun/winner.stm [accessed May 10, 2006].)

   Main Street and K Street were close behind these trends: in 2002, Selfridges ran a Bollywood-themed shopping month in their flagship store on Oxford Street, and when Webber's musical was set to arrive on Broadway, his first preview performance was for George W. Bush at a dinner the U.S. president hosted for Queen Elizabeth during a 2003 state visit to London. See Lawrence Gelder, "Arts Briefing," *New York Times*, November 20, 2003, C2.

6. *Monsoon Wedding*'s "foreign" (i.e., non-U.S.) gross was $16.9 million with a worldwide box office of $30.7 million; *Bride and Prejudice*'s "foreign" gross was $18.5 million for a worldwide box office of $25 million. More on these films follows later in the chapter. See www.boxofficemojo.com/movies/?id=monsoonwedding.htm; and www.boxofficemojo.com/movies/?id=brideandprejudice.htm (accessed October 3, 2006).

7. M. Madhava Prasad, "This Thing Called Bollywood," *Seminar* 525 (May 2003): 3.

8. It remains an important exercise to date *when* precisely the cinema of Bombay embraced excess as its constitutive mode. Raj Kapoor's dream sequence in *Awara*, for instance, is visually and cinematically spectacular, but its connection to the plot and to the characters is indisputable. One might say the same for Kapoor's 1964 hit, *Sangam*, with its long interlude in London, Venice, and Paris that is consistent with the plot (the couple are on their honeymoon) but is not necessary to advance it. By the 1970s, hits such as *Amar Akbar Anthony* (1977) and *Don* (1978) dispense with linearity and, with it, most visual unities. In some ways, these narrative disruptions and their extravagant expression are regarded as the "Bollywood" element, though again, *when* one could date their suffusion in the industry remains an exciting project. On the origins of the term Bollywood and the tensions around its usage, see Prasad, "This Thing Called Bollywood."

9. Bollywood does not include the films produced in other Indian languages, notably Tamil, Telugu, Malayalam, and Kannada that together comprise over 60 percent of India's annual film production, though these cinemas remain largely regional phenomena without Bombay's transnational reach. The question of language is hardly an issue: Bombay's films have traveled unsubtitled and undubbed in all reaches of India and many parts of the world; the same cannot be said even for Tamil or Telugu films whose vast popularity remains largely local. Exceptions such as Rajnikanth's *Muthu* (1995) and

Enthiran (The robot, 2010) are just that and have yet to characterize the reach of their wider industry. On Hindi cinema's "national" reach, see Ashish Rajadhyaksha, "The 'Bollywoodization' of the Indian Cinema: Cultural Nationalism in a Global Arena," *Inter-Asia Cultural Studies* 4.1 (2003): 25–39.

10. Farrukh Dhondy, "Keeping Faith: Indian Film and Its World." *Dædalus* 115.4 (Fall 1985): 131. Ashis Nandy made a similar argument over a decade later in his introduction to *The Secret Politics of Our Desires*, 11.

11. Ashis Nandy, "The Supermarket of Dreams," *The Illustrated Weekly of India*, March 16–22, 1986, 48.

12. The Kannada director Girish Karnad observed: "What saved the Indian film industry and made it invulnerable to Hollywood were the songs and dances. Hollywood could not match or beat them." Interview with the author, May 27, 2003, Nehru Center, London.

13. Data on Bollywood's worldwide grosses come from "International Business Overview Standard": see http://ibosnetwork.com/aso.actualalltime_worldwide (accessed June 2013).

14. Raj Kapoor, as quoted in Ritu Nanda, *Raj Kapoor: His Life and his Films*, 81. Kapoor records a slightly different version of the memory in the Siddharth Kak documentary, *Raj Kapoor Lives* (Bombay: Cinema Vision, 1987). Archie and Riverdale High influenced other Hindi blockbusters such as *Kuch Kuch Hota Hai* (Something happens, Karan Johar, 1998). As Sharmishta Roy, the film's art director, recalls of the look of the film: "It was meant to be an Archie comic. It was meant to be Riverdale High . . . because that was my briefing. I was told, 'It's Riverdale High.' It's not an ordinary college." As recorded in an interview with Tejaswini Ganti in *Producing Bollywood*, 104.

15. Kapoor recalls his first meeting with a teenage Nargis in which she answered the door with hands covered in batter that she wiped across her hair. The scene is reenacted in Raja's first meeting with Bobby, and the reminiscence is recorded in Siddharth Kak's documentary, *Raj Kapoor Lives*.

16. Scholarship by the historian Veena Talwar Oldenburg on the phenomenon of "dowry deaths" characterizes this form of gender violence as murder. "Bride burning . . . is murder, culpable on social, cultural, and legal grounds, executed privately, and often disguised as an accident or a suicide. Burning a wife is, perhaps, even more appalling than poisoning, drowning, strangling, shooting, or bludgeoning her, but it is patently chosen for the forensic advantage it has over the other methods" (xi). See Oldenburg, *Dowry Murder: The Imperial Origins of a Cultural Crime*.

17. Why Bombay was able to succeed over other Indian cinemas such as those from Calcutta, Madras, or Hyderabad remains a crucial question that few have been able to address adequately. The city itself might be one response, but from the outset motion pictures in India thrived in numerous cities, including Calcutta, Madras, and Lahore, among others. Bombay pulled talent from other regional film industries, but that talent also on occasion remained regional, as the Kannada and Tamil stories recount. Lahore's demise as a center for Pakistani film production is often blamed on the Partition, though that does not fully explain how Pakistan has become a thriving producer of serials televised on global cable, while its film industry relies on bootleg Bombay imports screened in decaying theaters.

18. See Rajagopalan, *Indian Films in Soviet Cinema*, 163, 164. Alongside public responses to Bollywood, the cinema's mythologization in the Soviet underground is equally notable. Alexandr Solzhenitsyn's *Cancer Ward* (1968) includes a revealing exchange when Zoya, the nurse, begins singing "Awara hun" from Kapoor's *Awara*.

    > Oleg's face instantly clouded. "No, don't! Not that song, Zoya, please . . ."
    > "It's from 'The Tramp,'" she said. "Haven't you see it?"
    > "Yes, I have."
    > "Isn't it a wonderful movie? I saw it twice." (In fact, she'd seen it four times, but she didn't quite like to admit it.)

    What follows is Oleg Kostoglotov's denunciation of life in Soviet Russia, cast as a critique of *Awara*, with the conclusion: "They are only too happy to kick a man when he's down, and then they have the nerve to wrap themselves up in a cloak of romanticism, while we help them create a legend, and even their songs are sometimes sung on the screen." Notable about this particular exchange is not just Oleg's denunciation of *Awara* but his use of *Awara*'s socialist themes (scripted by the Communist playwright K. A. Abbas) in order to denounce Soviet policies. From Alexandr Solzhenitsyn, *The Cancer Ward*, trans. Nicholas Bethell and David F. Burg, 170, as quoted in Gayatri Chatterjee, *Awara*, 133–35.

19. Brian Larkin, "Bollywood Comes to Nigeria," *Samar* 8 (Winter/Spring 1997). As reproduced in www.samarmagazine.org/archive/article.php?id=21.

20. The reports tend to vary quite considerably each year depending on the data and the respective industries' need to spin them in the most positive light. It is, therefore, best to regard the data as generally illustrative of rapidly evolving industries. Their general contours are indicative despite variations across the years.

21. "Bollywood Meets the Bankers," *Asiamoney* 16.5 (June 2005).

22. According to S. Narayanan, CEO of In2infotainment India, "Indian films were funded by the most unbelievable sources. There was a time when rich tobacco and rice farmers from the southern Indian state of Andhra Pradesh would make a good profit, travel to Madras and fund a film production. If the movie did well in the box office, the farmers would make another. Otherwise, they would return to their farms to try to get one more good harvest before investing in motion pictures again. Cinema had this kind of appeal" (as quoted by Gautam Bhaskaran, "India Gets Schooled in Film Finance," *Hollywood Reporter* 389.19 [International Edition], May 31, 2005). More recently, Subhash Chandra, a former rice trader who bested Rupert Murdoch in the Indian television market, founded Zee TV, a media giant producing TV shows, films, music, and internet sites in India and another 120 countries.

23. Other films since have vied for the "most expensive" honor, each overtaken seemingly within a year. See *Ghajini* (Aamir Khan, 2008, $13 million), *Don 2* (Farhan Akhtar, 2011, $14 million), and *Ra.One* (Anubhav Sinha, 2011, $27 million). Each of these "most expensive" productions has had palpably puny overall box office returns, even with the U.S. box office included. *Ra.One*'s U.S. returns were $2.5 million; *Don 2*, $3.7 million; and *Ghajini* did not even make the list of 100 top-grossing foreign-language films in the U.S. box office, according to Box Office Mojo (boxofficemojo.com; accessed June 2013). See also table 4.2.

24. The market for Hindi films is divided into six distribution territories: five in India and a sixth, overseas. Given the size of territories, distributors purchase rights for an entire territory and sell off subsidiary rights to smaller sections within. The sale of distribution rights funds a film's production and occurs at the very early stages of development.

25. Evening screenings in large theaters at 9 p.m. and midnight are generally reserved for B-films and for adult fare which can draw an unsavory and rowdy crowd given to tearing apart a theater at great cost to the owner. Theaters that show these films are often so ravaged by abuse that they can no longer draw a respectable audience to their regular shows.

26. Shyam Benegal, as recorded by William van der Heide, *Bollywood Babylon: Interviews with Shyam Benegal,* 39.

27. Raj Chopra, as quoted in Ratna Bhushan, "The Show Begins Here," *The Hindu Business Line* (Internet Edition), December 26, 2002; see: www.blonnet.com/catalyst/2002/12/26/stories/2002122600030100.htm (accessed May 19, 2006). See also Derek Bose, *Brand Bollywood: A New Global Entertainment Order;* and Athique and Hill, *The Multiplex in India.*

28. Ron Inden, "Transnational Class, Erotic Arcadia, and Commercial Utopia in Hindi Films," in Christiane Brosius and Melissa Butcher, eds., *Image Journeys: Audio-Visual Media and Cultural Change in India,* 62.

29. Athique and Hill, *The Multiplex in India,* 43, 42.

30. See Amit S. Rai, "On the Malltiplex Mutagen in India," in *Untimely Bollywood,* 133–78.

31. Father Dominic Emmanuel, spokesman for the Archdiocese of Delhi and producer of the film, observed, "In India, the one medium that attracts mass attention, whether literate or unlettered, rich or poor, small or big, low caste or upper caste, is cinema." See "Hooray for Bollywood," in *U.S. Catholic,* November 2005, 5.

32. Kaveri Bamzai and Sandeep Unnithan, "Show Business," *India Today International,* January 24, 2003, 48.

33. Salim-Javed's idea was expanded to a three-and-a-half hour epic in a month of sittings at the dimly lit "Sippy Writing Room" with Salim Khan, Javed Akhtar, and Ramesh Sippy. See Anupama Chopra, *Sholay: The Making of a Classic.*

34. The remarks were made by Komal Nahata, editor of the trade publication, *Film Information,* as quoted by Bhaskaran, "India Gets Schooled in Film Finance."

35. Kirloskar, quoted in ibid., 49.

36. Bhatnagar, quoted in ibid., 48.

37. In contrast, 2002 was a bumper year for Hollywood's box office receipts. John Fithian, head of the National Association of Theatre Owners, claims that part of the credit for this fiscal success belongs to "an important trend toward family-friendlier films. None of the top 20 films, all of which grossed over $100m, was rated R," he reported in the *Financial Times.* Fithian quoted in Christopher Parkes, "Family Films Give Hollywood Bumper Revenues," March 5, 2003, 6.

38. In contrast to Bombay's box office flops of 2002, the twenty-five major films released in the first half of 2003 earned $50 million in box office receipts, with *Chalte Chalte* (As we walk, Aziz Mirza) earning more than $7 million internationally in its first month of release. The figures come from Bryan Pearson, "Bollywood Writes Comeback Story," *Variety,* August 25, 2003, 18.

39. The figures on break-even occupancy in India versus in "developed" markets come from Ratna Bhushan, "The Show Begins Here."

40. See box office returns tabulated by ibosnetwork.com (accessed June 2013).

41. Eric Bellman, "Bollywood's Movies Are All the Rage but Stocks Draw Skeptical Audiences," *Wall Street Journal* (Eastern Edition), December 6, 2005, C1.

42. Corey Creekmur, *K3G*, in "Philip's Fil-ums"; see www.uiowa.edu/~incinema/K3G.html.

43. Anil Ambani's Reliance Big Pictures, which owns a stake in Steven Spielberg's Dream-Works, recognizes that the audience for Indian exports remains largely diasporic. Though it is moving rapidly into the U.S. screening market, Reliance Big's acquisitions of theaters is confined to what one report identified as "areas populated by Indian diasporic communities." See "Can the Indian Film Industry Go Global?," *The Hindu*, April 22, 2011 (hindu.com). KPMG's industry report on Indian film for 2011, *Hitting the High Notes*, rues that a decade of efforts later, "the market for overseas distribution has not opened up to the levels anticipated" (56).

    As the Indo-Canadian actor, Lisa Ray, echoes: "In terms of classic Bollywood, I don't think Western audiences are ready for that, other than as a novelty." As quoted in Shabnam Mahmood and Manjushri Mitra, "Bollywood Sets Sights on Wider Market," *BBC Business News*, June 24, 2011 (bbc.co.uk; accessed June 2013).

44. One is always likely to get in trouble when venturing views on what makes a "real" Bollywood film. Stars are clearly one component, but not the only one if *Monsoon Wedding* and *Bride and Prejudice* are taken into account. Lillette Dubey, Naseerudeen Shah, and Vasundhara Das (from *Monsoon Wedding*) have all appeared in enough blockbusters to make them "genuine" Bollywood figures, though they all have also appeared in enough alternates to the industry and, in the case of Shah, in the parallel cinema of the 1970s and 1980s, to be regarded in multiple ways. Meanwhile, Aishwarya Rai and Anupam Kher from *Bride and Prejudice* are seeped in Bollywood productions, so they would appear to be the genuine articles performing in Chadha's film. Yet the casting of stars is simply not enough to render a film a Bollywood production: its director, writers, sequencing, editing, production, dialogues, music, financing, and distribution go a long way in defining the film's provenance. While both of these films did well in the U.S. (and UK) box office, neither appears in the top 50 list of gross receipts for India.

45. See "International Business Overview Standard," at http://ibosnetwork.com/asp/actualalltime.asp (accessed in June 2013).

46. Nair, quoted in Adina Hoffman, "The Big-Bash Theory: Mira Nair's Latest Movie Revels and Reels," *The American Prospect* (March 25, 2002): 28.

47. Reviewing top box office earners for the 2000s including domestic and foreign returns, Sangita Gopal observes the prominence of Karan Johar's productions: *K3G*, *Kabhi Alvida Naa Kehna* (Never say goodbye, 2006), *Kal Ho Naa Ho* (Tomorrow may not be, 2003), and *Kuch Kuch Hota Hai* (Something happens, 1998). "Clearly, the overseas box office belongs to 'KJo,'" she concludes (Gopal, *Conjugations*, 64).

48. The anthropologist Tejaswini Ganti locates the erasure of labor in Hindi film in the industry's efforts to appear "cool" in the post-liberalization period. "Hindi cinema's social transformation, or path to 'coolness,' often lauded by filmmakers and journalists, began in the mid-1990s with the erasure of the signs and symbols of poverty, labor, and rural

life from films, and with the decline of plots that focused on class conflict, social injustice, and youthful rebellion." See Ganti, *Producing Bollywood*, 79.

49. See Meheli Sen, "'It's All About Loving Your Parents': Liberalization, Hindutva, and Bollywood's New Fathers," in Rini Bhattacharya Mehta and Rajeshwari V. Pandhiripande, eds., *Bollywood and Globalization: Indian Popular Cinema, Nation, Diaspora*, 149.

50. Mulling over *K3G* in the context of his *oeuvre*, director Karan Johar observed of *Kabhi Alvida Naa Kehna* (2006), his feature on marital infidelity among NRIs in New York: "This time I've given no candy floss. . . . I've matured. I've changed." See Johar's interview with Subhash K. Jha, "I Can't Go Back to Candy Floss: Johar," at www.ibnlive.com/printpage.php?id=20341§ion_id=8 (accessed September 11, 2006).

51. These remarks and those that follow come from Ratna Bhushan's account of the changing multiplex landscape in India, "The Show Begins Here."

52. The remarks come from Tarun Mehrotra of Satyam Cineplexes in response to a concern he acknowledged: "What if no good movies are made next year? Software is one area we have no control over." As quoted in Ratna Bhushan's industry survey, "The Show Begins Here."

53. The Hollywood film industry too once vertically integrated with studios owning production, distribution, and exhibition of films, till 1948 when a Supreme Court ruling forced studios to sell their stakes in exhibition halls. Today, productions by studios and independents in the United States compete for screens, with distributors apparently having the upper hand in bringing a film to screen.

54. See Satish Poduval's analysis of Hrishikesh Mukherjee's cinema characterized by what Poduval calls its "affable young man": "The Affable Young Man: Civility, Desire, and the Making of a Middle-Class Cinema in the 1970s," *South Asian Popular Culture* 10.1 (2012): 37–50.

55. In contrast, the U.S. has 117 screens per million people (or circa one screen per 8,500 people). See Motion Picture Association of America (MPAA), "Theatrical Market Statistics: Cinema Screens" (2012), 22.

EPILOGUE: ANTHEM FOR A NEW INDIA

1. See data compiled in KPMG-FICCI, *The Stage Is Set*, Indian Media and Entertainment Report (2014), 3. Television continues to lead media in India with revenues in 2013 of INR 417 billion; film comes third (behind TV and print) in revenues at INR 125 billion. KPMG-FICCI's 2013 report observes, "India is an outlier country where print is still a growth market" (see *The Power of a Billion: Realizing the Indian Dream*, Indian Media and Entertainment Report [2013], 10). While the data on film include cinema in all languages, the report is dominated by products coming out of Bombay, with fleeting references to the Tamil and Telugu film industries (which each generally produce more films than Bombay).

2. Yash Chopra, Karan Johar, and Jehil Thakkar, "Foreword," KPMG-FICCI, *Digital Dawn: The Metamorphosis Begins*, Indian Media and Entertainment Report (2012). Chopra and Johar served as 2012 Chair of the FICCI Media and Entertainment Committee and Co-Chair of FICCI Frames, respectively, and the emphasis on Bollywood themes throughout the report reflects the industry's still dominant place in the media ecology. (In 2013 and 2014, Ramesh Sippy took over Yash Chopra's chair duties.)

3. Anil Arjun and Siddharth Roy Kapur, as quoted in "Films: Spotlight on Growth," KPMG-FICCI, *Digital Dawn* (2012), 59.

4. "The Indian M&E Industry in 2013: An Introduction," in KPMG-FICCI, *The Power of a Billion* (2013), 11.

5. See KPMG-FICCI, *The Power of a Billion* (2013), 109–110.

6. Sanjay Gaikwad, CEO of UFO Moviez India, as quoted in KPMG-FICCI, *The Power of a Billion* (2013), 63. KPMG's 2014 report is even more cautious about the growth of multiplexes: "Going forward, multiplex growth is expected to slow down, in line with the overall delays and future expectations for retail sector and commercial real estate development, impacting box office growth in the short term." See KPMG-FICCI, *The Stage Is Set* (2014), 4.

7. Nukkad theaters are planned to serve as school classrooms outside screening hours, according to a program called "Nukkad ki Patshala" (Nukkad's Schools), taking the notion of "greater social good" to a new and very literal level. See http://nukkad.unitedmedia works.in/Nukkad-Ki-Pathshala.htm (accessed November 2013).

8. On the Indian middle classes and their contested numbers, see Leela Fernandes, *India's New Middle Class: Democratic Politics in an Era of Economic Reform*; Diana Farrell and Eric Beinhocker, "Next Big Spenders: India's Middle Class," McKinsey Global Institute (May 19, 2007, at www.mckinsey.com/Insights/MGI/In_the_news/Next_big _spenders_Indian_middle_class, accessed January 2014); Christian Meyer and Nancy Birdsall, "New Estimates of India's Middle Class: A Technical Note," Center for Global Development, Peterson Institute for International Economics, at www.cgdev.org/ doc/2013_MiddleClassIndia_TechnicalNote_CGDNote.pdf (accessed January 2014).

9. See Sangita Gopal, *Conjugations*, especially the claim that "New Bollywood cinema's address is deliberately narrow and aimed at a transnational, urban, middle class audience" (14).

10. See S. Ganesh, "*Lage Raho Munnabhai*: History as Farce," *Economic and Political Weekly* 41.41 (October 14–20, 2006), 4317–19.

11. The film scholar Rachel Dwyer insists that "the specific melodramatic mode and requirements of the Hindi film are not well suited to the character of Gandhi." See Dwyer, "The Case of the Missing Mahatma," *Public Culture* 23:2 (2011): 370. Earlier in the essay, Dwyer observes of *Lage Raho*: "Although Gandhi is back, it is not the historical Gandhi, a challenging and difficult figure urging the abandonment of consumerism, but a Gandhi of India's new middle classes" (Dwyer 353). Other critics, following Ashis Nandy's work on Gandhi, catalog Nandy's four Gandhis and conclude, as Arunabhava Ghosh and Tapan Babu do, that *Lage Raho*'s "Gandhigiri is perhaps closer to the fourth variety of [Nandy's] Gandhi," who has been refashioned to become an "icon of popular culture." See Ghosh and Babu, "*Lage Raho Munnabhai*: Unraveling Brand 'Gandhigiri,'" *Economic and Political Weekly* 41.51 (December 23–29, 2006): 5225–26.

12. Ashis Nandy, "The Lure of 'Normal' Politics: Gandhi and the Battle for Popular Culture of Politics in India," *South Asian Popular Culture* 5.2 (October 2007): 167. Dwyer's essay, "The Case of the Missing Mahatma," documents Gandhi's absence in popular cinema and the medium's selective treatment of his life.

13. Ashis Nandy recounts Gandhi's last lonely days when "Let Gandhi Die" was commonly heard around his last fast and, according to Nandy, "his mail usually brought a large

number of abusive letters. The attendance in his daily prayer meetings was dwindling, and most of those who came, some say, came ritually." Threats of assassination were known but ignored by a state largely tired of the man. See Nandy, "The Lure of 'Normal' Politics," 174 passim.

14. Ibid., 175.

15. In Vikram Chandra's novella, "Artha" (1997), a fabled wrestling teacher of the old school blames Bombay's frequent riots on the unrelenting demand for land that is inconveniently occupied by long-term residents. "Do you know, when I first opened this *akhara* here, forty years ago, this was all an open *maidan*? . . . Now everything is built up. Even this land they want. . . . Perhaps next time there is trouble in the city, I'll find all this gone, burnt down" (203). Later, the teacher connects the city's "unrest" to agitations manipulated by the criminal underworld for the purposes of grabbing land for developers: "The big fellows, all they're good for is scaring people. Destroying houses and huts and slums. Clearing land. If anyone dies, they die—it's incidental." See Vikram Chandra, "Artha," in *Love and Longing in Bombay*, 210.

16. See Inden, "Transnational Class, Erotic Arcadia, and Commercial Utopia in Hindi Films," in Brosius and Butcher, eds., *Image Journeys*, 41–68.

17. Bollywood remains the name for a cinema that however clumsily captures a wide(r) swathe of audience share than its producers predict, as the KPMG reports in note 1 of this chapter further underscore. It is also the name for the cinema that inspires widespread imitations. A discussion of the cinema's own references to its past would need to address the A-list blockbuster, *Om Shanti Om* (Farah Khan, 2007), in which the 1970s are not so much remade as reincarnated as a site of possibility that must be exhumed from a grave with the help of specters and spectacle. The sociologist Rajinder Dudrah observes the many remakes of 1970s Bollywood blockbusters in the 2000s and identifies them as an effort to rescript millennial history in a new way. Developing Elizabeth Guffey's work on retro, Dudrah names the remakes "retro Bollywood," which express both a "longing for the past with a suspicion of the new and current." See Rajinder Dudrah, "The Retro Noughties: 1970s Hindi Films in 2000s Bollywood Cinema" in Joshi and Dudrah, eds., *The 1970s and Its Legacies in India's Cinemas*, 102.

   Among recent low-budget remakes of 1970's Bollywood blockbusters, films such as *Malegaon ke Sholay* (Malegaon's Sholay, Nasir Shaikh, 2000), made and circulating in Malegaon, a poverty-stricken town outside Mumbai, reveal local experiments in production that enjoy passionate if narrow circulation and audiences. See the documentary, *Supermen of Malegaon* (Faiza Ahmad Khan, 2008) depicting the Malegaon phenomenon.

FILMOGRAPHY

Unless otherwise noted, all titles below were viewed on DVD in the version listed. Titles marked with an asterisk are treated at length in the study.

*3 Idiots. Dir. Rajkumar Hirani. Eros Entertainment, 2009.

*A Wednesday. Dir. Neeraj Pandey. MoserBaer, 2008.

Aag [Fire]. Dir. Raj Kapoor. Yash Raj Films, 1948.

Aaj ka Arjun [Today's Arjun]. Dir. K. C. Bokadia. B. M. B. Pictures, 1990.

*Ab Dilli Dur Nahin [Delhi is not far now]. Dir. Amar Kumar. Yash Raj Films, 1957.

Aisa Kyon Hota Hai? [Why does it happen like this?]. Dir. Ajay Kanchan. Vishesh Films, 2006.

All That Heaven Allows. Dir. Douglas Sirk. Criterion, 1955.

*Amar Akbar Anthony. Dir. Manmohan Desai. DEI Entertainment, 1977.

Andha Kanoon [Blind justice]. Dir. T. Rama Rao. Eagle DVDs, 1983.

Around the World in Eight Dollars. Dir. S. Pachhi. P.S. Pictures, 1967.

Aurat [Woman]. Dir. Mehboob Khan. National Studios, 1940. Film.

*Awara [The vagabond]. Dir. Raj Kapoor. Yash Raj Films, 1951.

Barsaat [Rain]. Dir. Raj Kapoor. Yash Raj Films, 1949.

*Bobby. Dir. Raj Kapoor. Yash Raj Films, 1973.

Bombay. Dir. Mani Ratnam. Eros Entertainment, 1995.

Bride and Prejudice. Dir. Gurinder Chadha. Pathé Pictures, 2004. Film.

Bunty aur Babli [Bunty and Babli]. Dir. Aditya Chopra. Yash Raj Films, 2005.

Chalte Chalte [As we walk]. Dir. Aziz Mirza. Eros Entertainment, 2003.

Chaudhvin ka Chand [Moon of the 14th day]. Dir. Mohammed Sadiq. Eros Entertainment, 1960.

*Deewaar [The wall]. Dir. Yash Chopra. Eros Entertainment, 1975.

Devdas. Dir. Sanjay Leela Bhansali. Eros Entertainment, 2002.

Dil Se [From the heart]. Dir. Mani Ratnam. Eros Entertainment, 1998.

Dilwale Dulhaniya le Jayenge [*DDLJ*, The man with the heart gets the bride]. Dir. Aditya Chopra. Yash Raj Films, 1995.

Don. Dir. Chandra Barot. Bollywood Entertainment, 1978.

Don 2. Dir. Farhan Akhtar. Excel Entertainment, 2011.

East Is East. Dir. Damien O'Donnell. Miramax, 1999.

Ghajini. Dir. A. R. Murugadoss. Reliance BigPictures, 2008.

Guru. Dir. Mani Ratnam. Eros Entertainment, 2007.

Hum Aapke Hain Kaun? [Who am I to you?]. Dir. Sooraj Barjatya. Eros Entertainment, 1994.

Inquilab [Revolution]. Dir. T. Rama Rao. Eagle DVDs, 1984.

Jai Santoshi Maa [Hail, Goddess Santoshi]. Dir. Vijay Sharma. Baba Traders, 1975.

Kabhi Alvida Naa Kehna [Never say goodbye]. Dir. Karan Johar. Yash Raj Films, 2006.

*Kabhi Khushi Kabhi Gham [K3G; Sometimes happy, sometimes sad]. Dir. Karan Johar. Yash Raj Films, 2001.

*Kahaani [Story]. Dir. Sujoy Ghosh. Shemaroo, 2012.

Kal Ho Naa Ho [Tomorrow may not be]. Dir. Nikhil Advani. Yash Raj Films, 2003.

Kissa Kursi Ka [The story of a chair]. Dir. Amrit Nahata. No distributor, 1977.

Kuch Kuch Hota Hai [Something happens]. Dir. Karan Johar. Yash Raj Films, 1998.

*Lage Raho Munnabhai [Keep at it, Munnabhai]. Dir. Rajkumar Hirani. Eros Entertainment, 2006.

Malegaon ke Sholay [Malegaon's Sholay]. Dir. Nasir Shaikh. 2000.

Mangal Pandey: The Rising. Dir. Ketan Mehta. Eros Entertainment, 2005.

Mera Nam Joker [My name is Joker]. Dir. Raj Kapoor. Yash Raj Films, 1971.

Mission Kashmir. Dir. Vidhu Vinod Chopra. Eros Entertainment, 2000.

Mohabattein [Lovers]. Dir. Aditya Chopra. Yash Raj Films, 2000.

*Monsoon Wedding. Dir. Mira Nair. IFC Productions, 2001.

*Mother India. Dir. Mehboob Khan. Eros Entertainment, 1957.

Mr. and Mrs. 1955. Dir. Guru Dutt. Yash Raj Films, 1955.

Mukti Chai [Cry for freedom]. Dir. Utpalendu Chakraborty, 1977,

Om Shanti Om. Dir. Farah Khan. Eros Entertainment, 2007.

Pakeeza [The pure one]. Dir. Kamal Amrohi. Shemaroo, 1971.

Pyaasa [The thirsty one]. Dir. Guru Dutt. Yash Raj Films, 1957.

Ra.One. Dir. Anubhav Sinha. Eros Entertainment, 2011.

*Raj Kapoor Lives. Dir. Siddharth Kak. Films Division, 1987.

Ram Ram Gangaram. Dir. Dada Kondke. Dada Kondke Productions, 1977.

Ram Teri Ganga Maili [Ram, your Ganges is dirty]. Dir. Raj Kapoor. Yash Raj Films, 1985.

Rang de Basanti [Color it saffron]. Dir. Rakeysh Omprakash Mehra. UTV, 2006.

Roti Kapda aur Makaan [Food clothing and housing]. Dir. Manoj Kumar. VIP Films, 1974.

Samay [When time strikes]. Dir. Robby Grewal. Spark Entertainment, 2003.

*Sangam [Union]. Dir. Raj Kapoor. Yash Raj Films, 1964.

Satya [Truth]. Dir. Ram Gopal Verma. Eros Entertainment, 1998.

*Shakti [Power]. Dir. Ramesh Sippy. Shemaroo, 1982.

*Sholay [Embers]. Dir. Ramesh Sippy. Eros Entertainment, 1975.

*Shree 420 [The gentleman cheat]. Dir. Raj Kapoor. Yash Raj Films, 1955.

*Slumdog Millionaire. Dir. Danny Boyle. Fox Searchlight Pictures, 2008.

Supermen of Malegaon. Dir. Faiza Ahmad Khan. KBS Productions, 2008.

Talaash [Search]. Dir. Reema Kagti. Excel Entertainment, 2012.

**Trishul* [Trident]. Dir. Yash Chopra. Eros Entertainment, 1978.

Zakhm [Wounds]. Dir. Mahesh Bhatt. Pooja Bhatt Productions, 1998.

Zanjeer [Chains]. Dir. Prakash Mehra. Eros Entertainment, 1973.

BIBLIOGRAPHY

"30,000 Cinemas?" *Filmfare* (November 12–25, 1976): 1.

Abbas, K. A. "A 'Film Pamphleteer's' Diary." *The Illustrated Weekly of India*, April 23, 1972, 42–43.

——. "Kamasutra Via Hollywood." *The Illustrated Weekly of India*, April 15, 1973, 48–51.

——. "Raj Kapoor and the Writer." *Cinema India International* (April–June 1985): 16ff.

——. "Thanks, Raj—and Damn You!" *Filmfare* 19.25 (December 4, 1970): 36–39.

Ahmed, Afsana. "*Awara* Years: The Legend Lives On." *Asian Age* (January 9, 1999): 23.

Ahmed, Akbar S. "Bombay Films: The Cinema as Metaphor for Indian Society and Politics." *Modern Asian Studies* 26.2 (1992): 289–320.

Ahmed, Rauf. "1978—Amitabh's Year." *The Illustrated Weekly of India*, January 28, 1979, 41–43.

——. "Who Will Be on Top?" *The Illustrated Weekly of India*, November 6, 1977, 20–27.

Ahmed, Saghir. "*Sholay*, Satyajit Ray and the Warring Clans of Indian Cinema." *Deep Focus* 5 (1993): 22–31.

Akbar, Khatija. *Madhubala: Her Life, Her Films*. New Delhi: UBSPD, 1997.

Akhtar, Javed. "From Ceiling Fans to A/C and Juice: Javed Akhtar in Conversation with Priya Joshi." *South Asian Popular Culture* 10.1 (2012): 103–110.

——. *Quiver: Poems and Ghazals*. Trans. David Matthews. New Delhi: HarperCollins, 2003.

Akhtar, Javed. Personal interview by author, Philadelphia, April 13–15, 2011.

Akhtar, Salman, and Komal Choksi. "Bollywood and the Indian Unconscious." In Salman Akhtar, ed., *Freud Along the Ganges: Psychoanalytic Reflections on the People and Culture of India*, 139–76. New York: Other Press, 2005.

Alessandrini, Anthony C. "'My Heart's Indian for All That': Bollywood Film between Home and Diaspora." *Diaspora* 10.3 (2001): 315–40.

Alter, Stephen. *Fantasies of a Bollywood Love Thief: Inside the World of Indian Moviemaking*. Orlando, FL: Harcourt, 2007.

"*Amar Akbar Anthony*: Blow to Prestige." *Film World* (August 1977): 18.

"*Amar Akbar Anthony*: Man's Master Blend." *Blitz* (June 4, 1977).

Amladi, K. L. "Blood, Sweat and Tears." *The Illustrated Weekly of India*, December 15, 1975, 28.

Anderson, Benedict. *Imagined Communities: Reflections on the Origin and Spread of Nationalism*. 2d rev. ed. New York: Verso, 1991.

Anjaria, Ulka. "'Relationships Which Have No Name': Family and Sexuality in 1970s Popular Film." *South Asian Popular Culture* 10.1 (2012): 23–36.

Appadurai, Arjun, and Carol A. Breckenridge. "Public Modernity in India." In Carol A. Breckenridge, ed., *Consuming Modernity: Public Culture in a South Asian World*, 1–20. Minneapolis: U of Minnesota P, 1995.

Armes, Roy. *Third World Film Making and the West.* Berkeley: U of California P, 1987.

Ashokamitran. "The Dream Bazaar." *The Illustrated Weekly of India*, October 13–19, 1985, 44–49.

——. "The Great Dream Bazaar." *The Illustrated Weekly of India*, July 21–27, 1985, 52–55.

Athique, Adrian, and Douglas Hill. *The Multiplex in India: A Cultural Economy of Urban Leisure.* London: Routledge, 2010.

Baig, Ali Asghar. "Sixty Years of Indian Cinema." *The Illustrated Weekly of India*, May 21, 1972, 6–15.

Balakrishnan, Ajit. "India's IT Industry: The End of the Beginning." *Social Research* 78.1 (Spring 2011): 1–20 (in a Special Issue titled *India's World*, ed. Arjun Appadurai).

Balakrishnan, Gopal, ed. *Mapping the Nation.* London: Verso, 1996.

Balaram, Gunvanthi. "Ashok Kumar: 50 Eventful Years on Screen." *Bombay* (June 7–21, 1986): 32–38.

Bamzai, Kaveri, and Sandeep Unnithan. "Show Business." *India Today International*, January 24, 2003, 48.

Banaji, S. J. "*Deewaar*: They're Hijacking the Matron." *Filmfare* 24.3 (1975): 35.

——. "*Zanjeer*: Busted Copper." *Filmfare* (June 1, 1973): 35.

Banaji, Shakuntala. *Reading Bollywood: The Young Audience and Hindi Film.* London: Palgrave Macmillan, 2006.

Banerjea, Koushik. "'Fight Club': Aesthetics, Hybridisation and the Construction of Rogue Masculinities in *Sholay* and *Deewar*." In Kaur and Sinha, eds., *Bollyworld*, 163–85.

Banerjee, Mukulika. "Election as Communitas." *Social Research* 78.1 (Spring 2011): 75–98 (in a Special Issue titled *India's World*, ed. Arjun Appadurai).

Banerjee, Purabi. "Rushdie's Homeland." *Patriot* (April 3, 1983): 2.

Banerjee, Shampa. "Raj Kapoor." *Profiles: Five Film-Makers from India*, 19–49. New Delhi: A. Viren Luther, 1985.

Banerjee, Shampa, and Anil Srivastava. *One Hundred Indian Feature Films: An Annotated Filmography.* New York: Garland, 1998.

Banerjee, Utpal K. "Myths in Indian Cinema." *The Illustrated Weekly of India*, April 25, 1982, 42–44.

Barnouw, Erik. "M. G. Ramachandran." *Media Marathon: A Twentieth-Century Memoir*, 155–66. Durham, NC: Duke UP, 1996.

Barnouw, Erik and S. Krishnaswamy. *Indian Film.* 2d ed. New York: Oxford UP, 1980.

Basu, Siddhartha, Sanjay Kak, and Pradip Krishen. "Cinema and Society: A Search for Meaning in a New Game." *India International Centre Quarterly. Indian Popular Cinema: Myth Meaning and Metaphor* 8.1 (March 1980): 57–76.

Batra, Bindu. "Kiss Kiss, Bang Bang." *India Today*, May 15, 1976, 31.

Beeman, William O. "The Use of Music in Popular Film: East and West." *India International Centre Quarterly. Indian Popular Cinema: Myth Meaning and Metaphor* 8.1 (March 1980): 77–88.

"Behind the Showman." *Filmfare* (December 4, 1970): 17–18.

Bellman, Eric. "Bollywood's Movies Are All the Rage but Stocks Draw Skeptical Audiences." *Wall Street Journal* (Eastern ed.), December 6, 2005, C1.

Bhagat, Dhiren. "Is the Film Biased?" *The Illustrated Weekly of India*, March 11–17, 1984, 12–13.

Bhagwat, Nakul. "*Awara*: The Triumph of a Tramp." *Movie* (1985): 95–99.

Bharatan, Raju. "1975: The Year of Violence and Sex in Films." *The Illustrated Weekly of India*, December 28, 1975, 24–29.

——. "*Prem Rog*: Raj Kapoor's Supreme Test." *The Illustrated Weekly of India*, May 2 1982, 24–27.

——. "*Sholay*: Anatomy of Violence." *The Illustrated Weekly of India*, August 31, 1975, 35.

Bharati, Agehananda. "Anthropology of Hindi Films." *The Illustrated Weekly of India*, January 30, 1977, 24–31.

——. "Anthropology of Hindi Films—2." *The Illustrated Weekly of India*, February 6, 1977, 22–27.

Bharucha, Rustom. "Haraam Bombay!" *Economic and Political Weekly* (June 10, 1989): 1275–79.

Bhaskaran, Gautam. "India Gets Schooled in Film Finance." *Hollywood Reporter* 3.19 (International Edition), May 31, 2005.

Bhatkal, Satyajit. *The Spirit of Lagaan*. Mumbai: Popular Prakashan, 2002.

Bhattacharya, Nandini. *Hindi Cinema: Repeating the Subject*. London: Routledge, 2013.

Bhushan, Ratna. "The Show Begins Here." *The Hindu Business Line* (Internet Edition), December 26, 2002.

Binford, Mira Reym. "Innovation and Imitation in the Contemporary Indian Cinema." In Dissanayake, ed., *Cinema and Cultural Identity*, 77–92.

——. "The Two Cinemas of India." In John D. H. Downing, ed., *Film and Politics in the Third World*, 145–66. New York: Praeger, 1987.

Bisplinghoff, Gretchen D., and Carol J. Sligo. "Eve in Calcutta: The Indianization of a Movie Madwoman." *Asian Cinema* 9.1 (Fall 1997): 99–110.

Bobb, Dilip. "*Kissa Kursi Ka*: The Case of the Missing Film." *India Today*, June 1–15, 1978, 24–33.

"Bollywood Meets the Bankers." *Asiamoney* 16.5 (June 2005).

Booth, Gregory D. *Behind the Curtain: Making Music in Mumbai's Film Studios*. Oxford: Oxford UP, 2008.

Bordwell, David. *Planet Hong Kong: Popular Cinema and the Art of Entertainment*. Cambridge: Harvard UP, 2000.

——. *Poetics of Cinema*. New York: Routledge, 2007.

Bose, Derek. *Brand Bollywood: A New Global Entertainment Order*. New Delhi: Sage, 2006.

Breuer, Josef, and Sigmund Freud. *Studies on Hysteria* (1893–1895). Trans. James Strachey with Anna Freud. Ed. James Strachey. New York: Basic Books, 1955.

Brosius, Christiane. "The Scattered Homelands of the Migrant: Bollywood through the Diasporic Lens." In Kaur and Sinha, eds., *Bollyworld*, 207–38.

Burke, Peter. "The 'Discovery' of Popular Culture." In Ralph Samuel, ed., *People's History and Socialist Theory*, 216–26. London: Routledge and Kegan Paul, 1981.

Cawelti, John. "Reflections on the Western since 1970." In Glenwood Irons, ed., *Gender, Language, and Myth: Essays on Popular Culture*, 83–102. Toronto: U of Toronto P, 1992.

Chakravarty, Sumita. "Fragmenting the Nation: Images of Terrorism in Indian Popular Cinema." In Hjort and MacKenzie, eds., *Cinema and Nation*, 222–37.

——. *National Identity in Indian Popular Cinema, 1947–1987*. Austin: U of Texas P, 1993.

Chandra, Nandini. "Merit and Opportunity in the Child-Centric Nationalist Films of the 1950s." In Manju Jain, ed., *Narratives of Indian Cinema*, 123–44.

Chandra, Vikram. "Artha." In *Love and Longing in Bombay*, 163–228. Boston: Little Brown, 1997.

Chatterjee, Gayatri. *Awara*. 2d ed. New Delhi: Penguin, 2003.

——. *Mother India*. New Delhi: Penguin, 2002.

Chatterjee, Partha. "When Melody Ruled the Day." In Vasudev, ed., *Frames of Mind*, 51–68.

——. "Whose Imagined Communities?" In Gopal Balakrishnan, ed., *Mapping the Nation*, 214–25.

Chattopadhyay, Saratchandra. *Devdas: A Novel*. Trans. Sreejata Guha. New Delhi: Penguin, 2002.

Chaubal, Devyani. "What the Stars Foretell." *The Illustrated Weekly of India*, January 13–19, 1985, 54–55.

Cheah, Pheng, and Bruce Robbins, eds. *Cosmopolitics: Thinking and Feeling Beyond the Nation*. Minneapolis: U Minnesota P, 1998.

Chinnaswami, R. "How Political Is Tamil Cinema?" *The Illustrated Weekly of India*, March 23, 1975, 36–41.

Chopra, Anupama. "Bollywood Is Big B.O. Overseas." *Variety*, November 29–December 5, 2004, 16.

——. *First Day First Show: Writings from the Bollywood Trenches*. New Delhi: Penguin, 2011.

——. *King of Bollywood: Shah Rukh Khan and the Seductive World of Indian Cinema*. New York: Warner Books, 2007.

——. *Sholay: The Making of a Classic*. Rev. paperback. New Delhi: Viking Penguin India, 2001.

Chopra, B. R. "Film City or Duplicity?" *The Illustrated Weekly of India*, April 11, 1982, 38–39.

Chute, David. "The Big B: The Rise and Fall and Rebirth of Bollywood Superstar Amitabh Bachchan." *Film Comment* (2005): 50–56.

Creekmur, Corey. "Bombay Boys: Dissolving the Male Child in Popular Hindi Cinema." In Murray Pomerance and Frances Gateward, eds., *Where the Boys Are: Cinemas of Masculinity and Youth*, 345–76. Detroit: Wayne State UP, 2005.

Culler, Jonathan, and Pheng Cheah, eds. *Grounds of Comparison: Around the Work of Benedict Anderson*. London: Routledge, 2003.

Das Gupta, Chidananda. "How Indian Is Our Cinema?" *Indian Express*, August 2, 1987, 3.

——. "The Painted Face of Politics: The Actor Politicians of South India." In Dissanayake, ed., *Cinema and Cultural Identity*, 127–48.

——. *Talking About Films*. New Delhi: Orient Longman, 1981.

Das, Veena. "The Mythological Film and Its Framework of Meaning: An Analysis of *Jai Santoshi Ma*." *India International Centre Quarterly. Indian Popular Cinema: Myth Meaning and Metaphor* 8.1 (March 1980): 43–56.

Datta, Sangeeta. *Shyam Benegal*. London: British Film Institute, 2002.

Davis, Richard H., ed. *Picturing the Nation: Icononographies of Modern India*. New Delhi: Orient Longman, 2007.

Deep, Mohan. *The Mystery and Mystique of Madhubala*. Bombay: Magna, 1996.

Del Giudice, Luisa, and Gerald Porter, eds. *Imagined States: Nationalism, Utopia, and Longing in Oral Cultures*. Logan: Utah State UP, 2001.

Derné, Steve. *Globalization on the Ground: Media and the Transformation of Culture, Class, and Gender in India*. New Delhi: Sage , 2008.

——. *Movies, Masculinity, and Modernity*. Westport, CT: Greenwood Press, 2000.

Desai, Jigna. *Beyond Bollywood: The Cultural Politics of South Asian Diasporic Film*. New York: Routledge, 2004.

Desai, Jigna, Rajinder Dudrah, and Amit Rai. "Bollywood Audiences Editorial." *South Asian Popular Culture* 3.2 (2005): 79–82.

Deshpande, Sudhanva. "The Consumable Hero of Globalised India." In Kaur and Sinha, eds., *Bollyworld*, 186–206.

——. "What's So Great About *Lagaan?*" In Geeti Sen, ed., *India: A National Culture?*, 236–45.

Devereux, George. "Why Oedipus Killed Laius: A Note on the Complementary Oedipus Complex in Greek Drama." *International Journal of Psycho-analysis* 34.2 (1953): 132–41.

Dhir, Anurag. "The World According to Bollywood." *Ascent Magazine* (2005): 27–31.

Dhondy, Farrukh. "Keeping Faith: Indian Film and Its World." *Dædalus* 115.4 (Fall 1985): 125–40.

Dickey, Sara. *Cinema and the Urban Poor in South India*. New Delhi: Cambridge UP, 1993.

——. "Opposing Faces: Film Star Fan Clubs and the Construction of Class Identities in South India." In Dwyer and Pinney, eds., *Pleasure and the Nation*, 212–46.

Dirks, Nicholas. "The Home and the Nation: Consuming Culture and Politics in *Roja*." In Dwyer and Pinney, eds., *Pleasure and the Nation*, 161–86.

Dissanayake, Wimal. "Globalization and Cultural Narcissism: Note on Bollywood Cinema." *Asian Cinema* 15.1 (2004): 143–50.

——. "Nationhood, History, and Cinema: Reflections on the Asian Scene." In Dissanayake, ed., *Colonialism and Nationalism in Asian Cinema*, ix–xxix.

Dissanayake, Wimal, ed. *Cinema and Cultural Identity: Reflections on Films from Japan, India, and China*. Lanham, MD: University Press of America, 1988.

——. *Colonialism and Nationalism in Asian Cinema*. Bloomington: Indiana UP, 1994.

Dissanayake, Wimal, and Malti Sahai. *Raj Kapoor's Films: Harmony of Discourses*. New Delhi: Vikas, 1988.

——. *Sholay: A Cultural Reading*. New Delhi: Wiley Eastern, 1992.

Dogra, Bharat B. "*Sholay*: The Tragedy of Commercial Films." *Filmfare* (November 12–25, 1976): 23.

Donner, Henrike, ed. *Being Middle Class in India: A Way of Life*. London: Routledge, 2011.

Doraiswamy, Rashmi. "Image and Imagination: Reconstructing the Nation in Cinema." In Geeti Sen, ed., *India: A National Culture?*, 211–23.

Dudrah, Rajinder. *Bollywood: Sociology Goes to the Movies*. New Delhi: Sage, 2006.

——. *Bollywood Travels: Culture, Diaspora and Border Crossings in Popular Hindi Cinema*. London: Routledge, 2012.

——. "The Retro Noughties: 1970s Hindi Films in 2000s Bollywood Cinema." In Joshi and Dudrah, eds., *The 1970s and Its Legacies in India's Cinemas*, 101–119.

Duncan, Ian. *Modern Romance and Transformations of the Novel: The Gothic, Scott, Dickens*. Cambridge: Cambridge UP, 1992.

Dutta, Sangeeta. "Small Dreams, Big City: A Comparative Analysis of *Shree 420* and *Raju Ban Gaya Gentleman.*" *Cinema in India* 3.12 (December 1992): 60–66.

Dutta, Siddhartha. "Cinema in the Marketplace." *Deep Focus* 5 (1993): 48–53.

Dwyer, Rachel. *All You Want Is Money, All You Need Is Love: Sex and Romance in Modern India.* London: Cassell, 2000.

——. "Bollywood's India: Hindi Cinema as a Guide to Modern India." *Asian Affairs* 41.3 (2010): 381–98.

——. "The Case of the Missing Mahatma: Gandhi and the Hindi Cinema." *Public Culture* 23.2 (2011): 349–76.

——. "The Erotics of the Wet Sari in Hindi Film." *South Asia* 23.1 (2000): 143–59.

——. *Yash Chopra: Fifty Years in Indian Cinema.* New Delhi: Roli Books, 2002.

——. "*Zara hatke* ('somewhat different'): The New Middle Classes and the Changing Forms of Hindi Cinema." In Donner, ed., *Being Middle Class in India: A Way of Life*, 184–208.

Dwyer, Rachel, and Divia Patel. *Cinema India: The Visual Culture of Hindi Film.* New Brunswick: Rutgers UP, 2002.

Dwyer, Rachel, and Christopher Pinney, eds. *Pleasure and the Nation: The History, Politics, and Consumption of Public Culture in India.* New Delhi: Oxford UP, 2001.

Dwyer, Rachel, and Jerry Pinto, eds. *Beyond the Boundaries of Bollywood: The Many Forms of Hindi Cinema.* New Delhi: Oxford UP, 2011.

Eagleton, Terry. "Nationalism: Irony and Commitment." *Nationalism, Colonialism, Literature.* Minneapolis: U of Minnesota P, 1988.

Edmunds, Lowell, and Alan Dundes, eds. *Oedipus: A Folklore Casebook.* New York: Garland, 1983.

Ewing, Anjali. "Showbiz Showdown." *The Illustrated Weekly of India*, January 2, 1983, 8–13.

Eye, Lens. "Cut to Politics: An Interview with Ramesh Sippy." *Times of India Sunday Review*, November 19, 1989.

Farrell, Diana, and Eric Beinhocker. "Next Big Spenders: India's Middle Class." McKinsey Global Institute. May 19, 2007. See mckinsey.com.

Fernandes, Leela. *India's New Middle Class: Democratic Politics in an Era of Economic Reform.* Minneapolis: U of Minnesota P, 2006.

Fernandes, Naresh. "Remembering Anthony Gonçalves." *Seminar* 543 (November 2004).

Freitag, Sandria. "Visions of the Nation: Theorizing the Nexus between Creation, Consumption, and Participation in the Public Sphere." In Dwyer and Pinney, eds., *Pleasure and the Nation*, 35–75.

Freud, Sigmund. "Family Romances" (1909). Trans. James Strachey. In vol. 9 of *The Standard Edition of the Complete Psychological Works of Sigmund Freud*, 236–41. Ed. James Stratchey. London: Hogarth Press, 1959.

"Fundamental Blunder." In Ayaz Memon and Ranjona Bannerji. eds., *India 50: The Making of a Nation*, 130–32. Bombay: Book Quest, 1997.

Gabriel, Karen. *Melodrama and the Nation: Sexual Economies of Bombay Cinema, 1970–2000.* New Delhi: Women Unlimited/Kali for Women, 2010.

Gahlot, Deepa. "Look Back in Anger." *Cinema in India* 3.12 (1992): 52–55.

Ganesh, S. "*Lage Raho Munnabhai*: History as Farce." *Economic and Political Weekly* 41.41 (October 14–20, 2006): 4317–19.

Gangar, Amrit, and V. K. Dharamsey. "The Way We Were." *Cinema in India* 3.9 (1992): 9–17.

Ganti, Tejaswini. *Bollywood: A Guidebook to Popular Hindi Cinema.* New York: Routledge, 2004.

——. *Producing Bollywood: Inside the Contemporary Hindi Film Industry.* Durham, NC: Duke UP, 2012.

Garga, B. D. *So Many Cinemas: The Motion Picture in India.* Bombay: Eminence, 1996.

——. "The Turbulent Thirties." In Vasudev, ed., *Frames of Mind,* 17–28.

Geetha, J. "The Mutating Mother: From *Mother India* to *Ram Lakhan.*" *Deep Focus* 3.3 (1990): 9–15.

Gehlawat, Ajay. "The Construction of 1970s Femininity, or Why Zeenat Aman Sings the Same Song Twice." *South Asian Popular Culture* 10.1 (2012): 51–62.

——. *Reframing Bollywood: Theories of Popular Hindi Cinema.* New Delhi: Sage, 2010.

Gelder, Lawrence. "Arts Briefing." *New York Times,* November 20, 2003, C2.

Gellner, Ernst. "The Coming of Nationalism and Its Interpretation: The Myths of Nation and Class." In Gopal Balakrishnan, ed., *Mapping the Nation,* 98–145.

George, T. J. S. *The Life and Times of Nargis.* New Delhi: HarperCollins India, 1994.

Georgekutty, A. L. "The Sacred, the Secular, and the Nation in *Bombay.*" *Deep Focus* 6 (1996): 77–81.

Ghatak, Ritwik. *Rows and Rows of Fences.* Calcutta: Seagull Books, 2000.

Ghosh, Amitav. "A Day in Calcutta." In Spinelli, ed., *Indian Summer,* 33–35.

Ghosh, Arunabhava, and Tapan Babu. "*Lage Raho Munnabhai*: Unraveling Brand 'Gandhigiri.'" *Economic and Political Weekly* 41.51 (December 23–29, 2006): 5225–26.

Ghosh, Bishnupriya. "Sensate Outlaws: The Recursive Social Bandit in Indian Popular Cultures." In Sen and Basu, eds., *Figurations in Indian Film,* 21–43.

"Giver and Taker of Royalties." *Filmfare* (December 4, 1970): 35.

Godse, Nathuram. *May It Please Your Honour: Statement of Nathuram Godse.* Rpt., Pune: Vitasta Prakashan, 1977.

Gokulsing, K. Moti, and Wimal Dissanayake. *Indian Popular Cinema: A Narrative of Cultural Change.* New Delhi: Orient Longman, 1998.

Gokulsing, K. Moti, and Wimal Dissanayake, eds. *Popular Culture in a Globalised India.* London: Routledge, 2009.

Goldman, R. P. "Fathers, Sons, and Gurus: Oedipal Conflict in the Sanskrit Epics." *Journal of Indian Philosophy* 6 (1978): 325–92.

Gooptu, Sharmishtha. *Bengali Cinema: "An Other Nation."* London: Routledge, 2011.

Gopal, Sangita. "The Afterlives of 1970s Hindi Cinema." In Joshi and Dudrah, eds., *The 1970s and Its Legacies in India's Cinemas,* 120–35.

——. *Conjugations: Marriage and Form in New Bollywood Cinema.* Chicago: U of Chicago P, 2011.

Gopal, Sangita, and Sujata Moorti, eds. *Global Bollywood: Travels of Hindi Song and Dance.* Minneapolis: U of Minnesota P, 2008.

Gopal, Sarvepalli. *Jawaharlal Nehru: A Biography.* Abridged ed. Delhi: Oxford UP, 1989.

Gopalan, Lalitha. *Cinema of Interruptions: Action Genres in Contemporary Indian Cinema.* London: British Film Institute, 2002.

Gramsci, Antonio. *Selections from Cultural Writings.* Ed. David Forgacs and Geoffrey Nowell-Smith. Trans. William Boelhower. Cambridge: Harvard UP, 1985.

Griffiths, Alison. "Discourses of Nationalism in Guru Dutt's *Pyaasa*." *Deep Focus* 6 (1996): 24–31.

Guffey, Elizabeth. *Retro: The Culture of Revival*. London: Reaktion Books, 2006.

Guha, Ramachandra. *India After Gandhi: The History of the World's Largest Democracy*. New York: Ecco/HarperCollins, 2007.

Guneratne, Anthony R. "Religious Conflict, Popular Culture and the Troubled Spectators of Recent Indian Film." *Contemporary South Asia* 6.2 (1997): 177–89.

Habermas, Jürgen. "The European Nation-State—Its Achievements and Its Limits: On the Past and Future of Sovereignty and Citizenship." In Gopal Balakrishnan, ed., *Mapping the Nation*, 281–95.

Hall, Stuart. "In Defense of Theory." In Ralph Samuel, ed., *People's History and Socialist Theory*, 378–85. London: Routledge and Kegan Paul, 1981.

——. "Notes on Deconstructing 'the Popular.'" In Ralph Samuel, ed., *People's History and Socialist Theory*, 227–41. London: Routledge and Kegan Paul, 1981.

Halstead, Narmala. "Belonging and Respect Notions Vis-À-Vis Modern East Indians: Hindi Movies in the Guyanese East Indian Diaspora." In Kaur and Sinha, eds., *Bollyworld*, 261–83.

Hansen, Thomas Blom. "In Search of the Diasporic Self: Bollywood in South Africa." In Kaur and Sinha, eds., *Bollyworld*, 239–60.

Haque, Anisul. "Bollywood and Indian Society." *Deep Focus* 4.1 (1992): 59–63.

Hariharan, K. "Revisiting Sholay A.K.A. Flames of the Sun." *Asian Cinema* (Spring/Summer 1999): 151–54.

Hayward, Susan. "Framing National Cinemas." In Hjort and MacKenzie, eds., *Cinema and Nation*, 88–102.

Higson, Andrew. "The Limiting Imagination of National Cinema." In Hjort and MacKenzie, eds., *Cinema and Nation*, 63–74.

Hjort, Mette, and Scott MacKenzie, eds. *Cinema and Nation*. London: Routledge, 2000.

Hobsbawm, Eric. *Nations and Nationalism since 1780: Programme, Myth, Reality*. 2d ed. Cambridge: Cambridge UP, 1990.

Hobsbawm, Eric, and Terence Ranger, eds. *The Invention of Tradition*. Cambridge: Cambridge UP, 1983.

Hoffman, Adina. "The Big-Bash Theory: Mira Nair's Latest Movie Revels and Reels." *The American Prospect* (March 25, 2002): 28–29.

Hogan, Patrick Colm. *Understanding Indian Movies: Culture, Cognition, and Cinematic Imagination*. Austin: U of Texas P, 2008.

"Hooray for Bollywood." *U.S. Catholic*, November 2005, 5.

Horkheimer, Max, and Theodor W. Adorno. *The Dialectic of Enlightenment* (1947). Trans. John Cumming. Rpt., New York: Continuum, 1988.

Hunt, Lynn. *The Family Romance of the French Revolution*. Berkeley: U of California P, 1992.

Hussain, Akhtar. "On Nargis." *Super* (June 1981): 29–30.

Hyder, Aurratulain. "Bobby." *The Illustrated Weekly of India*, October 14, 1973, 41.

Inden, Ronald. "Transcending Identities in Modern India's World." In Kathryn Dean, ed., *Politics and the Ends of Identity*, 64–102. Aldershot, Eng.: Ashgate, 1997.

——. "Transnational Class, Erotic Arcadia, and Commercial Utopia in Hindi Films." In Christiane Brosius and Melissa Butcher, eds., *Image Journeys: Audio-Visual Media and Cultural Change in India*, 41–68. New Delhi: Sage, 1999.

Iordanova, Dina. "Bollywood Calling: Marketing in the Global Diaspora as Exemplified in Bollywood Cinema." *Springerin* (Austria) 1.2 (2002): 1–5.

"Is the Super Star the Man in the Street." *Film World* 16.4 (April 1979): 31–32.

Ismail, Qadri. "Constituting Nation, Contesting Nationalism: The Southern Tamil (Woman) and Separatist Tamil Nationalism in Sri Lanka." In Partha Chatterjee and Pradeep Jeganathan, eds., *Community, Gender, and Violence*, 212–82. Subaltern Studies 11. New York: Columbia UP, 2000.

Iyer, Shilpa Bharatan. "Bollywood Helmer Eyes IPO for Pix." *Daily Variety Gotham*, December 8, 2005, 34.

Jaikumar, Priya. "Bollywood Spectaculars." *World Literature Today* (October–December 2003): 24–29.

——. *Cinema at the End of Empire: A Politics of Transition in Britain and India*. Durham, NC: Duke UP, 2006.

Jain, Madhu. *The Kapoors: The First Family of Indian Cinema*. New Delhi: Penguin/Viking, 2005.

Jain, Manju, ed. *Narratives of Indian Cinema*. Delhi: Primus Books, 2009.

Jameson, Fredric. *The Political Unconscious: Narrative as Socially Symbolic Act*. Ithaca, NY: Cornell UP, 1981.

Jarvie, I. C. *Towards a Sociology of the Cinema: A Comparative Essay on the Structure and Functioning of a Major Entertainment Industry*. London: Routledge & Kegan Paul, 1970.

Javadeva, M. U. "Family Matters: The Good and the Bad in HAHK." *Deep Focus* 16 (1996): 83–85.

Jha, Priya. "Lyrical Nationalism: Gender, Friendship, and Excess in 1970s Hindi Cinema." *The Velvet Light Trap* 51 (Spring 2003): 43–53.

Jha, Subhash K. "I Can't Go Back to Candy Floss: Interview with Karan Johar" (2006). Web. Accessed September 11, 2006.

Joshi, Lalit Mohan. "The Power of Popular Hindi Cinema." In Spinelli, ed., *Indian Summer*, 75–81.

Joshi, Priya. "Bollylite in America." *South Asian Popular Culture* 8.3 (2010): 245–59.

——. "Cinema as Family Romance." *South Asian Popular Culture* 10.1 (2012): 7–22.

Joshi, Priya, and Rajinder Dudrah. "The 1970s and Its Legacies in India's Cinemas." In a Special Issue of *South Asian Popular Culture* 10.1 (2012): 1–5.

Joshi, Priya, and Rajinder Dudrah, eds. *The 1970s and Its Legacies in India's Cinemas*. New York and London: Routledge, 2014.

Kaarsholm, Preben, ed. *City Flicks: Indian Cinema and the Urban Experience*. Calcutta: Seagull Books, 2004.

Kabir, Ananya Jahanara. "Allegories of Alienation and Politics of Bargaining: Minority Subjectivities in Mani Ratnam's *Dil Se*." *South Asian Popular Culture* 1.2 (2003): 141–59.

——. "Nipped in the Bud? Pleasure and Politics in the 1960s 'Kashmir Films.'" *South Asian Popular Culture* 3.2 (October 2005): 83–100.

Kabir, Nasreen Munni. *Bollywood: The Indian Cinema Story*. London: Chanel 4 Books, 2001.

——. *Guru Dutt: A Life in Cinema*. New Delhi: Oxford UP, 1997.

——. *Talking Films: Conversations on Hindi Cinema with Javed Akhtar*. New Delhi: Oxford UP, 1999.

——. *Talking Songs: Javed Akhtar in Converation with Nasreen Munni Kabir*. New Delhi: Oxford UP, 2005.

Kadir, Djelal, ed. *Questing Fictions: Latin America's Family Romance*. Minneapolis: U of Minnesota P, 1986.

Kak, Siddharth. *Raj Kapoor Lives*. Bombay: Films Division, 1987. DVD.

Kakar, Sudhir. "The Cinema as Collective Fantasy." In Vasudev and Lenglet, eds., *Indian Cinema Superbazaar*, 89–97.

——. *Intimate Relations: Exploring Indian Sexuality*. New Delhi: Penguin, 1988.

——. "The Ties That Bind: Family Relationships in the Mythology of Hindi Cinema." *India International Centre Quarterly* 8.1 (March 1980): 11–22.

Kapoor, Prithviraj. "A Father Remembers." *Filmfare* (December 4, 1970): 24–26.

Kapoor, Raj. "In Defense of the Commercial Cinema." *Debonair* (March 1977): 49–51.

——. "Leaves from My Diary." *Filmfare* (June 21, 1957): 5–7.

——. "My Films and I." *Filmfare* 9.22 (October 21, 1960): 49–51.

——. "Self Portrait." *Filmfare* 15.24 (November 23, 1956): 5–7.

Kapoor, Randhir. Personal interview by author, RK Studios, Chembur, Mumbai, June 19, 2003.

Kapoor, Rishi. Personal interview by author, RK Studios, Chembur, Mumbai, June 19, 2003.

Kapoor, Shashi. "My Father Prithviraj." *The Illustrated Weekly of India*, October 16–22, 1983, 35–39.

——. "He Hit Me Twice." *Filmfare* (December 4, 1970): 26.

Kapoor, Shashi. Personal interview by author, Atlas Apartments, Mumbai, June 20, 2003.

Kapse, Anupama. "What Happened to Khadi? Dress and Costume in Bombay Cinema." In Sen and Basu, eds., *Figurations in Indian Film*, 44–66.

Kapur, Anuradha. "The Representation of Gods and Heroes: Parsi Mythological Drama of the Early Twentieth Century." *Journal of Arts and Ideas* 23–24 (January 1993).

Kapur, Geeta. "Articulating the Self into History: Ritwik Ghatak's *Jukti Takko Ar Gappo*." In Pines and Willemen, eds., *Questions of Third Cinema*, 179–94.

Karanjia, B. K. "Are Cinema Audiences to Blame?" *The Illustrated Weekly of India*, April 2, 1978, 16–19.

——. *Blundering in Wonderland*. New Delhi: Vikas, 1990.

——. "One India, One Film Policy." *The Illustrated Weekly of India*, November 6, 1977, 19.

——. "Rebels of Indian Cinema." *The Illustrated Weekly of India*, October 17, 1971, 21–25.

Karnad, Girish. Personal interview by author, Nehru Center, London, May 27, 2003.

Kasbekar, Asha. "Hidden Pleasures: Negotiating the Myth of the Female Ideal in Popular Hindi Cinema." In Dwyer and Pinney, eds., *Pleasure and the Nation*, 286–308.

Kaul, Gautam. *Cinema and the Indian Freedom Struggle*. New Delhi: Sterling, 1998.

Kaur, Ravinder. "Viewing the West through Bollywood: A Celluloid Occident in the Making." *Contemporary South Asia* 11.2 (2002): 199–209.

Kaur, Raminder, and Ajay J. Sinha, eds. *Bollyworld: Popular Indian Cinema through a Transnational Lens*. New Delhi: Sage, 2005.

Kaushal, Kamini. "'Filmi' Envy." *The Illustrated Weekly of India*, July 22, 1973, 29–31.

Kaviraj, Sudipta. "The Imaginary Institution of India." In Partha Chatterjee and Gyanendra Pandey, eds., *Writing on South Asian History and Society*, 1–39. Subaltern Studies 7. Delhi: Oxford UP, 1992.

——. "Reading a Song of the City: Images of the City in Literature and Film." In Kaarsholm, ed., *City Flicks*, 60–82.

Kavoori, Anandam P., and Aswin Punathambekar, eds. *Global Bollywood*. New York: New York UP, 2008.

Kazmi, Fareed. *The Politics of India's Conventional Cinema*. New Delhi: Sage, 1999.

———. *Sex in Cinema: A History of Female Sexuality in Indian Films*. New Delhi: Rupa, 2010.

Kazmi, Nikhat. *The Dream Merchants of Bollywood*. New Delhi: UBSPD, 1998.

Keating, H. R. F. *Filmi, Filmi, Inspector Ghote* (1976). New York: Doubleday Crime Club, 1977.

Khambatta, J. M. "Sholay." *Filmfare* (October 17, 1975): 46.

Khanna, Anil. "Limits of Anger: A Look at the Persona of the Anti-Hero in Popular Hindi Cinema over the Decades." *Cinema in India* 3.6 (1992): 4–9.

Khanna, K. C. "All That Glitters Is Black." *The Illustrated Weekly of India*, January 12, 1975, 6–10.

Khanna, Rajbans. "'My Wajid Is Not Effete or Effeminate!'" *The Illustrated Weekly of India*, December 31, 1978, 49–52.

———. "Ray's Wajid Ali Shah." *The Illustrated Weekly of India*, October 22, 1978, 49–53.

Khilnani, Sunil. *The Idea of India*. New York: Farrar, Straus, and Giroux, 1997.

Khubchandani, Lata. *Raj Kapoor: The Great Showman*. New Delhi: Rupa, 2003.

Kohli, Suresh. "Middle of the Road Cinema." *The Illustrated Weekly of India*, December 19, 1982, 46–47.

Kothari, Komal. "Myth, Tales and Folklore: Exploring the Substratum of Cinema." *India International Centre Quarterly. Indian Popular Cinema: Myth Meaning and Metaphor* 8.1 (March 1980): 31–42.

KPMG-FICCI. *Digital Dawn: The Metamorphosis Begins*. Indian Media and Entertainment Industry Report. 2012. See kpmg.com.in.

———. *Hitting the High Notes*. Indian Media and Entertainment Industry Report. 2011. See kpmg.com.in.

———. *The Power of a Billion: Realizing the Indian Dream*. Indian Media and Entertainment Industry Report. 2013. See kpmg.com.in.

———. *The Stage Is Set*. Indian Media and Entertainment Industry Report. 2014. See kpmg .com.in.

Kripalani, Coonoor. "Coming of Age: Bollywood Productions in the Nineties." *Asian Cinema* 12.1 (2001): 29–48.

Kripalani, Manjeet. "Bollywood: Can New Money Create a World-Class Film Industry in India?" *Business Week Online* (December 22, 2002).

Krishen, Pradip. "Knocking on the Doors of Public Culture: India's Parallel Cinema." *Public Culture* 4.1 (1991): 25–42.

Krishna, Akbar. "The Politics of Cinema." *The Illustrated Weekly of India*, April 13–19, 1986, 52.

Krishna, Nanditha. "Cinema of Power." *The Illustrated Weekly of India*, April 30, 1978, 20–22.

Kumar, Seetha. "Partition." *The Illustrated Weekly of India*, August 16–22, 1987, 48–49.

Kumar, Shanti. "Politics After Television: Hindu Nationalism and the Reshaping of the Public in India." *Screen* 44.1 (2003): 123–28.

Kumar, Vijay. "Nargis: Yesterday, Today, and Tomorrow." *Nagpur Times* (1979).

Lahiri, Monojit. "With Japani Juta and a Rusi Topi He Walked into the Hearts of Millions." *Asian Age* (June 2, 1995): 14.

Lal, Vinay. *Deewaar: The Footpath, the City, and the Angry Young Man*. New Delhi: Harper-Collins & India Today, 2011.

——. "The Impossibility of the Outsider in the Modern Hindi Film." In Ashis Nandy, ed., *The Secret Politics of Our Desires*, 228–59.

Larkin, Brian. "Bandiri Music, Globalisation and Urban Experience in Nigeria." In Kaur and Sinha, eds., *Bollyworld*, 284–308.

——. "Bollywood Comes to Nigeria." *Samar* 8 (Winter/Spring 1997).

——. "Colonialism and the Built Space of Cinema in Nigeria." In Kaarsholm, ed., *City Flicks*, 183–210.

——. "Indian Films and Nigerian Lovers: Media and the Creation of Parallel Modernities." *Africa* 67.3 (1997): 406–439.

——. "Itineraries of Indian Cinema: African Videos, Bollywood, and Global Media." In Ella Shohat and Robert Stam, eds., *Multiculturalism, Postcoloniality, and Transnational Media*, 170–92. New Brunswick: Rutgers UP, 2003.

Laul, Brian. "Where Cinema Is Politics and Politics Is Cinema." *The Illustrated Weekly of India*, January 16, 1983, 16–19.

Laxminarayan, Sunki. "Hindi Films." *Sunday Standard* (London), February 12, 1978, n.p.

Lulla, Arjun. Personal interview by author, telephone, March 17, 2003.

Lutgendorf, Philip. *"Jai Santoshi Maa* Revisited: On Seeing a Hindu 'Mythological' Film." In S. Brent Plate, ed., *Representing Religion in World Cinema: Mythmaking, Culture Making, Filmmaking*, 19–42. New York: Palgrave, 2003.

——. "Ritual Reverb: Two 'Blockbuster' Hindi Films." *South Asian Popular Culture* 10.1 (2012): 63–76.

Magal, Uma. "Indian Cinema Fifty Years After Independence: A Cinema of Ferment." *Asian Cinema* 10.1 (Fall 1998): 193–97.

Maitra, Prabodh, ed. *100 Years of Cinema*. Calcutta: Nandan, 1995.

Majumdar, Neepa. "Doubling, Stardom, and Melodrama in Indian Cinema: The 'Impossible' Role of Nargis." *Post Script* 22.3 (Summer 2003): 89–105.

——. "The Embodied Voice: Song Sequences and Stardom in Popular Hindi Cinema." In Pamela Robertson Wojcik and Arthur Knight, eds., *Soundtrack Available: Essays on Film and Popular Music*. Durham, NC: Duke UP, 2001.

——. *Wanted Cultured Ladies Only! Female Stardom and Cinema in India, 1930s–1950s*. Urbana and Chicago: U of Illinois P, 2009.

Majumdar, Rochona, and Dipesh Chakrabarty. "Mangal Pandey: Film and History." *Economic and Political Weekly* 42:19 (May 12–18, 2007): 1771–78.

Malcolm, Derek. "Monarch of the Indian Cinema's Royal Family." *The Guardian*, June 4, 1988, 34.

Malhotra, Inder. *Indira Gandhi: A Personal and Political Biography*. Boston: Northeastern UP, 1991.

Malik, Amita. "Nargis Symbolized the Ideal Indian Woman." *The Statesman* (Delhi), May 5, 1981.

——. "The Showman Supreme." *The Statesman* (Delhi), May 15, 1988.

Mankekar, Purnima. "Brides Who Travel: Gender, Transnationalism, and Nationalism in Hindi Film." *positions* 7.3 (1999): 731–61.

——. *Screening Culture, Viewing Politics: An Ethnography of Television, Womanhood, and Nation in Postcolonial India*. Durham, NC: Duke UP, 1999.

Manto, Saadat Hasan. *Stars from Another Sky: The Bombay Film World of the 1940s*. Trans. Khalid Hasan. New Delhi: Penguin, 1998.

Manuel, Peter. *Cassette Culture: Popular Music and Technology in North India*. Chicago: U of Chicago P, 1993.

Masud, Iqbal. *Dream Merchants, Politicians and Partition: Memoirs of an Indian Muslim*. New Delhi: HarperCollins India, 1997.

——. "Genesis of Popular Cinema." *Cinema in India* (January 1987): 10–17.

——. "The Great Four of the Golden Fifties." In Vasudev, ed., *Frames of Mind*, 29–42.

——. "Nationalism and Hindi Cinema." *Deep Focus* 6 (1996): 21–23.

Mazumdar, Ranjani. *Bombay Cinema: An Archive of the City*. Minneapolis: U of Minnesota P, 2007.

——. "From Subjectification to Schizophrenia: The 'Angry Man' and the 'Psychotic Hero' of Bombay Cinema." In Vasudevan, ed., *Making Meaning in Indian Cinema*, 238–66.

Mehra, Vishwa (Mamaji). Personal interview by author, RK Studios, Chembur, Mumbai, June 19, 2003.

Mehta, Monika. "Globalizing Bombay Cinema: Reproducing the Indian State and Family." *Cultural Dynamics* 17 (2005): 135–54.

Mehta, Rini Bhattacharya. "Bollywood, Nation, Globalization: An Incomplete Introduction." In Mehta and Pandhiripande, eds., *Bollywood and Globalization*, 1–14.

Mehta, Rini Bhattacharya, and Rajeshwari V. Pandhiripande, eds. *Bollywood and Globalization: Indian Popular Cinema, Nation, Diaspora*. London: Anthem Press, 2011.

Mehta, Suketu. *Maximum City: Bombay Lost and Found*. New York: Knopf, 2004.

Mehta, Vinod. "Life and Loves of Meena Kumari." *The Illustrated Weekly of India*, November 5, 1972: 40–49.

Menon, Raghava R. *K. L. Saigal: The Pilgrim of the Swara*. New Delhi: Hind Pocket Books, 1989.

Meyer, Christian, and Nancy Birdsall. "New Estimates of India's Middle Class: A Technical Note." Center for Global Development, Peterson Institute for International Economics. November 2012. Web.

Miller, Barbara Stoler. "Contending Narratives: The Political Life of Indian Epics." *Journal of Asian Studies* 50.4 (1991): 783–92.

Mishra, Sumant, ed. *Main Amitabh Bachchan Bol Raha Hoon (I'm Amitabh Bachchan Speaking)*. Bombay: Egmont Imagination, 2002.

Mishra, Vijay. *Bollywood Cinema: Temples of Desire*. London: Routledge, 2002.

——. "Decentering History: Some Versions of Bombay Cinema." *East-West Film Journal* 6.1 (1992): 111–55.

——. "Towards a Theoretical Critique of Bombay Cinema." *Screen* 26.3–4 (May-August 1985): 133–46.

Mishra, Vijay, Peter Jeffery, and Brian Shoesmith. "The Actor as Parallel Text in Bombay Cinema." *Quarterly Review of Film & Video* 11 (1989): 49–67.

Mistry, Rohinton. *A Fine Balance*. New York: Vintage, 1995.

Mitra, Shibani. "'The Empire Strikes Back.'" *The Illustrated Weekly of India*, July 19, 1981, 36–39.

Mohamed, Khalid. "The Babies That *Sholay* Spawned." *Filmfare* (October 16–31, 1978): 45.

——. "Fatal Attraction." *The Illustrated Weekly of India*, November 13–19, 1988, 8–17.

——. "Finished!" *The Illustrated Weekly of India*, January 8–14, 1989, 10–19.

——. "Heaven Can't Wait." *The Illustrated Weekly of India*, November 20–26, 1988, 38–45.

——. "The King of Hearts." *Times of India Sunday Review*, June 12, 1988.

——. "Those Days of Challenge: An Interview with Ramesh Sippy." *Cinema in India* 3.5 (May 1992): 20–32.

Mohan, Jag. *S. Sukhdev: Filmmaker*. Pune: National Film Archive of India, 1984.

Morcom, Anna. "Film Songs and the Cultural Synergies of Bollywood in and Beyond South Asia." In Dwyer and Pinto, eds., *Beyond the Boundaries of Bollywood*, 156–87.

Motion Picture Association of America (MPAA). "Theatrical Market Statistics: Cinema Screens" (2002–2013). See www.mpaa.org/policy/industry.

Mulvey, Laura. "Afterthoughts on 'Visual Pleasure and Narrative Cinema' Inspired by King Vidor's *Duel in the Sun* (1946)" (1981). In *Visual and Other Pleasures*, 29–38. Rpt., Bloomington: Indiana UP, 1989.

——. "'It Will Be a Magnificent Obsession': The Melodrama's Role in the Development of Contemporary Film Theory." In Jacky Bratton, Jim Cook, and Christine Gledhill, eds., *Melodrama: Stage Picture Screen*, 121–33. London: British Film Institute, 1994.

——. "Notes on Sirk and Melodrama" (1977). In *Visual and Other Pleasures*, 39–44. Rpt., Bloomington: Indiana UP, 1989.

——. "Visual Pleasure and Narrative Cinema" (1975). In *Visual and Other Pleasures*, 14–28. Rpt., Bloomington: Indiana UP, 1989.

Nair, P. K. "Partition in Cinema." *South Asian Cinema* 5–6 (2004): 9–14.

Nair, P. K. Personal interview by author, National Film Archive of India, Pune, June 11–12 and 18, 2003.

Nanda, Ritu, ed. *Raj Kapoor: His Life and His Films*. Bombay and Moscow: RK Films and Studio, Iskusstvo Publishers, 1991.

Nanda, Ritu, ed. *Raj Kapoor Speaks*. New Delhi: Penguin India, 2002.

Nandy, Ashis. "Final Encounter: The Politics of the Assassination of Gandhi." *At the Edge of Psychology: Essays in Politics and Psychology*, 70–98. New Delhi: Oxford UP, 1980.

——. "An Intelligent Critic's Guide to Indian Cinema." *The Savage Freud and Other Essays on Possible and Retrievable Selves*, 196–236. New Delhi: Oxford UP, 1995.

——. "Invitation to an Antique Death: The Journey of Pramathesh Barua as the Origin of the Terribly Effeminate, Maudlin, Self-Destructive Heroes of Indian Cinema." In Dwyer and Pinney, eds., *Pleasure and the Nation*, 139–60.

——. "The Lure of 'Normal' Politics: Gandhi and the Battle for Popular Culture of Politics in India." *South Asian Popular Culture* 5.2 (October 2007): 167–78.

——. "Notes toward an Agenda for the Next Generation of Film Theorists in India." *South Asian Popular Culture* 1.1 (2003): 79–84.

——. "The Popular Hindi Film: Ideology and First Principles." *India International Centre Quarterly. Indian Popular Cinema: Myth Meaning and Metaphor* 8.1 (March 1980): 89–96.

——. "Satyajit Ray's Secret Guide to Exquisite Murders: Creativity, Social Criticism, and the Partitioning of the Self." *The Savage Freud and Other Essays on Possible and Retrievable Selves*, 237–66. New Delhi: Oxford UP, 1995.

———. "The Split Within: Imran Khan, Sherlock Holmes, and Amitabh Bachchan." *The Illustrated Weekly of India*, April 5, 1987, 38–41.

———. "The Supermarket of Dreams." *The Illustrated Weekly of India*, March 16–22, 1986, 48–51.

Nandy, Ashis, ed. *The Secret Politics of Our Desires: Innocence, Culpability, and Indian Popular Cinema*. New Delhi: Oxford UP, 1998.

Nandy, Pritish. "Of Beautiful Housewives and Their Lonely Lives." *The Illustrated Weekly of India*, January 22–28, 1984, 36–39.

———. "Requeim for the Tramp." *Filmfare* (December 1–15, 1984): 34–35.

Nargis. "I Am a Hindusthani First." *Sunday*, May 17, 1981.

———. "The Postman Knocks at the Ivory Tower." *Filmfare* (January 3, 1958): 8–9, 11.

National Film Development Corporation. *Indian Cinema: A Visual Voyage*. New Delhi: NFDC, 1998.

Nayar, Ranvir. "Cannes Goes Ga-Ga over Raj Kapoor." *Asian Age* (April 2, 2002): 1.

Nayar, Sheila J. "Invisible Representation: The Oral Contours of a National Popular Cinema." *Film Quarterly* 57.3 (2004): 13–23.

Nehru, Jawaharlal. "Tryst with Destiny" (1947). In Salman Rushdie and Elizabeth West, eds., *The Vintage Book of India Writing, 1947–1997*, 1–2. London: Vintage, 1997.

Nigam, Aditaya. *The Insurrection of Little Selves: The Crisis of Secular-Nationalism in India*. New Delhi: Oxford UP, 2006.

Niranjana, Tejaswini. "Cinema, Femininity, and Economy of Consumption." *Economic and Political Weekly* (October 26, 1991): 85–86.

———. "Integrating Whose Nation? Tourists and Terrorists in *Roja*." *Economic and Political Weekly* (January 15, 1994): 79–82.

———. "Nationalism Refigured: Contemporary South Indian Cinema and the Subject of Feminism." In Partha Chatterjee and Pradeep Jeganathan, eds., *Community, Gender, and Violence*, 138–66. Subaltern Studies 11. New York: Columbia UP, 2000.

———. "Vigilantism and the Pleasures of Masquerade: The Female Spectator of Vijayasanthi Films." In Kaarsholm, ed., *City Flicks*, 237–54.

Nutan. "Hey Grandpop." *Filmfare* (December 4, 1970): 26, 31.

O'Flaherty, Wendy Doniger. "The Mythological in Disguise: An Analysis of *Karz*." *India International Centre Quarterly. Indian Popular Cinema: Myth Meaning and Metaphor* 8.1 (March 1980): 23–30.

Oldenburg, Ray. *The Great Good Place: Cafés, Coffee Shops, Community Centers, Beauty Parlors, General Stores, Bars, Hangouts, and How They Get You through the Day*. New York: Paragon House, 1989.

Oldenburg, Veena Talwar. *Dowry Murder: The Imperial Origins of a Cultural Crime*. New York: Oxford UP, 2002.

Oommen, T. K. "Demystifying the Nation and Nationalism." In Geeti Sen, ed., *India: A National Culture?*, 259–74.

Pandian, Anand. "Imagination: Cinematic, Anthropological." *Social Text* 30.4 (Winter 2012): 127–41.

Pandian, M. S. S. *The Image Trap: M.G. Ramachandran in Film and Politics*. New Delhi: Sage, 1992.

Parkes, Christopher. "Family Films Give Hollywood Bumper Revenues." *Financial Times*, March 5, 2003, 6.

Pearson, Bryan. "Bollywood Writes a Comeback Story." *Variety*, August 25, 2003, 18.

Pendakur, Manjunath. *Indian Popular Cinema: Industry, Ideology, and Consciousness.* Cresskill, NJ: Hampton Press, 2003.

——. "India's National Film Policy: Shifting Currents in the 1990s." In Albert Moran, ed., *Film Policy: International, National, and Regional Perspectives*, 148–71. London: Routledge, 1996.

Phillips, Maha Khan. "Backing Bollywood." *Global Investor* (April 2004): 171ff.

Pillai, Swarnavel Eswaran. "The 1970s Tamil Cinema and the Post-Classical Turn." *South Asian Popular Culture* 10.1 (2012): 77–90.

Pines, Jim, and Paul Willemen, eds. *Questions of Third Cinema.* London: British Film Institute, 1989.

Pinney, Christopher. "Introduction: Public, Popular, and Other Cultures." In Dwyer and Pinney, eds., *Pleasure and the Nation*, 1–34.

Pitalwalla, Yassir A. "Hollywood vs. Bollywood." *Fortune* 152.10 (Europe), November 28, 2005.

Poduval, Satish. "The Affable Young Man: Civility, Desire, and the Making of a Middle-Class Cinema in the 1970s." *South Asian Popular Culture* 10.1 (2012): 37–50.

Porter, Henry, ed. *Vanity Fair Salutes Bollywood.* London: Condé Nast, 2002.

Power, Carla, and Sudip Mazumdar. "Bollywood Goes Global." *Newsweek*, February 28, 2000.

Pradhan, Shalini. "*Amar Akbar Anthony*: Birds of the Same Blood Group." *Filmfare* (June 10–23, 1977): 41.

Prakash, Gyan. *Mumbai Fables.* Princeton, NJ: Princeton UP, 2010.

Prasad, M. Madhava. "Cinema and the Desire for Modernity." *Journal of Arts and Ideas* 25–26 (December 1993): 71–86.

——. *Cine-Politics: Film Stars and Political Existence in South India.* New Delhi: Orient Black-Swan, 2014.

——. *Ideology of the Hindi Film: A Historical Construction.* Delhi: Oxford UP, 1998.

——. "Realism and Fantasy in Representations of Metropolitan Life in Indian Cinema." In Kaarsholm, ed., *City Flicks*, 83–99.

——. "Surviving Bollywood." In Kavoori and Punathambekar, eds., *Global Bollywood*, 41–51.

——. "This Thing Called Bollywood." *Seminar* 525 (May 2003). Web.

Qureshi, Pushkin M. "View from the Gallery: *Amar Akbar Anthony*." *Filmfare* (August 5–18, 1977): 45.

Raghavendra, M. K. "Deewaar." *Fifty Indian Film Classics*, 186–92. New Delhi: HarperCollins, 2009.

——. *Seduced by the Familiar: Narration and Meaning in Indian Popular Cinema.* New Delhi: Oxford UP, 2008.

Rai, Amit S. "An American Raj in Filmistan: Images of Elvis in Indian Films." *Screen* 35.1 (1994): 51–77.

——. *Untimely Bollywood: Globalization and India's New Media Assemblage.* Durham, NC: Duke UP, 2009.

"Raj Kapoor's *Shree 420*: Impressively Spectacular Production." *Filmfare* (November 11, 1955): 37.

Rajadhyaksha, Ashish. "Beyond Orientalism." *Sight and Sound* 2.4 (1992): 32–35.

——. "The 'Bollywoodization' of the Indian Cinema: Cultural Nationalism in a Global Arena." *Inter-Asia Cultural Studies* 4.1 (2003): 25–39.

——. *Indian Cinema in the Time of Celluloid: From Bollywood to the Emergency.* Bloomington: Indiana UP, 2009.

——. "Rethinking the State After Bollywood." *Journal of the Moving Image* 3 (June 2004): 47–90.

——. "Viewership and Democracy in the Cinema." In Vasudevan, ed., *Making Meaning in Indian Cinema*, 267–96.

Rajadhyaksha, Ashish, and Paul Willemen, eds. *Encyclopedia of Indian Cinema* (1994). Rev. ed. New Delhi: Oxford UP, 1999.

Rajagopal, Arvind. "The Emergency as Prehistory of the New Indian Middle Class." *Modern Asian Studies* 45.5 (2011): 1003–1049.

——. *Politics After Television: Religious Nationalism and the Shaping of the Indian Public.* Cambridge: Cambridge UP, 2001.

Rajagopalan, Sudha. *Indian Films in Soviet Cinema: The Culture of Movie-Going After Stalin.* Bloomington: Indiana UP, 2008.

Rajendran, Girija. "Amitabh Then and Now Is the Same Man." *Film World* (October 1978): 20–22.

——. "Shooting for Films: Then and Now." *The Illustrated Weekly of India*, July 5, 1981, 42–43.

Rajhans, P. "That's Entertainment." *Cinema in India* 3.6 (1992): 10–15.

Ramachandran, T. M., and S. Rukmini, eds. *70 Years of Indian Cinema (1913–1983).* Bombay: Cinema India-International, 1985.

Ramanujan, A. K. "The Indian Oedipus" (1983). In *The Collected Essays of A. K. Ramanujan*, 377–97. Ed. Vinay Dharwadker. New Delhi: Oxford UP, 1999.

Rangoonwalla, Firoze. *Bimal Roy, Life and Work: A Critical Study.* Bombay: Media 90's, 1991.

——. *Indian Films Index.* Bombay: J. Udeshi, 1968.

——. "Kissing—Hindi Film Style." *The Illustrated Weekly of India*, May 26, 1974, 26–29.

——. *A Pictorial History of Indian Cinema.* London: Hamlyn, 1979.

Rangoonwalla, Firoze. Personal interview by author, Parsi Gym, Mumbai, June 24, 2003.

Ray, Satyajit. *Childhood Days: A Memoir.* Trans. Bijoya Ray. New Delhi: Penguin India, 1999.

——. "What Is Wrong with Indian Films." *Our Films, Their Films*, 19–24. New Delhi: Orient Longman, 1976.

Renan, Ernst. "What Is a Nation?" (1882). Trans. Martin Thom. In Homi Bhabha, ed., *Nation and Narration*, 8-22. New York: Routledge, 1990.

Reuben, Bunny. *Mehboob, India's Demille: The First Biography.* New Delhi: HarperCollins India, 1994.

——. "An Open Letter to Raj Kapoor." *Star and Style*, April 30, 1971, 10–11.

——. *Raj Kapoor, the Fabulous Showman: An Intimate Biography.* New Delhi: Indus, 1995.

RK Studios Staff. Personal interviews by author, RK Studios, Chembur, Mumbai, June 2003.

Roberge, Gaston. "The Cinema of Subversion." *The Illustrated Weekly of India*, October 13–19, 1985, 38–41.

Robinson, Andrew. *Satyajit Ray: The Inner Eye.* Berkeley: U of California P, 1989.

Rogin, Michael. "*Kiss Me Deadly*: Communism, Motherhood, and Cold War Movies." *Ronald Reagan, the Movie and Other Episodes in Political Demonology*, 236–71. Berkeley: U of California P, 1987.

Roy, Anjali Gera, and Huat, Chua Beng, eds. *Travels of Bollywood Cinema: From Bombay to LA*. New Delhi: Oxford UP, 2012.

Roy, Paroma. "Figuring Mother India: The Case of Nargis." *Indian Traffic: Identities in Question in Colonial and Postcolonial India*, 152–73. Berkeley: U of California P, 1998.

Rushdie, Salman. *Midnight's Children*. New York: Avon, 1981.

Saari, Anil. "Abbas on Raj Kapoor." *The Hindustan Times Sunday Supplement*, September 28, 1986, 12.

——. *Hindi Cinema: An Insider's View*. New Delhi: Oxford UP, 2009.

——. "Raj Kapoor: A Legend in Montage." *Hindustan Times*, June 12, 1988, 5.

Sadagopan, Shobha. "Interview with Ramesh Sippy." *The Sunday Observer*, August 21, 1988.

Sahgal, Nayantara. *Rich Like Us*. New York: New Directions, 1985.

Samant, Sapna. "Appropriating Bollywood Cinema: Why the Western World Gets Bollywood So Wrong." *Metro* 145 (Winter 2005): 82–86.

Sardar, Ziauddin. "Dilip Kumar Made Me Do It." In Ashis Nandy, ed., *The Secret Politics of Our Desires*, 19–91.

Sarkar, Avek, and Barun Sengupta. "*Awara* Beats Mao Music." *Business Standard* (July 4, 1979).

Sarkar, Bhaskar. *Mourning the Nation: Indian Cinema in the Wake of Partition*. Durham, NC: Duke UP, 2009.

Sarkar, Kobita. *Indian Cinema Today: An Analysis*. New Delhi: Sterling, 1975.

Sastry, K. N. T. *L.V. Prasad: A Monograph*. New Delhi: Wiley Eastern, 1993.

"Selling Dreams." *Asiaweek*, May 4, 1984, 39–44.

Sen, Geeti, ed. *India: A National Culture?* New Delhi: Sage and India International Centre, 2003.

Sen, Meheli. "'It's All About Loving Your Parents': Liberalization, Hindutva, and Bollywood's New Fathers." In Mehta and Pandhiripande, eds., *Bollywood and Globalization*, 145–68.

Sen, Meheli, and Anustup Basu, eds. *Figurations in Indian Film*. Houndmills, Basingstoke: Palgrave Macmillan, 2013.

Seth, Vikram. *From Heaven Lake*. New York: Vintage, 1983.

Sethi, Sunil. "The Kapoors: Filmdom's First Family." *India Today*, August 15, 1982, 120–28.

Shahani, Kumar, Mani Kaul, and Girish Karnad. "Comments from the Gallery." *India International Centre Quarterly. Indian Popular Cinema: Myth Meaning and Metaphor* 8.1 (March 1980): 97–107.

Shailendra. "Raj Kapoor: Man of Surprises." *Filmfare* (October 2, 1964): 7–9.

Shantaram, V. "It's Up to Us to Mould Public Taste." *The Illustrated Weekly of India*, October 1, 1978, 40–43.

——. "Why This Sex Excess?" *The Illustrated Weekly of India*, July 27, 1980, 6–13.

Sharma, Ashwani. "Blood, Sweat and Tears: Amitabh Bachchan, Urban Demi-God." In Pat Kirkham and Janet Thumin, eds., *You Tarzan: Masculinity, Movies, and Men*, 167–80. New York: St. Martin's, 1993.

Shetty, Sandhya. "(Dis)Figuring the Nation: Mother, Metaphor, Metonymy." *differences: A Journal of Feminist Cultural Studies* 7.3 (1995): 51–74.

"*Shree 420*: An Anti-Social Picture and Pathetic Burlesque of a Noisy Producer." *Filmindia* (November 1955): 34–36.

Simon, Bryant. *Everything but the Coffee: Learning About America from Starbucks*. Berkeley: U of California P, 2009.

Singh, Bikram. "'Amar Akbar Anthony': Absurd, but Funny." *Times of India*, May 29, 1977.

Singh, Khushwant. "'We Sell Them Dreams.'" *New York Times Magazine*, October 31, 1975, 42, 90–98.

Singhal, Rahul, ed. *Devdas: The Eternal Saga of Love*. New Delhi: Pentagon Paperbacks, 2002.

Sinha, Shatrughan. "'I Want Justice.'" *The Illustrated Weekly of India*, October 13–19, 1985, 42–43.

——. "Villainy—Film Institute Style." *The Illustrated Weekly of India*, October 29, 1972, 40–43.

Sippy, Ramesh. Personal interview by author, Sathe House, Khar, June 21, 2003.

Solzhenitzyn, Alexandr. *The Cancer Ward*. Trans. Nicholas Bethell and David F. Berg. New York: Bantam, 1969.

Somaaya, Bhavana, Jigna Kothari, and Supriya Madangarli. *Mother Maiden Mistress: Women in Hindi Cinema, 1950–2010*. New Delhi: HarperCollins and India Today, 2012.

Somaaya, Bhawana. *Amitabh Bachchan: The Legend*. New Delhi: Macmillan India, 1999.

——. *Salaam Bollywood: The Pain and the Passion*. South Godstone: Spantech & Lancer, 1999.

Sood, B. S., and B. K. Karanjia. *An Alien in Bollywood: An Autobiography*. New Delhi: UBSPD, 2000.

Sophocles. *Oedipus Tyrannus*. Trans. Luci Berkowitz and Theodore F. Brunner. Norton Critical Edition. New York: Norton, 1970.

Spinelli, Italo, ed. *Indian Summer: Films, Filmmakers and Stars between Ray and Bollywood*. Milan: Edizioni Olivares, 2002.

Srinivas, K. "Amitabh Bachchan: From Stone Bench to Stardom and Beyond." *Bombay* (August 7–21, 1985): 36–42.

Srinivas, Lakshmi. "The Active Audience: Spectatorship, Social Relations and the Experience of Cinema in India." *Media, Culture & Society* 24 (2002): 155–73.

——. "Imaging the Audience." *South Asian Popular Culture* 3.2 (2005): 101–16.

Srinivas, S. V. "Researching Indian Audiences." *Cultural Dynamics* 13.1 (2001): 117–23.

Subramaniam, K. N. "A Thousand and Fifty Nights of *Sholay*." *Filmfare* (October 16–31, 1978): 40–45.

Subramanian, Babu. "Film Review: Desi Villain, Pardesi Hero." *Deep Focus* 6 (1996): 95–96.

Sukumar, Padmini. "*Kissa Kursi Ka*, End of a Controversy." *The Illustrated Weekly of India*, June 16–22, 1985, 40–41.

Swamy, Anand. "Distributor's Dilemma: An Interview with Distributor Ramesh Sippy." *Free Press*, February 18, 1979.

Tagore, Rabindranath. *Nationalism: Three Lectures*. New Delhi: Rupa, 2002.

Taneja, Roshan. "Actors Are Made, Never Born." *The Illustrated Weekly of India*, March 20, 1983, 38–39.

Tarbouriech, Nadine. "Interview with Mani Ratnam." In Spinelli, ed., *Indian Summer*, 180–85.

Tarlo, Emma. *Unsettling Memories: Narratives of the Emergency in Delhi*. Berkeley: U of California P, 2003.

Taylor, Charles. "Nationalism and Modernity." In Ronald Beiner, ed., *Theorizing Nationalism*, 219–46. Albany: State U of New York P, 1996.

Taylor, Woodman. "Penetrating Gazes: The Poetics of Sight and Visual Display in Popular Indian Cinema." *Contributions to Indian Sociology* 36.1–2 (2002): 297–322.

Tharoor, Shashi. *Show Business: A Novel.* New Delhi: Penguin, 1991.

Tharu, Susie. "Third World Women's Cinema: Notes on Narrative, Reflections on Opacity." *Economic and Political Weekly* (May 17, 1986): 864–66.

Thomas, Rosie. *Bombay Before Bollywood: Film City Fantasies.* New Delhi: Orient BlackSwan, 2014.

——. "Indian Cinema—Pleasures and Popularity." *Screen* 26.3–4 (1985): 116–32.

——. "Sanctity and Scandal: The Mythologization of Mother India." *Quarterly Review of Film and Video* 11.3 (1989): 11–30.

Thoraval, Yves. *The Cinemas of India, 1896–2000.* New Delhi: Macmillan India, 2000.

Tompkins, Jane. *Sensational Designs: The Cultural Work of American Fiction, 1790–1860.* New York: Oxford UP, 1985.

——. "West of Everything." In Glenwood Irons, ed., *Gender, Language, and Myth: Essays on Popular Culture*, 103–26. Toronto: U of Toronto P, 1992.

Tremblay, Reeta Chowdhari. "Representation and Reflection of Self and Society in the Bombay Cinema." *Contemporary South Asia* 3.3 (1996): 303–18.

Tripathi, Salil. "Reminiscences: A Sentimental Father." *India Today*, June 30, 1988, 140.

Uberoi, Patricia. "Imagining the Family: An Ethnography of Viewing *Hum Aapke Hain Koun*." In Dwyer and Pinney, eds., *Pleasure and the Nation*, 309–52.

"The Vagabond (*Awara*)." *Monthly Film Bulletin* 21.247 (1954): 119.

Valicha, Kishore. *The Moving Image: A Study of Indian Cinema.* New Delhi: Orient Longman, 1988.

van der Heide, William. *Bollywood Babylon: Interviews with Shyam Benegal.* New York: Berg, 2006.

Vander Steene, Gwenda. "Bollywood Films and African Audiences." In Roy and Huat, eds., *Travels of Bollywood Cinema*, 302–20.

Vanier, Fiona. "Bollywood Distributor Eros Overtakes Yash Raj." *Screen Finance* 16.16 (2003): 5.

Vasudev, Aruna. *Frames of Mind: Reflections on Indian Cinema.* New Delhi: UBSPD, 1995.

Vasudev, Aruna, and Philippe Lenglet, eds. *Indian Cinema Superbazaar.* New Delhi: Vikas, 1983.

Vasudev, Aruna, Latika Padgaonkar, and Rashmi Doraiswamy, eds. *Being and Becoming: The Cinemas of Asia.* New Delhi: Macmillan India, 2002.

Vasudevan, Ravi. "*Bombay* and Its Public." *Journal of Arts and Ideas* 29 (January 1996): 44–65.

——. "Film Studies, New Cultural History and Experience of Modernity." *Economic and Political Weekly* 30.44 (November 4, 1995): 2809–14.

——. "The Meanings of 'Bollywood.'" In Dwyer and Pinto, eds., *Beyond the Boundaries of Bollywood*, 3–29.

——. *The Melodramatic Public: Film Form and Spectatorship in Indian Cinema.* New York: Palgrave Macmillan, 2011.

——. "Shifting Codes, Dissolving Identities: The Hindi Social Film of the 1950s as Popular Culture." *Journal of Arts and Ideas* 23–24 (January 1993): 51–84.

Vasudevan, Ravi, ed. *Making Meaning in Indian Cinema*. New Delhi: Oxford UP, 2000.

Vergès, Françoise. *Monsters and Revolutionaries: Colonial Family Romance and Métissage*. Durham, NC, and London: Duke UP, 1999.

Virani, Pinkie. "The Inheritors." *Sunday* (August 9–15, 1992): 72–74.

Virdi, Jyotika. *The Cinematic ImagiNation: Indian Popular Films as Social History*. New Brunswick, NJ: Rutgers UP, 2003.

——. "*Deewaar*: Fact, Fiction, and the Making of a Superstar." In Kaur and Sinha, eds., *Bollyworld*, 223–39.

——. "*Deewaar*: 'Fiction' of Film and 'Fact' of Politics." *Jump Cut* 38 (1993): 26–32.

——. "*Mr. And Mrs. 1955*: Comedy of Gender, Law, and the Nation." *Jump Cut* 43 (2000): 76–85.

Vitali, Valentina. *Hindi Action Cinema: Industries, Narratives, Bodies*. New Delhi: Oxford UP, 2008.

Weber, Max. *Politics as a Vocation*. Trans. H. H. Gerth and C. Wright Mills. Philadelphia: Fortress Press, 1965.

"What's So Special?" *Filmfare* (December 4, 1970).

Wilson, Dominic, and Roopa Purushothaman. "Dreaming with BRICS: The Path to 2050." Global Economics Paper #99. Goldman Sachs, October 2003. See www.goldmansachs.com/ceoconfidential/CEO-2003–12.pdf.

Windsor, D. A. "Nargis, Ray, Rushdie and the Real." *South Asia* 21.1 (1998): 229–42.

Wlaschin, Ken. "Birth of the 'Curry' Western: Bombay '76." *Films and Filming* 22.7 (April 1976): 20–23.

Zaman, Rana Siddiqui. "Blast from the Past: *Ab Dilli Door Nahin*." *The Hindu*, October 4, 2004 (Web ed.: np).

"*Zanjeer*: Rebel-in-Law versus the Law-Breakers." *Star and Style*, June 8, 1973, 35.

Zutshi, Somnath. "Woman, Nation and the Outsider in Contemporary Hindi Cinema." In Tejaswini Niranjana and Vivek Dhareshwar, eds., *Interrogating Modernity: Culture and Colonialism in India*, 83–142. Eds. Tejaswini Niranjana and Vivek Dhareshwar. Calcutta: Seagull, 1993.

INDEX

bold denotes photo

Aag (Fire) (film), 23

Aaj ka Arjun (Today's Arjun) (film), 60

Abbas, K. A., 24

Ab Dilli Dur Nahin (Delhi is not far now)
(film), 16, 23, 24, 33–42, **34**, **35**, 58, 128

adolescent passion, 104. *See also Bobby*
(film)

aesthetic of mobilization, 51. *See also* Prasad,
Madhava

ahimsa (nonviolence), 56, 129. *See also*
Gandhi, M. K.

Ahmed (character in *Sholay*), 54, 56

Aisa Kyon Hota Hai? (Why does it happen
like this?) (film), 110

Akhtar, Javed, 44, 61, 63, 64, 65, 67, 77–78,
81, 82, 85, 86, 87, 110, 145–46n10. *See also*
Salim-Javed

Allahabad, 24, 28, 29, 30, 37, 49, 61, 141n14.
See also Bachchan, Amitabh; Gandhi,
Indira; Nehru, Jawaharlal

Allahabadi, Akbar (character in *Amar Akbar
Anthony*), 29, **29**

All That Heaven Allows (film), 117

Amar (character in *Dil Se*), 12

Amar Akbar Anthony (film), 9, 29, **29**, 76,
77, 95, 96, 113

Amélie (film), 92

Anand, Dev, 19, **20**

Anandbabu (character in *Deewaar*), 64, **69**,
70, 72, 75, 80, 82

Anderson, Benedict, 136n4

Andha Kanoon (Blind justice) (film), 60

Anita (character in *Deewaar*), 70, 72

Archie comic book, xix, 96, **97**, 110, 150n14.
See also Bobby (film); Kapoor, Raj

Arjun, Anil, 125, 126

Around the World in Eight Dollars (film), 13

Athique, Adrian, 109–100

Aurat (Woman) (film), 48, 143n38. *See also*
Khan, Mehboob; *Mother India* (film)

Awara (The vagabond) (film), 2, 14, 16, 23,
24, 30–31, **31**, 33, 36, 37, 38, 81, 111, 118,
119, **119**

B4U, 110

Bachchan, Amitabh, 9, 49, 60, 61, 64, 66,
70, 91, 115, **121**, 124

Banerjee, Mukulika, 139n25

Barsaat (Rain) (film), 23

Baruah, Dev Kant, 147n19

Basanti (character in *Sholay*), 49, 51

Basu, Bipasha, 110

Batra, Bindu, 43, 44

Benegal, Shyam, 109